I0822990

NEW YORK FASHION ICONS

First published in 2026 by Welbeck

An Imprint of HEADLINE PUBLISHING GROUP LIMITED

1

Cataloguing in Publication Data is available from the British Library

ISBN 9781035430345

Printed and bound in China

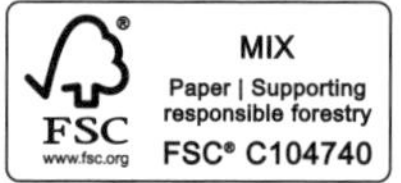

Headline's policy is to use papers that are natural, renewable and recyclable products and made from wood grown in well-managed forests and other controlled sources. The logging and manufacturing processes are expected to conform to the environmental regulations of the country of origin.

HEADLINE PUBLISHING GROUP LIMITED

An Hachette UK Company
Carmelite House
50 Victoria Embankment
London EC4Y 0DZ

The authorised representative in the EEA is Hachette Ireland, 8 Castlecourt Centre, Dublin 15, D15 XTP3, Ireland (email: info@hbgi.ie)

www.headline.co.uk
www.hachette.co.uk

50 STYLE LEGENDS OF NEW YORK CITY

NEW YORK FASHION ICONS

KRISTEN BATEMAN

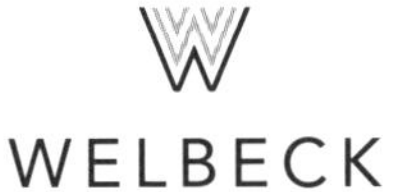

WELBECK

Contents

Chapter 4: The Megawatts 114

Chapter 5: Fashion Insiders

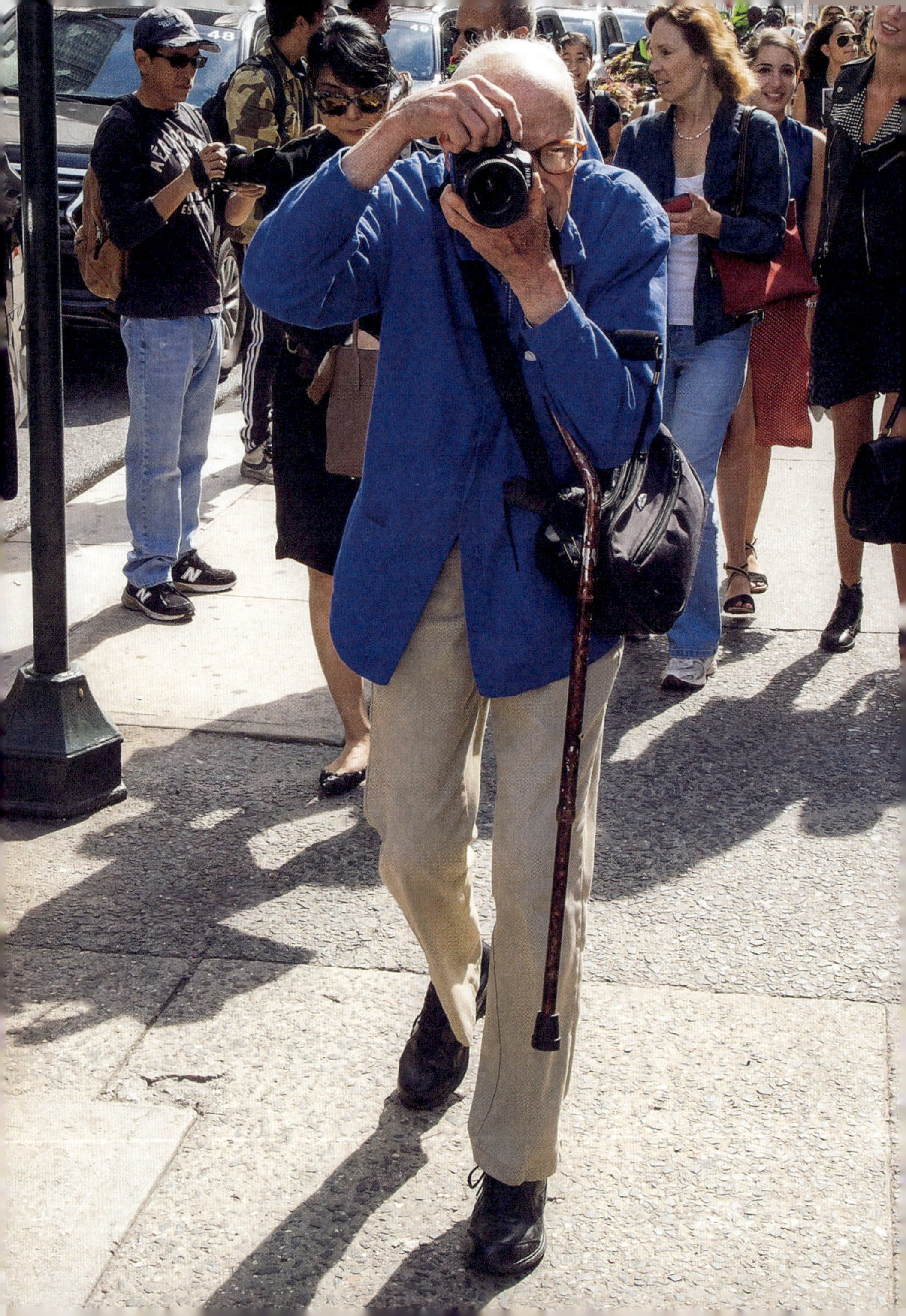
48

INTRODUCTION

No other place in the world has style like New York. Musicians, actors, stylists, designers, artists and tastemakers have walked these city streets for hundreds of years, culminating in the perfect storm of proud and unapologetic individuality fuelled with powerful sartorial flair. Unlike other major fashion capitals, in New York anything goes; even the most extreme, formal or informal looks – everything from subway to sidewalk.

But what makes a New York fashion icon? Our definition includes those who were either born, lived, or made their biggest fashion statements in and around the New York Metropolitan area. New York is a walking city through and through, and even celebrities take public transportation here, resulting in a certain art of one dressing for public display with a sense of unique practicality. Along with that, the weather brings seismic style changes that are as interesting to watch as a designer runway show. As the well-loved New York street-style photographer Bill Cunningham (an icon himself) once said: "When it rains, it's a whole different scene. Things happen. People forget about you. If they see you, they don't go putting on airs. They're the way they are."

Opposite: The late photographer Bill Cunningham was once the most recognizable street-style photographer in New York City.

In a city where as many as 800 different languages are spoken every single day, it's impossible not to notice the vast diversity when it comes to dressing. One can walk down the street and see sequins, feathers and sweatpants all at the same time. Vintage, designer and handmade pieces mix with everyday down-to-earth items. You'll see museum-level fashion alongside the most amazing DIY designs that the world has ever seen. Even the very stylistic codes that go deep into New York's roots are endlessly reinterpreted. Take, for instance, the colour black, which is so essential to the city when it comes to blending in and becoming invisible or standing out with structure, texture and panache.

It's part of the reason why New York has turned out icon after icon when it comes to style. From maximalist to minimalist, there are so many different forces of inspiration present from day to night. But New Yorkers can all agree on one thing: here, you can be anyone. You can dress however you want. There are no rules, no customs and above all else, self-expression is celebrated.

This book recounts some of the most memorable New York style icons of all time – from the fictional and fantastical icons of film and television to the real-world people who continue to inspire with their legacies today. These are the stories of the muses who make New York fashion what it is.

Opposite: The concept of the little black dress was born in New York, shaped by the ever-iconic Audrey Hepburn in her role in *Breakfast at Tiffany's*.

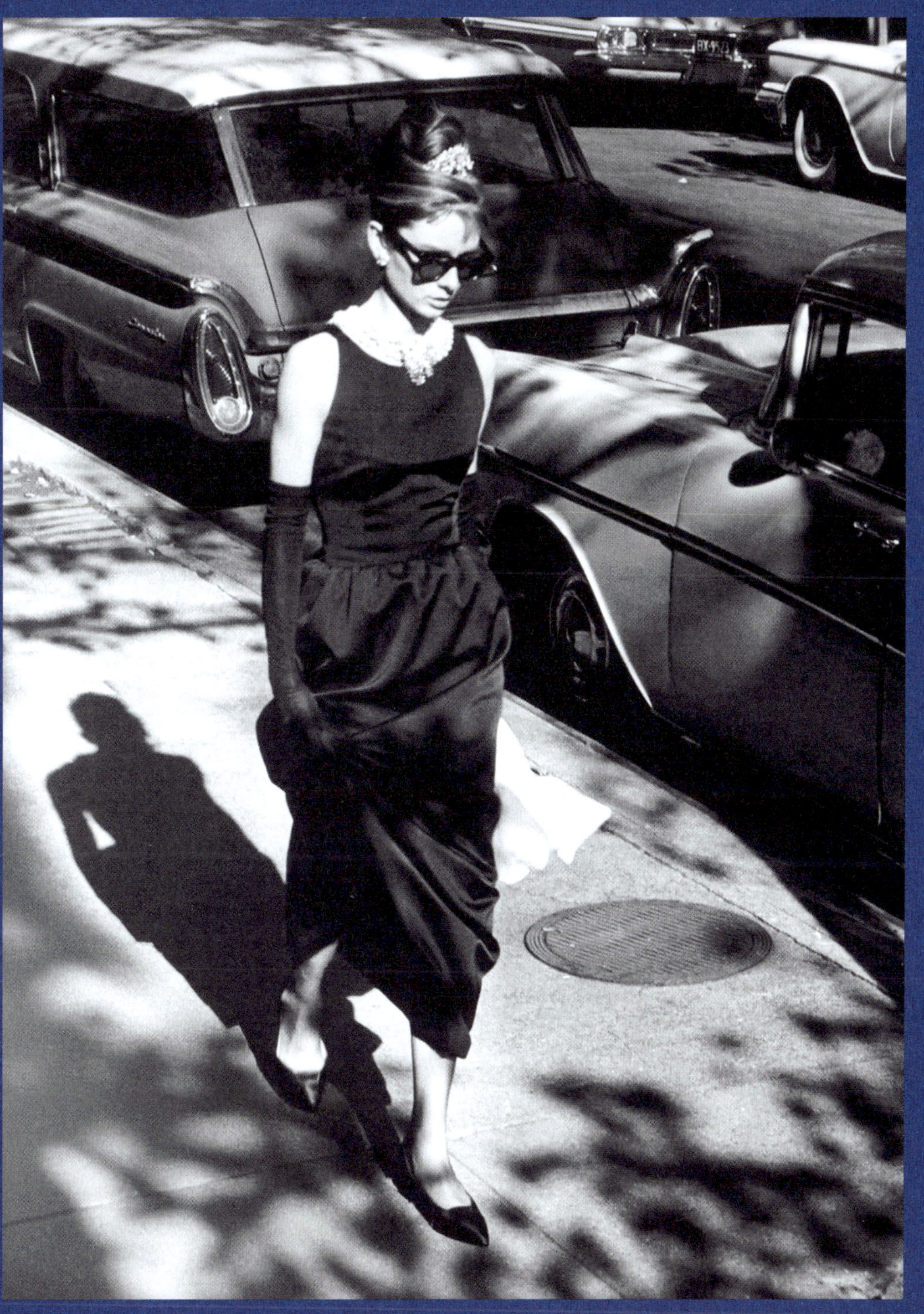

CHAPTER 1: THE FICTIONAL FANTASIES

In a city as vast as New York, so many icons have forged their own paths, forever inspiring those who may have never even set foot on its streets. Whether by way of TV or the familiar flick, it's impossible not to see the direct influence of fabulous fictional stars on our everyday wardrobes. These fashionable tastemakers are forever in our minds and on our screens, ever present in the collective consciousness of fashion history. They live on and they never die – part of the magical, never-ending fantasy behind icons that are purely fictional. Our style story starts here, with the characters who dared viewers at home to dream and dress differently.

CARRIE BRADSHAW

Who could forget the oddball combinations of tutus, tube tops, big belts, brooches and polka dots that Carrie Bradshaw (Sarah Jessica Parker) wore in HBO's *Sex and the City*? Hands down, Bradshaw is one of the most influential New York fashion characters of all time.

Her style, deeply saturated in Y2K designers, from Vivienne Westwood to Moschino and Jean Paul Gaultier, is anchored with poppy accessories, like Manolo Blahnik Mary Janes and playful pearls, huge rosettes and newsprint Dior Galliano dresses or sequin Fendi Baguette bags. All of this is combined with vintage finds for a unique high-low look. Case in point? The $5 tutu paired with the palest pink sheer tank top and leopard-print Jimmy Choos in the show's famous opening credits.

Sex and the City originally aired from 1998 to 2004, and at the time there had never been a TV character with such a strong tie to designer fashion. Bradshaw, a New York writer who was often seen walking the sidewalks, hailing cabs and hanging out in trendy restaurants, actively shopped and celebrated high-end fashion by name. It was a decadent fantasy that a newspaper columnist could afford that much high fashion. Bradshaw also visited the legendary *Vogue* fashion closet, and the series showcased fashion phenomena in New York in a way never before seen on TV. In one scene, Bradshaw's Manolo Blahniks disappear from a house party where she begrudgingly has to remove her shoes at the host's request. In another, she gets mugged and the assailant demands her shoes (Manolos, again) by name. Her friends, Miranda Hobbes, Samantha

Opposite: Carrie Bradshaw of *Sex and the City* is one of New York's most famous fictional style icons, well known for bold fashion choices, like the white tutu worn in the opening credits of the show.

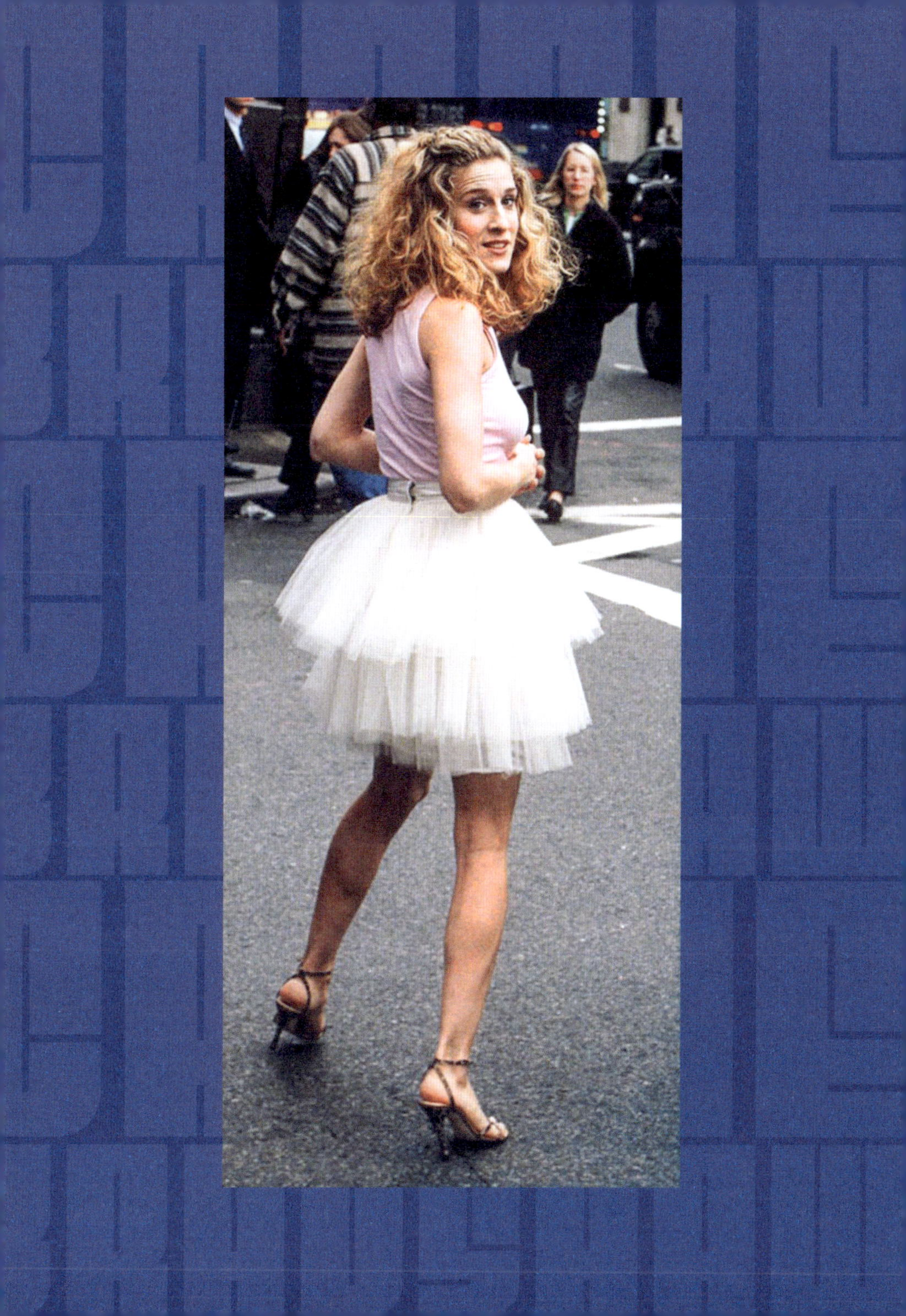

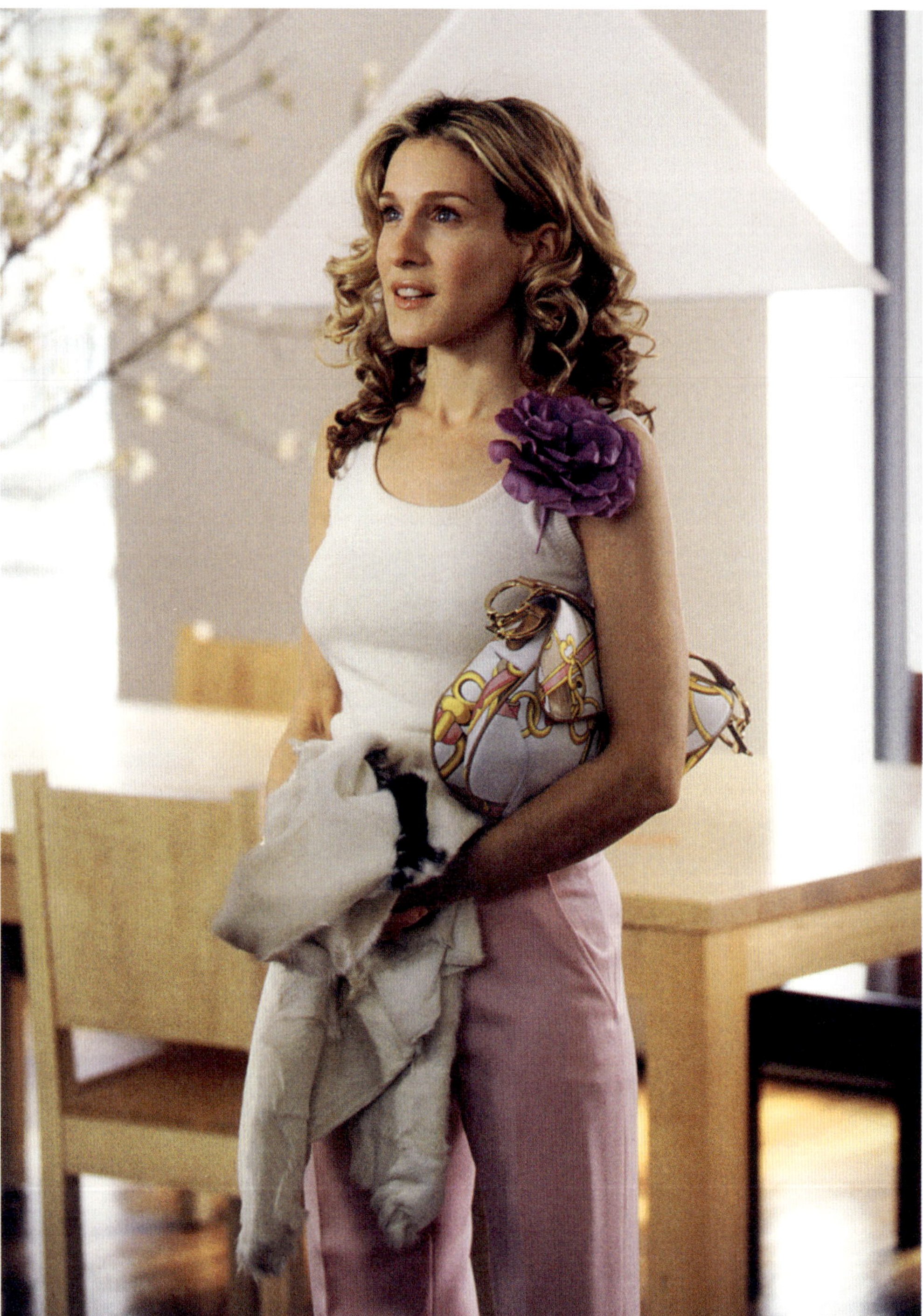

Jones and Charlotte York, also represent different kinds of New York archetypes and styles in the show, from corporate androgyny to Park Avenue Princess. However, Bradshaw's unique style has been the most loved, hated and imitated, all at once.

True to the most fashionable New Yorkers' narratives, Bradshaw took risks and dressed unconventionally. She also – groundbreakingly – played with high and low trends seen in the city at the time, from her most popular designer handbags to the show's appropriated nameplate logo necklaces that were spotted around the necks of everyday New Yorkers. Stylist Patricia Field was key to developing the style on screen. As a native New Yorker and style icon of the city herself, she often wears loud colours and sports a mane of vivid scarlet-red hair. "New York was my palette, but I never really made a conscious connection between the city and the wardrobe as such," she told *Vogue*. Carrie Bradshaw and her friends' fashion legacies live on in the later *Sex and the City* movies and the revival sequel, *And Just Like That*.

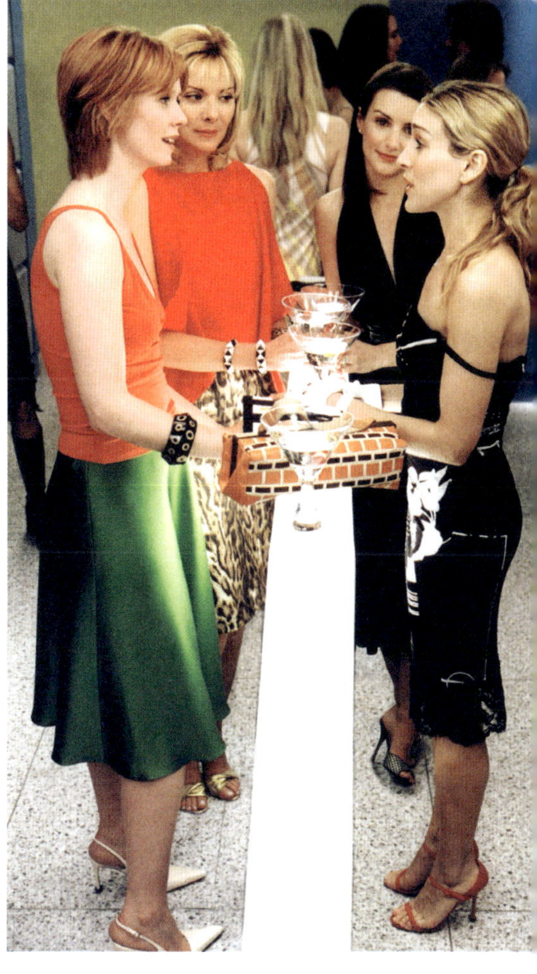

Opposite: In *Sex and the City*, Carrie Bradshaw popularized bold designer fashion, particularly designer handbags like Dior Saddles (as seen opposite) along with Fendi Baguettes.

Above: Carrie Bradshaw and her group of friends each represented a different sort of New York archetype, but all of them had a love for designer fashion and trends.

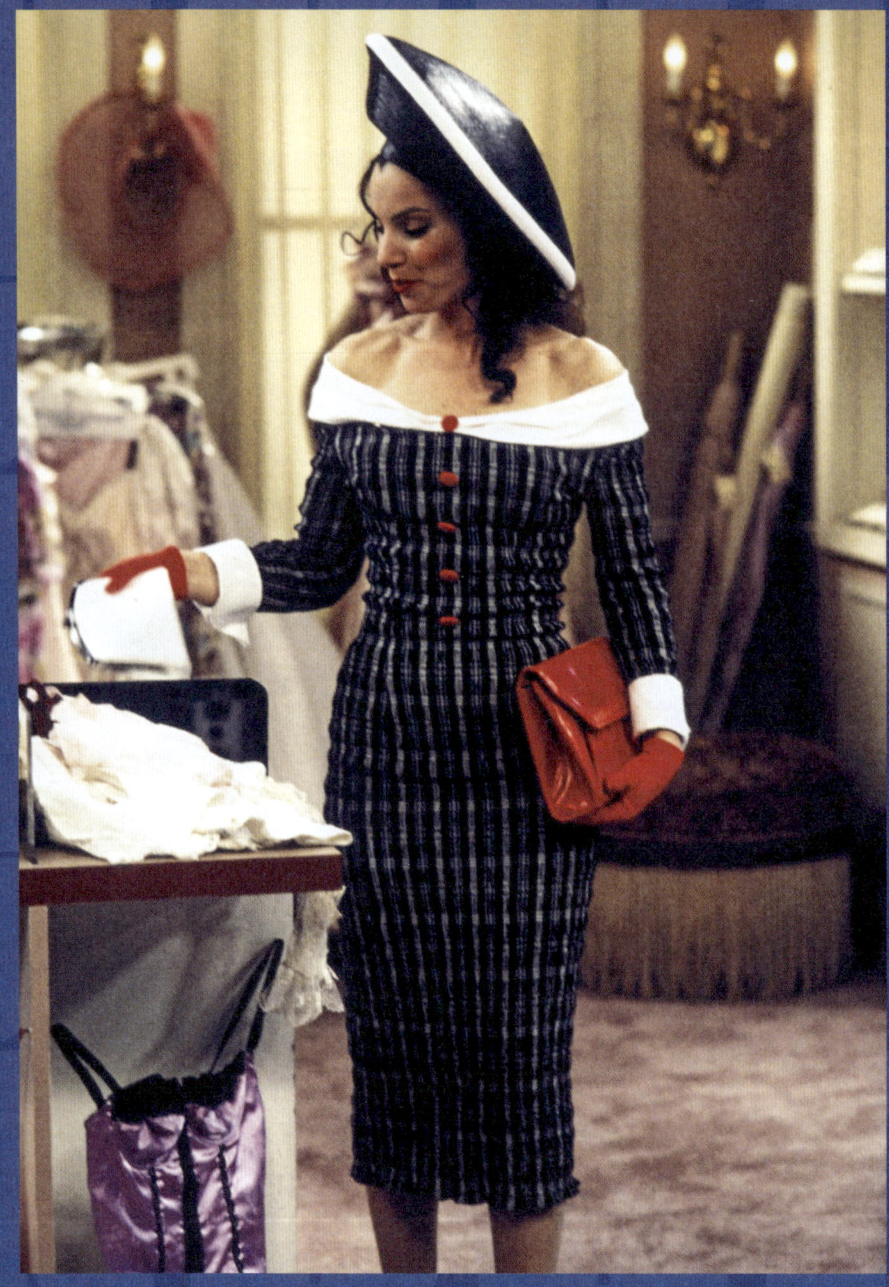

FRAN DRESCHER

Fans of Carrie Bradshaw and *SATC* can't deny the influence of one very important New York style icon who came before it all: Fran Drescher of *The Nanny* (1993–99).

The pink newsprint pantsuit she wore pre-dates Carrie's iconic Dior moment. And even though the show didn't delve as deep into designer name-dropping dialogue the way *SATC* did, *The Nanny* was pure fashion fantasy in a way that hadn't been seen before – and, on a so-called "flashy girl from Flushing", Queens, no less. Fashionista Fran becomes the nanny of three children uptown and doesn't compromise her loud, maximalist, over-the-top style. She wore Dolce & Gabbana, Bob Mackie, Versace, Todd Oldham and Anna Sui. She loved bold Moschino polka-dot skirt suits and the iconic, heart-shaped bag from the brand, wore copious amounts of leopard print, black-and-white chequerboard mini-skirts, fabulous fluffy coats, ample crop tops and iconic, impactful accessories. Think gold chain belts, cloth headbands and, always, big, big hair. She was unafraid of bold colours, mixed prints or layering and her dynamic, loud aesthetic makes the contrast between her and the uptown family she nannied for even more interesting. Costume designer Brenda Cooper won an Emmy for her work on the show. The pieces that Drescher wore have been highly documented by fans on social media, and have also become incredibly collectible.

Opposite: Fran Fine of *The Nanny* fame was famously one of New York fashion's most expressive characters, wearing a uniform of funky suits, bold hats, gloves and fun accessories.

FASHION FAN GIRLS

GOSSIP GIRL

In the same vein as Fran Drescher, the New York cast of *Gossip Girl* (2007–2012) had an epic influence on an entire generation of fashion lovers. Like *Sex and the City*, these characters dominated the streets of New York and their outfits came directly from the real world of the upper echelons of New York society.

Unsurprisingly, the stylist of the series, Eric Daman, worked on *Sex and the City* as assistant to the highly influential Patricia Field. Daman transformed the cast of *Gossip Girl* characters into archetypes of young, fashionable New Yorkers the likes of which the TV-watching general public had never ever seen before.

In the *Gossip Girl* universe, viewers saw the good, the bad and the ugly side of the exclusive Upper East Side and all the style that went with it. There was Blair Waldorf, the ultra-girly, feminine prepster with a love of A-line dresses, headbands, pearls, berets and floaty little Old Hollywood dresses with heels and gloves. And then there was Serena van der Woodsen, the It-girl bohemian icon who wore jeans, ties, mini-skirts, sequin blazers and printed silk dresses. The two served as sartorial opposites that lit up the screen and presented a play-by-play of top-tier personal style as imagined through the lens of New York private high schoolers. Every character in the original *Gossip Girl* series (a revival series debuted in 2021) had style. Jenny Humphrey served as the younger, rock 'n' roll, emo-fuelled It-girl who went through style phases, but eventually gained her own toughened-up, high-fashion grunge aesthetic and ended up going to the city's premier fashion school, Parsons.

Opposite: *Gossip Girl*'s Blair and Serena defined an entire generation of It-girl fashion through the lens of Manhattan's elite private school cool girls during the mid-2000s.

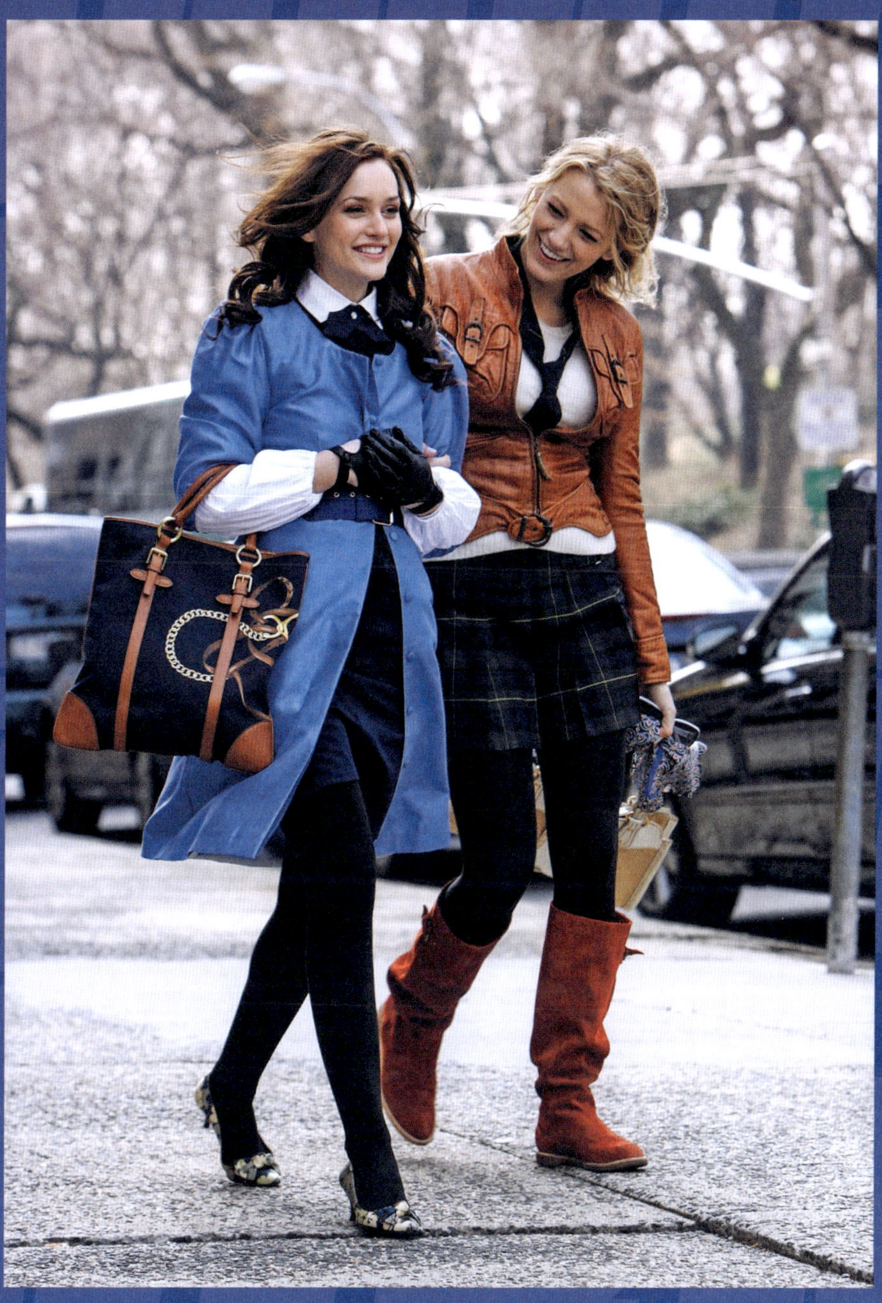

The original *Gossip Girl* was perhaps the first time an entire generation was exposed to high fashion beyond the pages of a magazine. In a time when social media didn't yet exist in the way it does today, here was New York style in all its glory, from the preppy get-ups of the Upper East Siders to the hipster-inspired, Brooklynite style of the Humphreys. "New York style and being a New Yorker for 25-plus years definitely influenced how the cast dressed and the look of the girls," Daman, who would camp outside the private schools of the Upper East Side to get ideas, once told me for an interview with *Town & Country*. "It made sense to use a lot of high-end labels and mix in downtown designers. The essence of New York fashion DNA was essential in creating those characters." Much like *Sex and the City*, the characters became deeply associated with certain brands. Think Jennifer Behr headbands, Roger Vivier heels, Marc Jacobs dresses.

Take fashion designer Anna Sui, for example (yet another New York style icon herself), who first met Daman in the 1990s when he modelled for some of her runway shows. Sui released a *Gossip Girl*-inspired collaboration with mass retailer, Target, in 2009. "I love the fact that it was encouraging people to dress up again," she says. "Instead of being casual, they were wearing dresses with shoes and headbands, and it was just encouraging people to really put a lot more effort into their outfits. I thought that was really, really, really such a great thing for fashion. Instead of going so casual and wearing denim, they were wearing dresses and coats and jackets and party dresses."

Even decades later, there has been no other show quite like *Gossip Girl* that showcased private school personal style in quite the same way. Most of all, both Blair and Serena remain as their own kind of archetypes. The clothing that they wore – whether it was a fun, beaded Marc Jacobs top or a Hervé Léger bandage dress – defined generations of style. Some of the looks worn by the OG *Gossip Girl* characters have become incredibly collectible, as documented by social media fans and serious collectors alike.

Opposite: The cast of *Gossip Girl* gave viewers at home a taste of the New York style icon palette. We saw the preps, the jocks, the hipsters, the alternative girls and more re-envisioned as New York fashion icons.

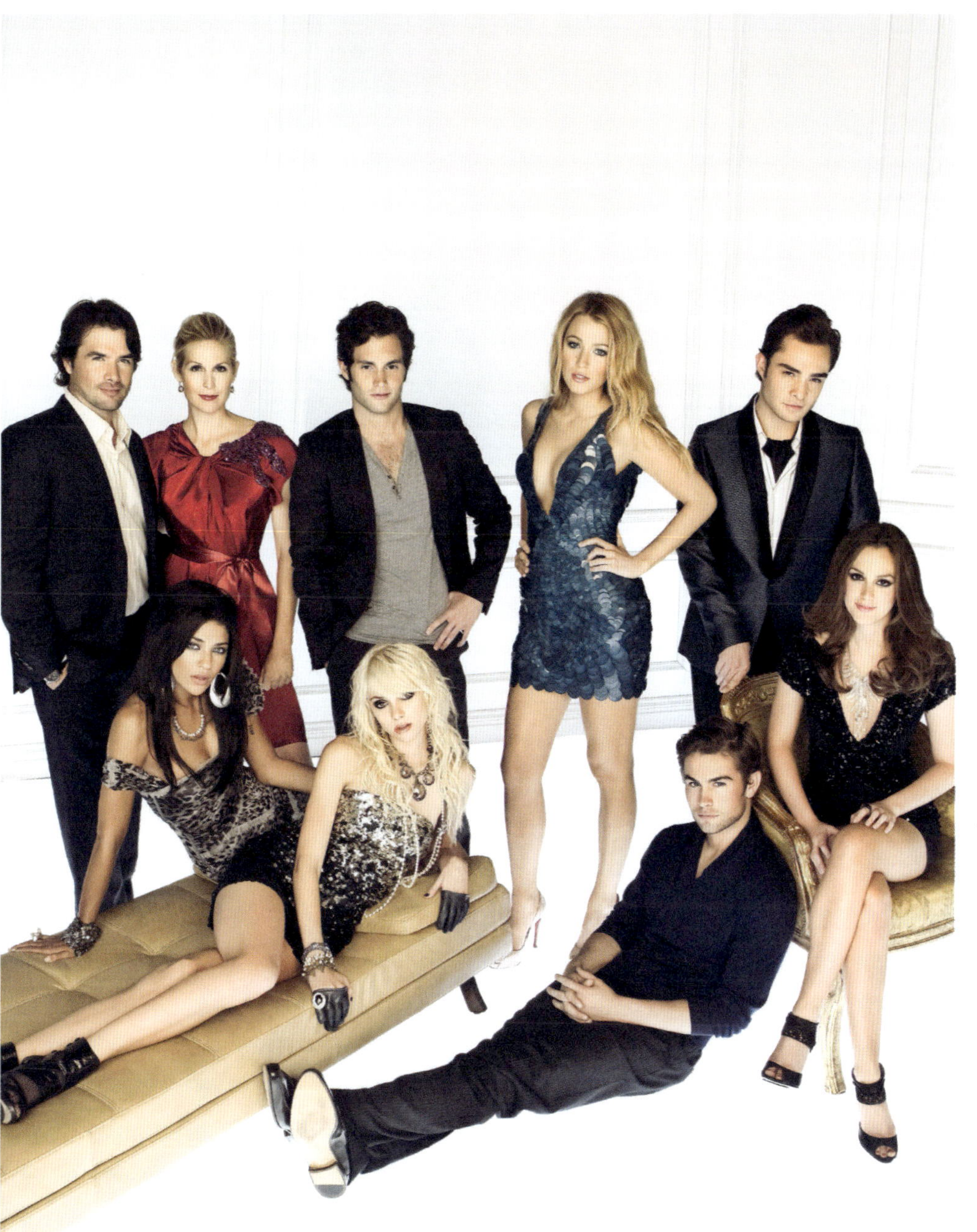

HOLLY GOLIGHTLY

If New York style had to be distilled down to a single scene, one might immediately think of the opening scene of *Breakfast at Tiffany's* (1961).

"Moon River" plays softly as a yellow taxicab speeds down a lonely Fifth Avenue. Out comes Audrey Hepburn as Holly Golightly, wearing a floor-length black gown, crystal tiara, opera-length gloves, sunglasses and stacks of pearls. She stares forlornly into the window of Tiffany's, while eating her croissant and sipping from her paper coffee cup. The scene helped immortalize the glamour and isolation of New York, and locked in the little black dress as a style signifier of the city. Hubert de Givenchy designed the costumes, while other pieces were provided by the Paramount wardrobe department, supervised by legendary costume designer Edith Head. Movies like *Breakfast at Tiffany's* were visions of a New York fashion fantasy that changed the definition of what style in the city was.

The little black dress here doesn't just define New York style. It also echoes an entire era of fashion history. Just a few years earlier, Hubert de Givenchy met Audrey Hepburn, and thus began their lifelong friendship as collaborators and muses. Givenchy had previously dressed Jacqueline Kennedy, the Duchess of Windsor and Grace Kelly in refined, elegant and ladylike attire. He took his aesthetic a step further with Hepburn, solidifying the never-ending quest for the perfect silhouette and the ideal fabric. "Audrey was someone who knew perfectly how to dress, and knew perfectly what she should wear," Givenchy told the journalist Dana Thomas. "What counted was her eyes, her face and her silhouette. We refined, purified, cleared away for her face. We had to, as I would say, surround Audrey. The results were extraordinary because her face and her style became my style."

Opposite: Perhaps there is no other fictional New York fashion icon as well known as Holly Golightly, with her little black dress and pearls.

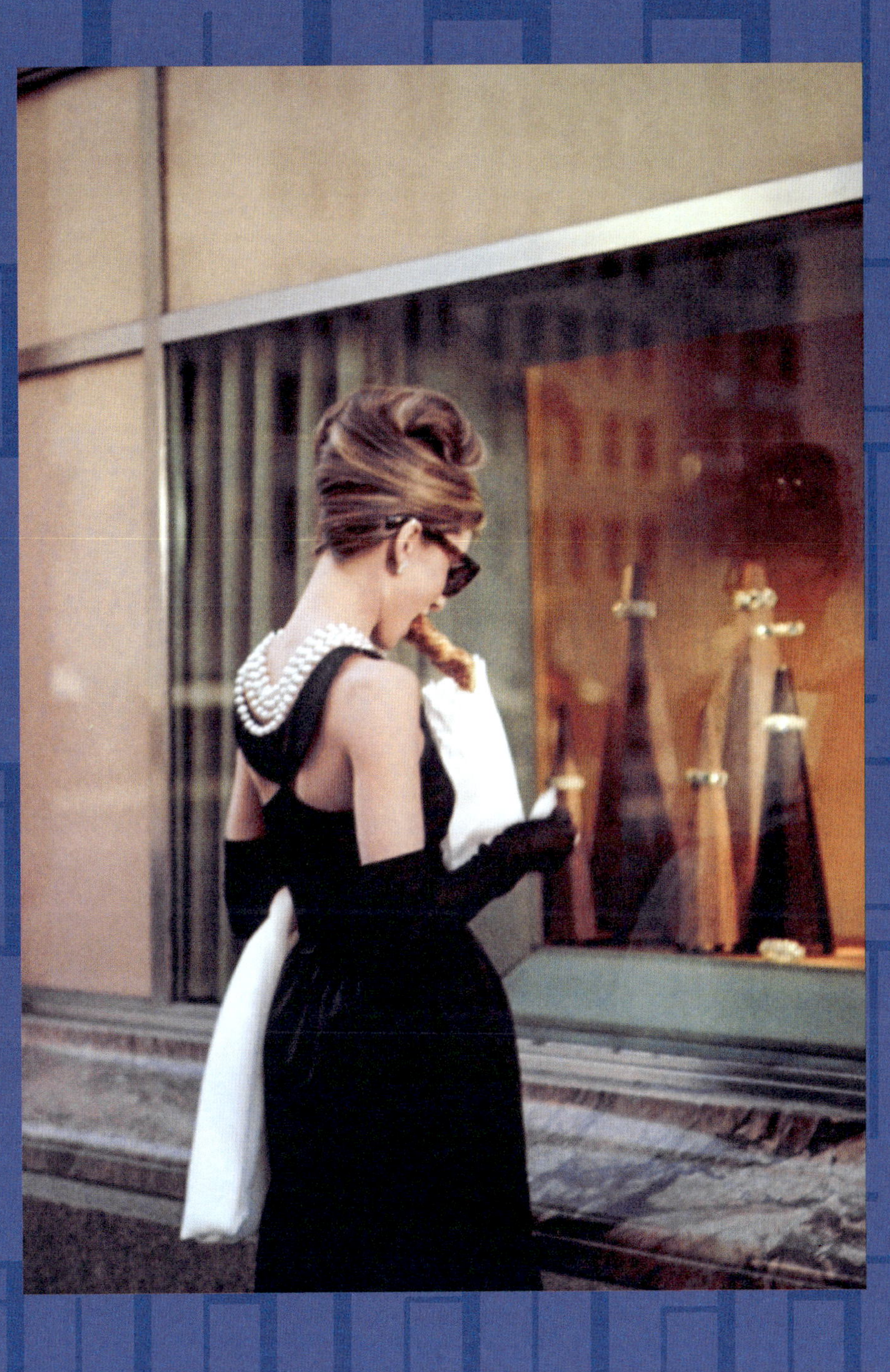

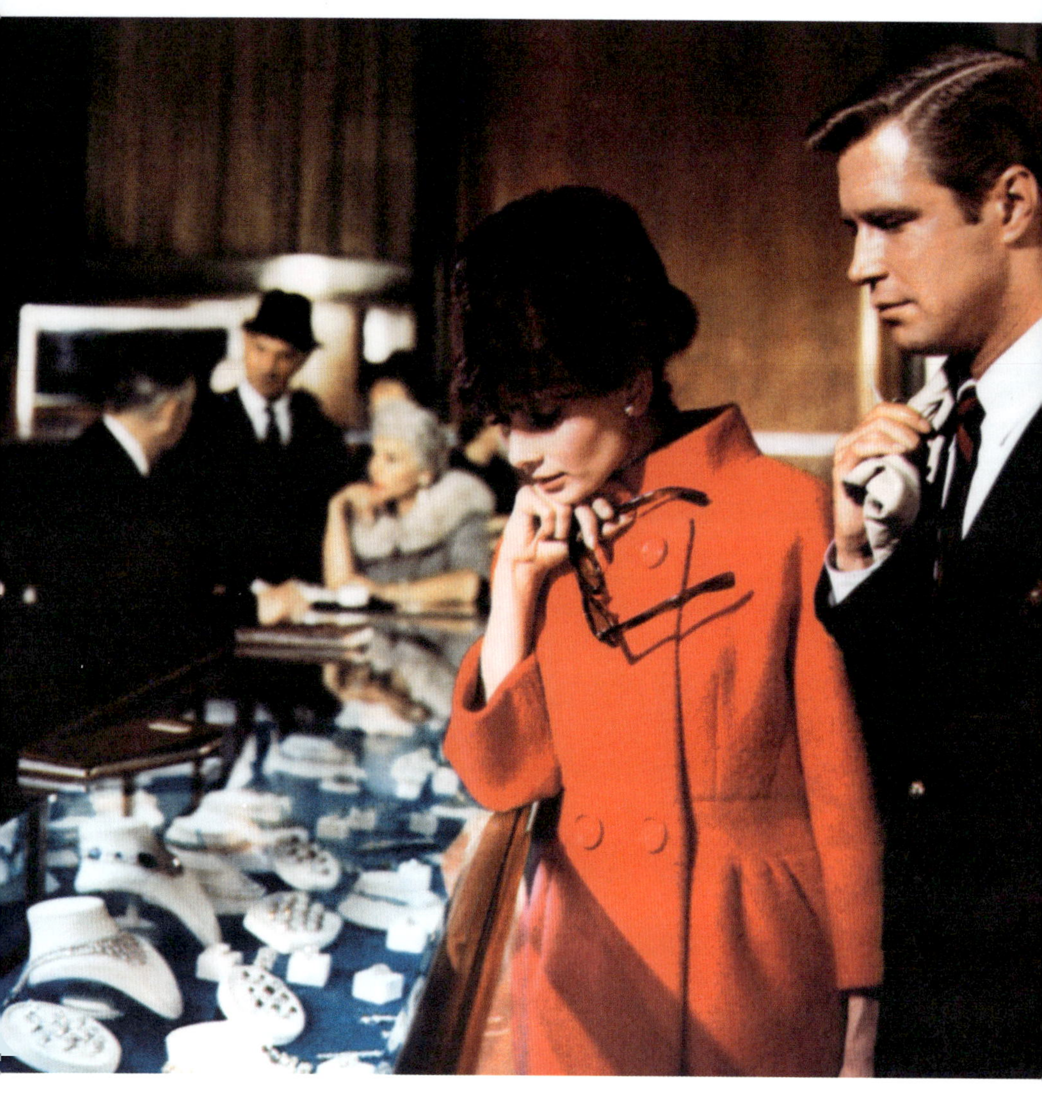

Above: In the film *Breakfast at Tiffany's*, Audrey Hepburn's character Holly Golightly wears a classic, feminine wardrobe with a New York twist. Accessories pop and silhouettes have dramatic cuts.

Opposite: Hubert de Givenchy designed the costumes for *Breakfast at Tiffany's* and it's easy to see his soft yet streamlined aesthetic in everything Holly wears.

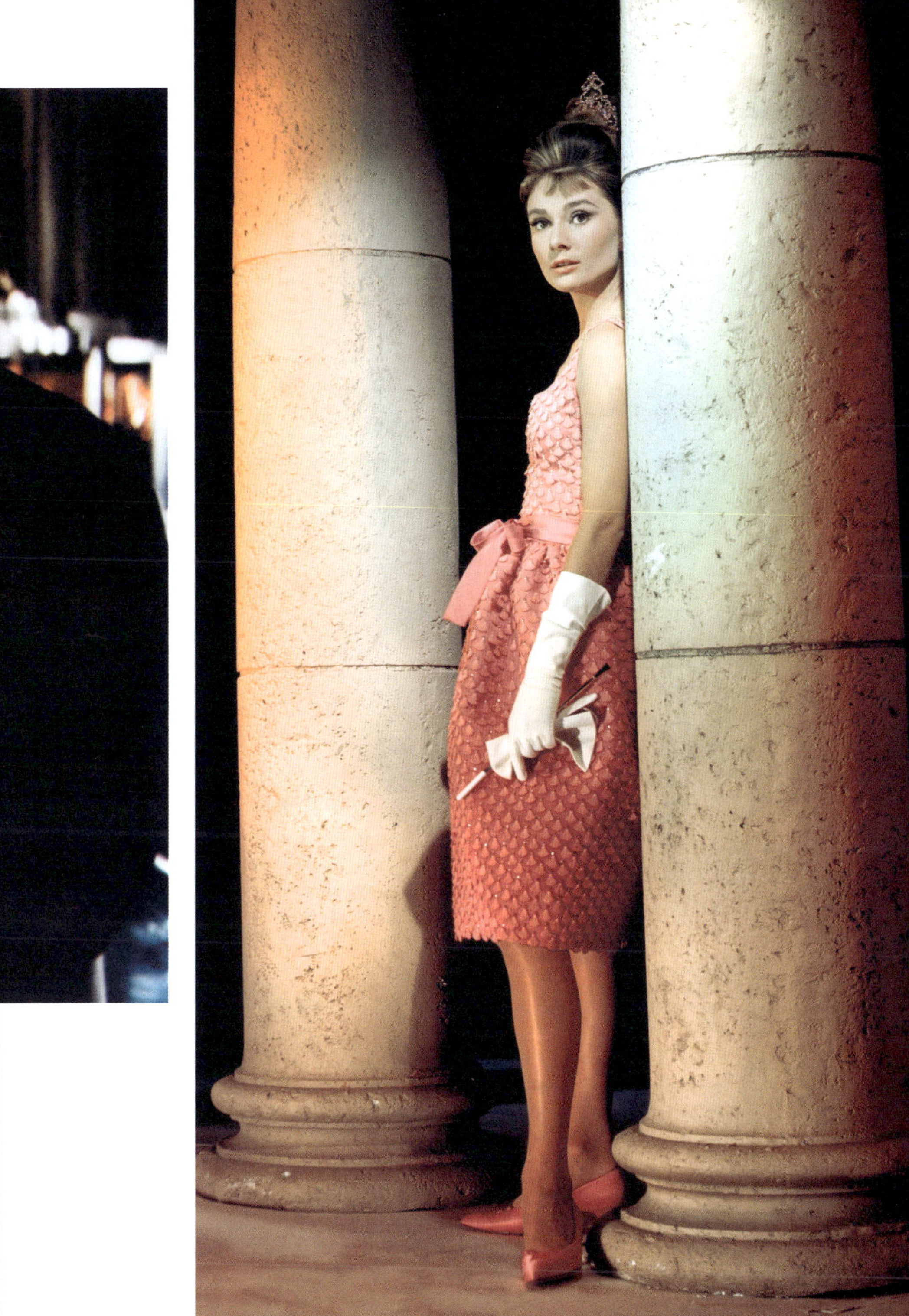

THE FASHION INDUSTRY ON SCREEN

Another prime example of defining style icons on screen is *The Devil Wears Prada* (2006). Based on the novel by Lauren Weisberger, the movie follows Andrea Sachs (Anne Hathaway), who gets a job as an assistant working under the notoriously tough fashion magazine editor-in-chief, Miranda Priestly (Meryl Streep) in New York.

Several scenes live on in fashion history – most notably when Sachs's look is transformed by art director Nigel (Stanley Tucci). He takes away her fuzzy, cable-knit sweaters and mid-length skirts and delivers her to glory with stacks of gold chains, a tailored Chanel blazer and thigh-high Chanel boots.

The Devil Wears Prada takes a cue from a legacy of campy, dramatized films about the fashion industry in New York. *Funny Face* (1957) is a good example. Taking place between New York and Paris, the film follows Audrey Hepburn and Fred Astaire on wild adventures in the context of a top-tier fashion magazine. It has been rumoured that Maggie Prescott, the fictionalized editor-in-chief of the made-up *Quality* magazine, was based on New York fashion icon and editor Diana Vreeland. The film brought real-life heavy hitters of the 1950s fashion industry to the cast and production, such as noted photographer Richard Avedon, who designed the pop art visual opening credits, and top supermodel of the time, Dovima, who posed in a scene. Other models, Suzy Parker and Sunny Harnett, have dancing cameos. Likewise, in the campy horror thriller, *The Eyes of Laura Mars* (1978), Faye Dunaway stars as a glam New York City photographer who specializes in controversial imagery, decked in billowy blouses, fur-trimmed coats, heeled boots and big hair.

Opposite: In *The Devil Wears Prada*, Andy Sachs (Anne Hathaway) solidified herself as a forever fashion icon in the fictional world of New York magazines when she stepped out in runway Chanel.

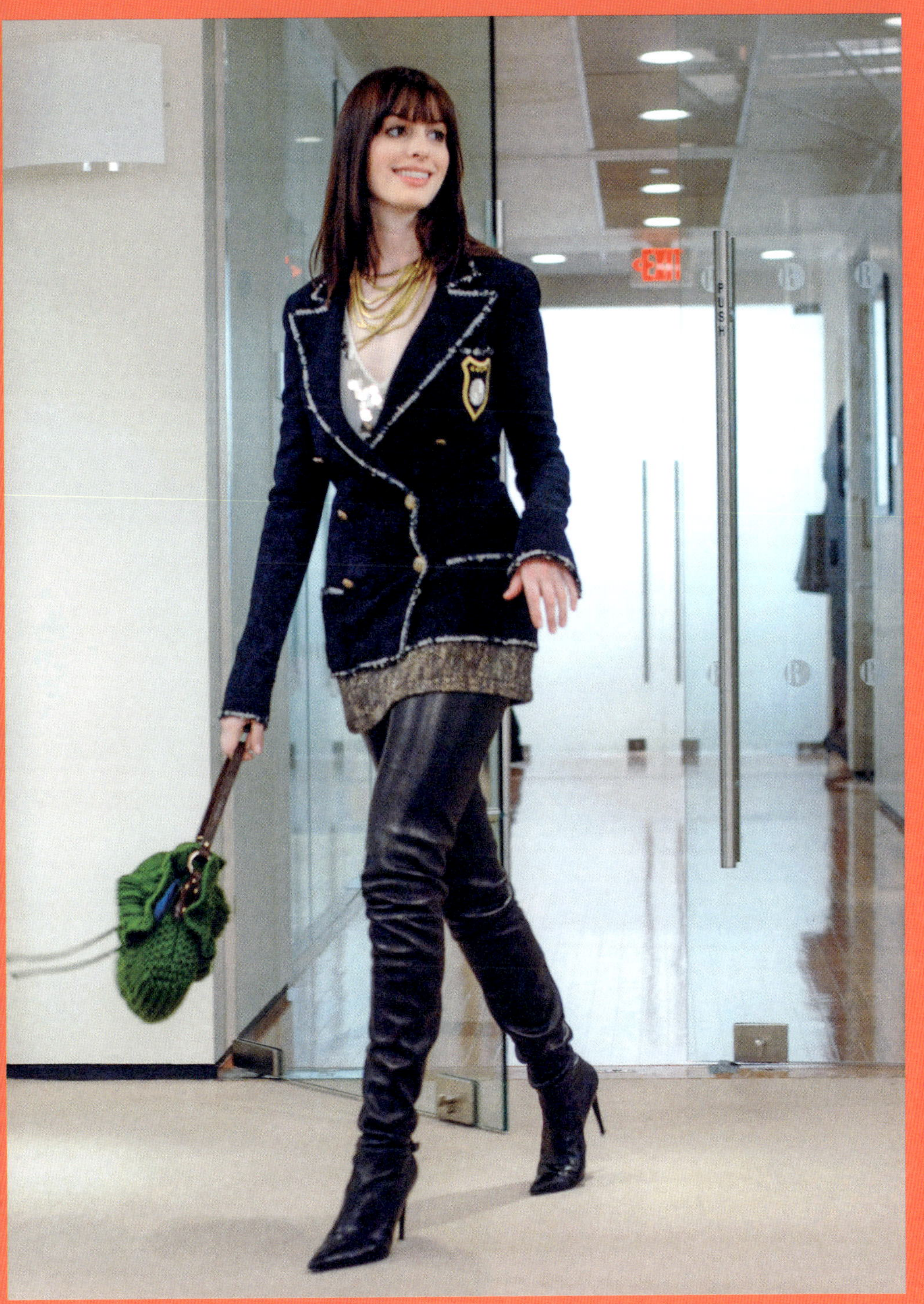
PUSH

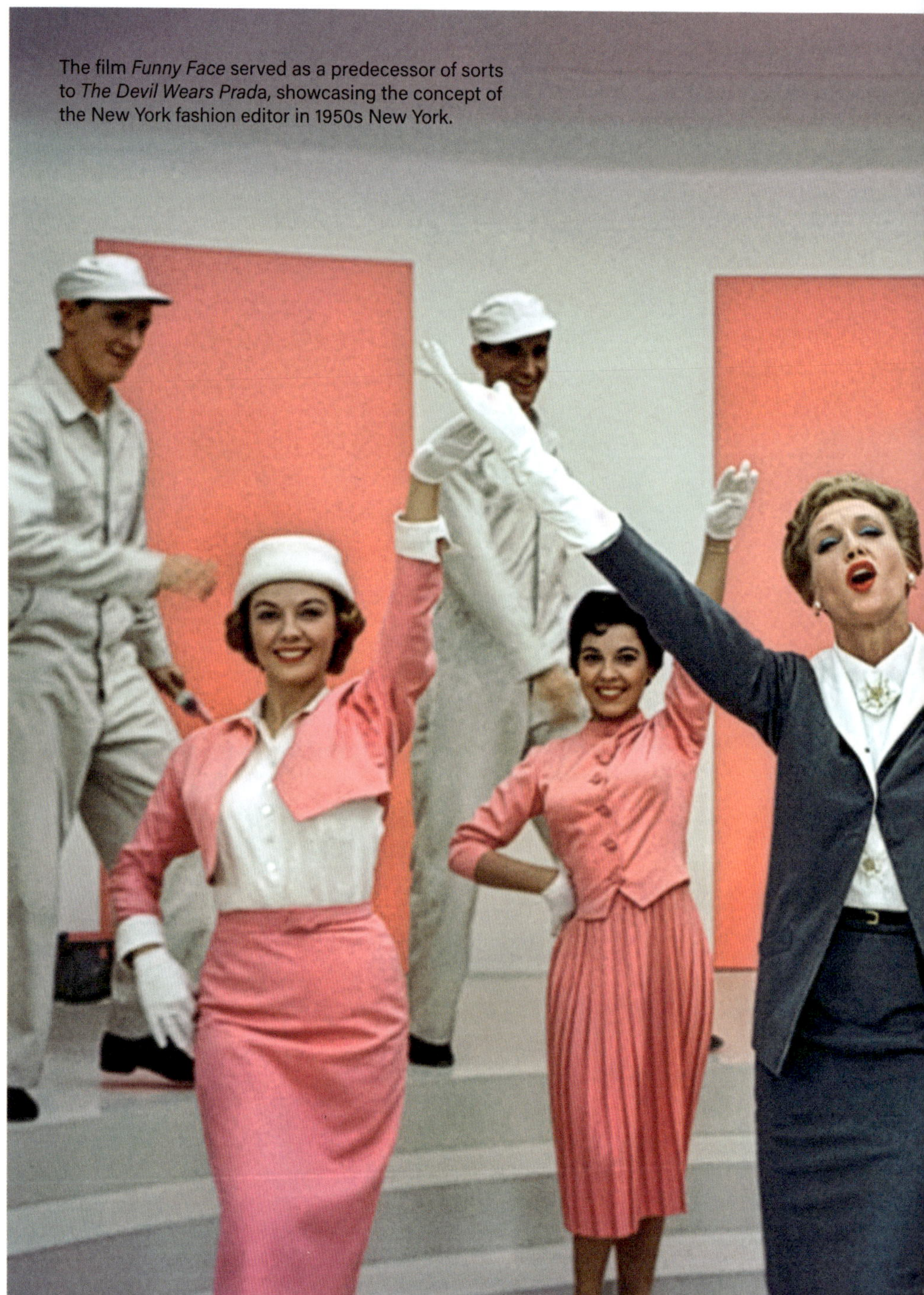

The film *Funny Face* served as a predecessor of sorts to *The Devil Wears Prada*, showcasing the concept of the New York fashion editor in 1950s New York.

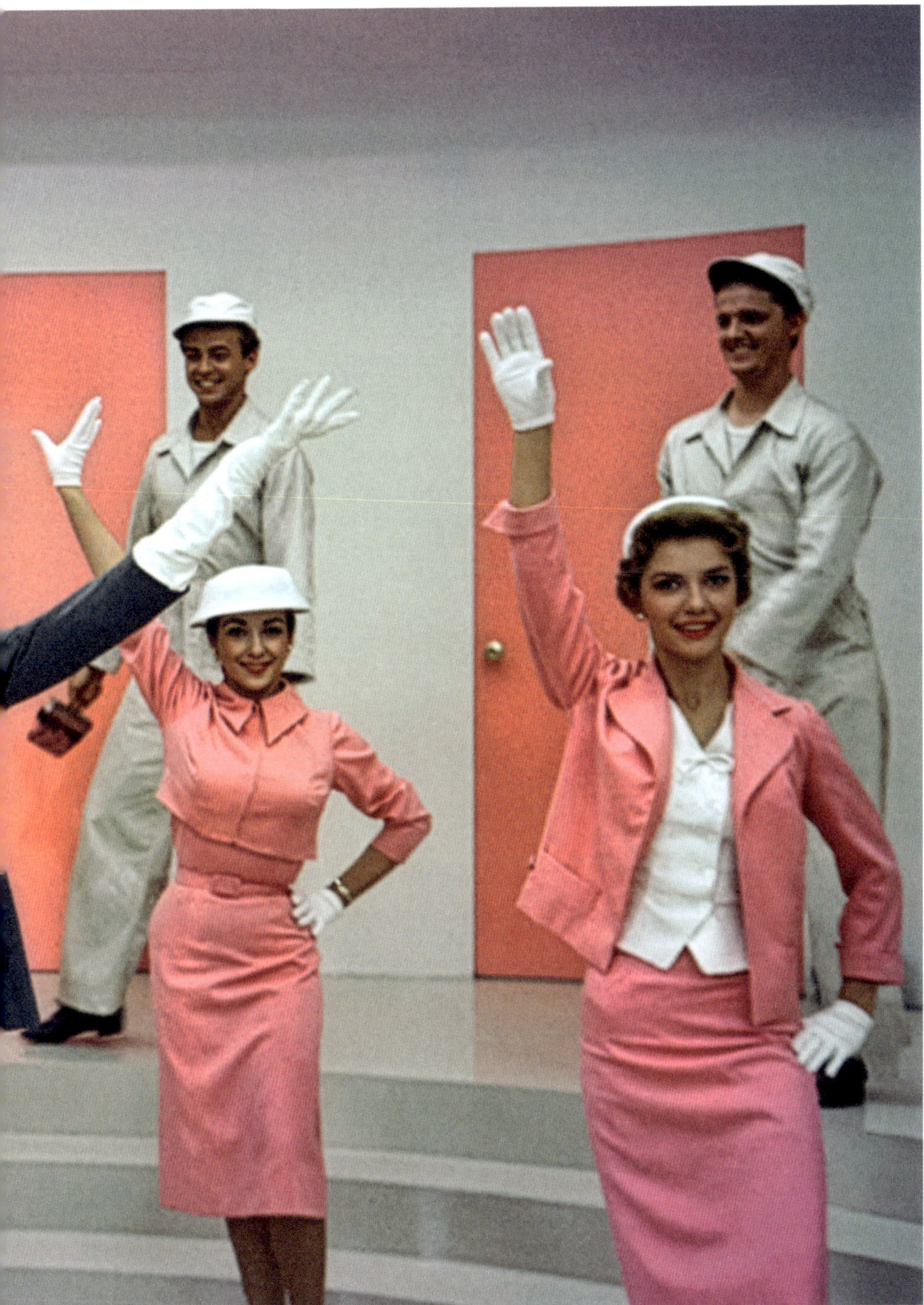

REAL LIFE TO SCREEN ICONS

DIANE KEATON AS ANNIE HALL

Certain New York-centric films created style icons based on real-life characters. Like *Annie Hall*. The 1977 film is set in New York City and stars the late Diane Keaton in the eponymous role written just for her, with a personal style ethos that was directly taken from the way she dressed in real life.

Keaton was known for wearing lots of menswear and androgynous pieces, as icons of the past such as Katharine Hepburn once did. In the film, she wore much of her own clothing, with a helping hand from designer Ralph Lauren and costume stylist Ruth Morley. She donned hats, ties, tailored vests, button-downs, wide-leg trousers and more. She has said that in the 1970s she was finding herself, her career and her personal style slowly. So, it's interesting that her character Annie Hall is a real-life reflection of herself, now canonized in cinematic history. Later in her career, she favoured suits, cross necklaces, pocket squares, hats and thick-rimmed glasses.

But most importantly, in Annie Hall, Keaton took inspiration from the real women she saw in the SoHo neighbourhood of New York in the 1970s. Back then, pre-gentrification, the area was filled with artists and outsiders who did their own thing. "I look back on *Annie Hall* and can't talk about that movie without talking about the fashion, it was everything to me," she once said. "I loved being able to dress like myself. My muses were the women of New York City who were walking the streets of SoHo in baggy trousers and a blazer. I was layering pieces."

Opposite: *Annie Hall* was groundbreaking because the aesthetic of the character was lifted from real-life icon Diane Keaton who, at the time, took inspiration from style setters in 1970s SoHo.

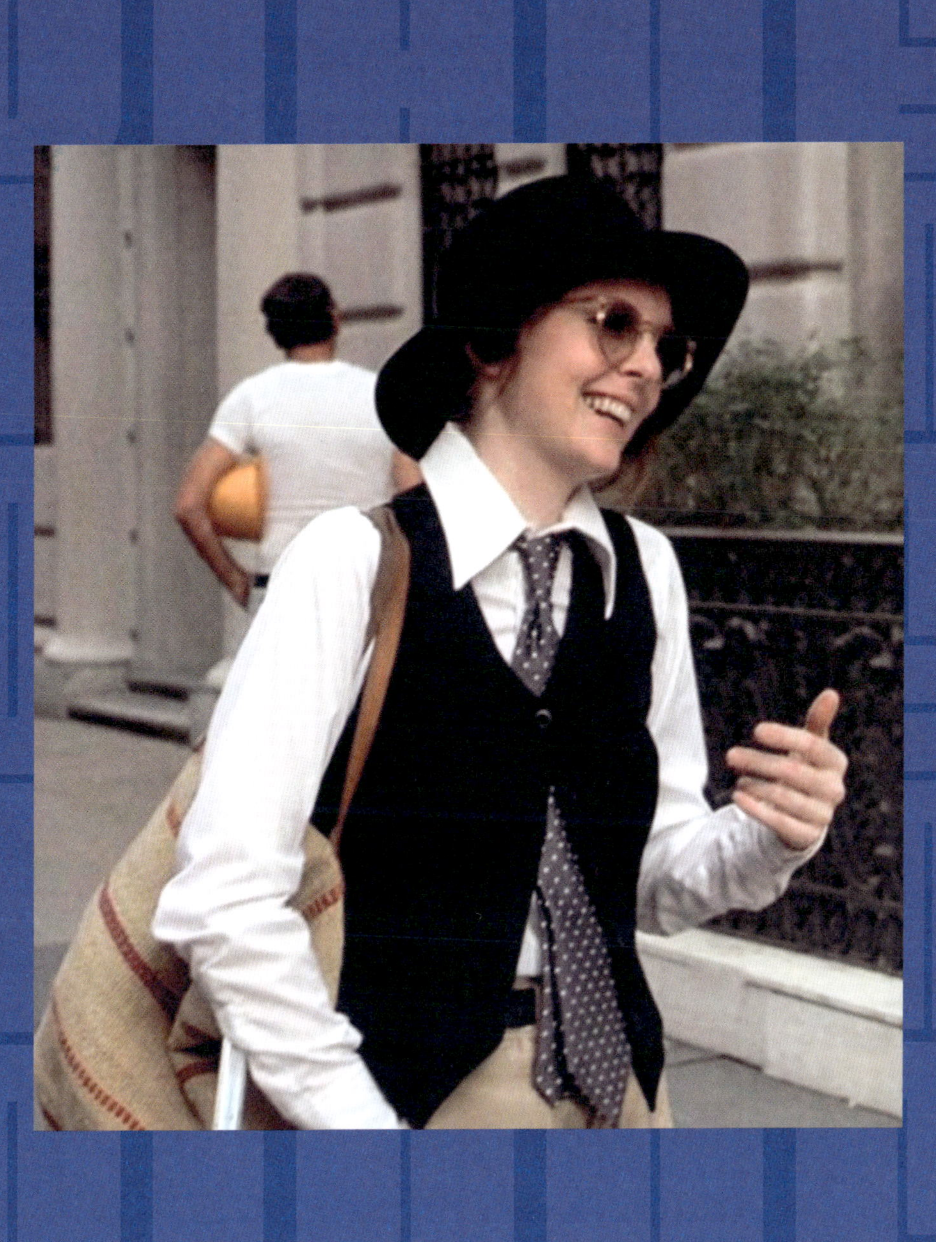

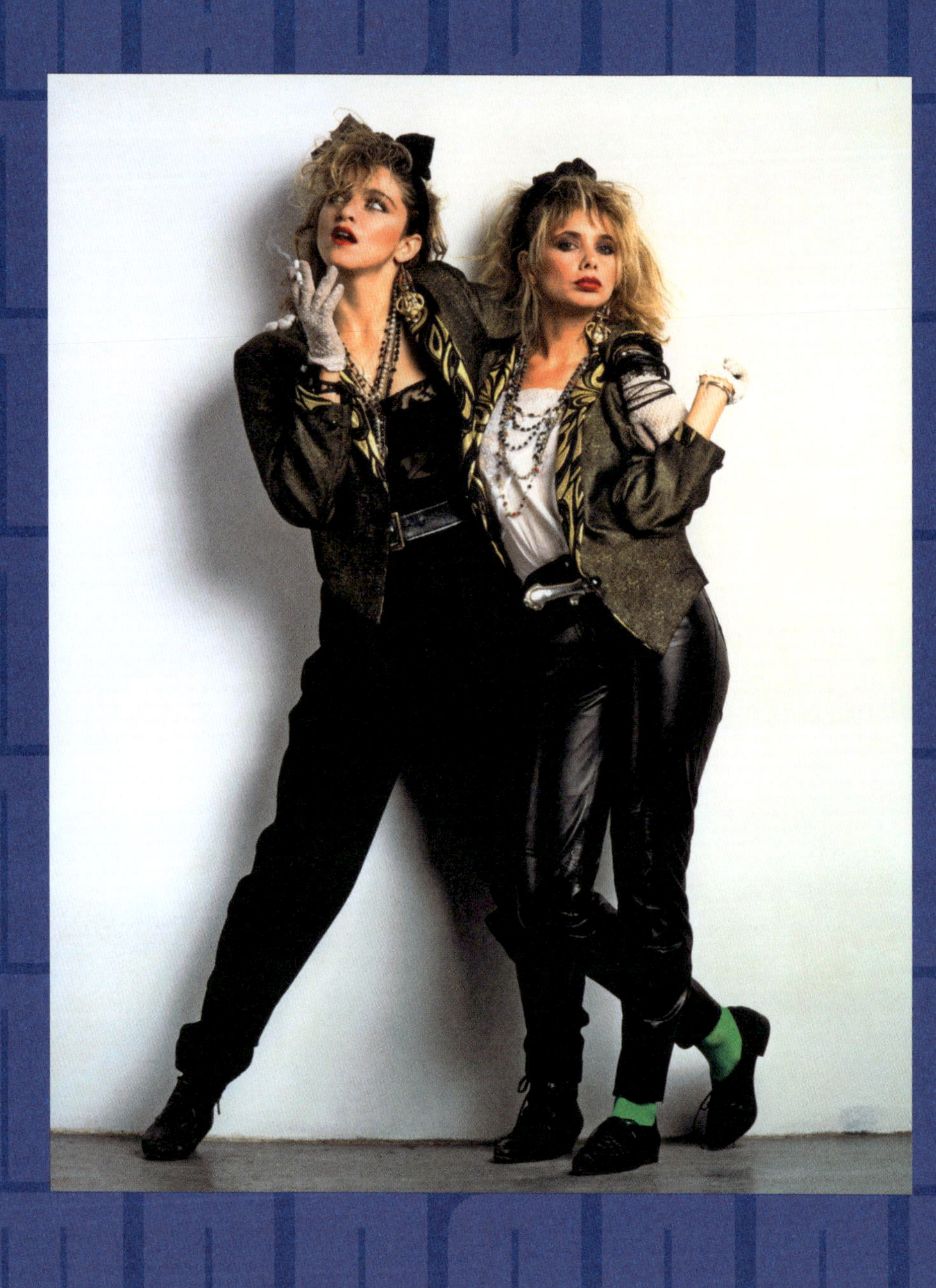

MADONNA AS SUSAN

In *Desperately Seeking Susan* (1985) honorary New York fashion icon Madonna essentially plays herself at the height of her fame. Much like Annie Hall, Madonna's style on screen is decidedly similar to the looks she lives in real life: tonnes of chunky jewellery, underwear as outerwear, black lace and structured, experimental shapes.

In the film, Rosanna Arquette stars as a bored housewife (Roberta) who meets Madonna (Susan) through a newspaper's personal ads.

Costume and production designer Santo Loquasto pulled pieces from his own mother's wardrobe to get Madonna's eccentric, downtown look. The star herself dropped out of college and came to the city to start her career with $35 in her pocket. *Desperately Seeking Susan* is shot in Manhattan, including Chelsea, Battery Park and East Village. The underlying theme? Transformation and reinvention, which Madonna herself has used time and time again in her own career and her mind-blowing, boundary-breaking fashion choices that literally changed history.

The film didn't just cement Madonna as a style icon: it introduced her fashion lexicon to the masses in a new way, with New York as the backdrop. Back then, she didn't have any acting experience and was chosen as a way to add authenticity to the film. Inspiration was also pulled from her own real-life style at the time. Think lace tights, boxer shorts, huge earrings, even bigger bows, studded boots, mesh, pearls, crop tops and crosses! "We didn't want actors putting on costumes and playing downtown," director Susan Seidelman told the *New York Times*.

Opposite: Madonna is a fashion icon through and through, but in *Desperately Seeking Susan*, she brings an unexpected dose of downtown New York to her look.

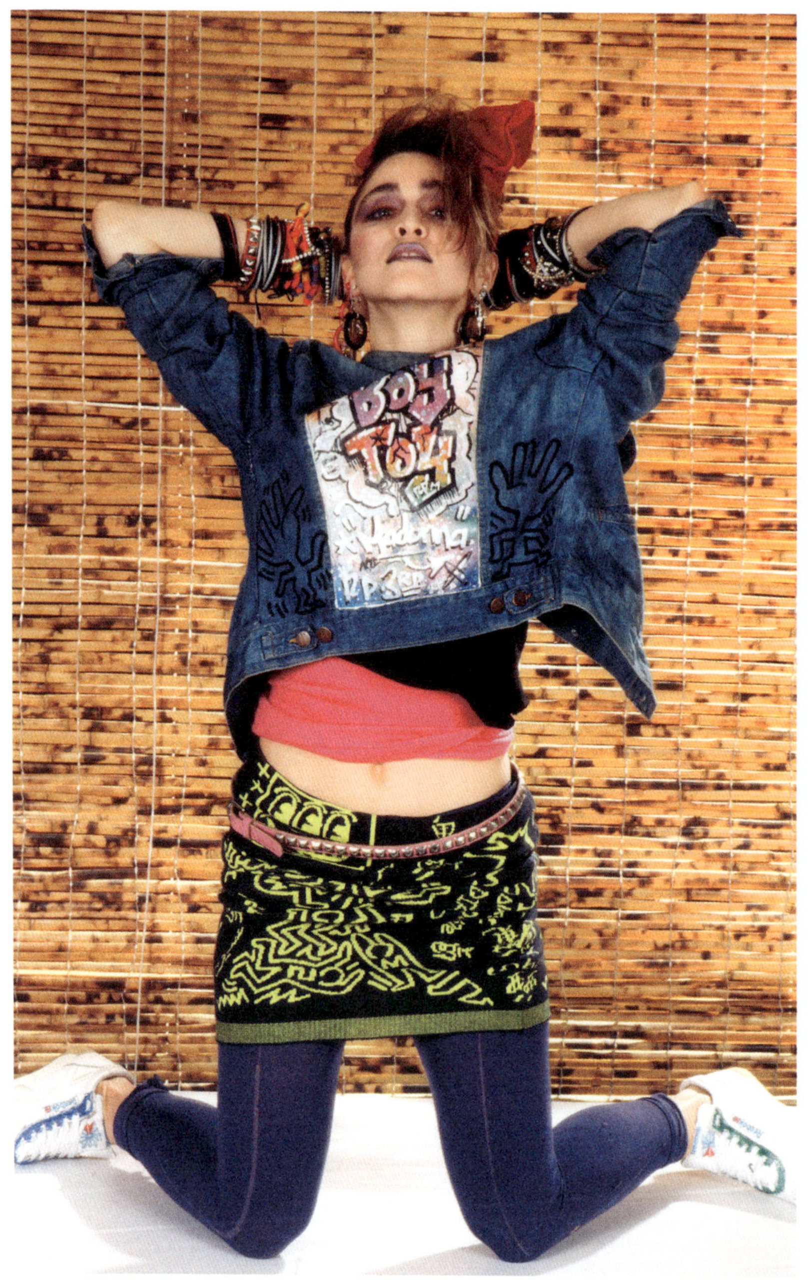
BOY TOY

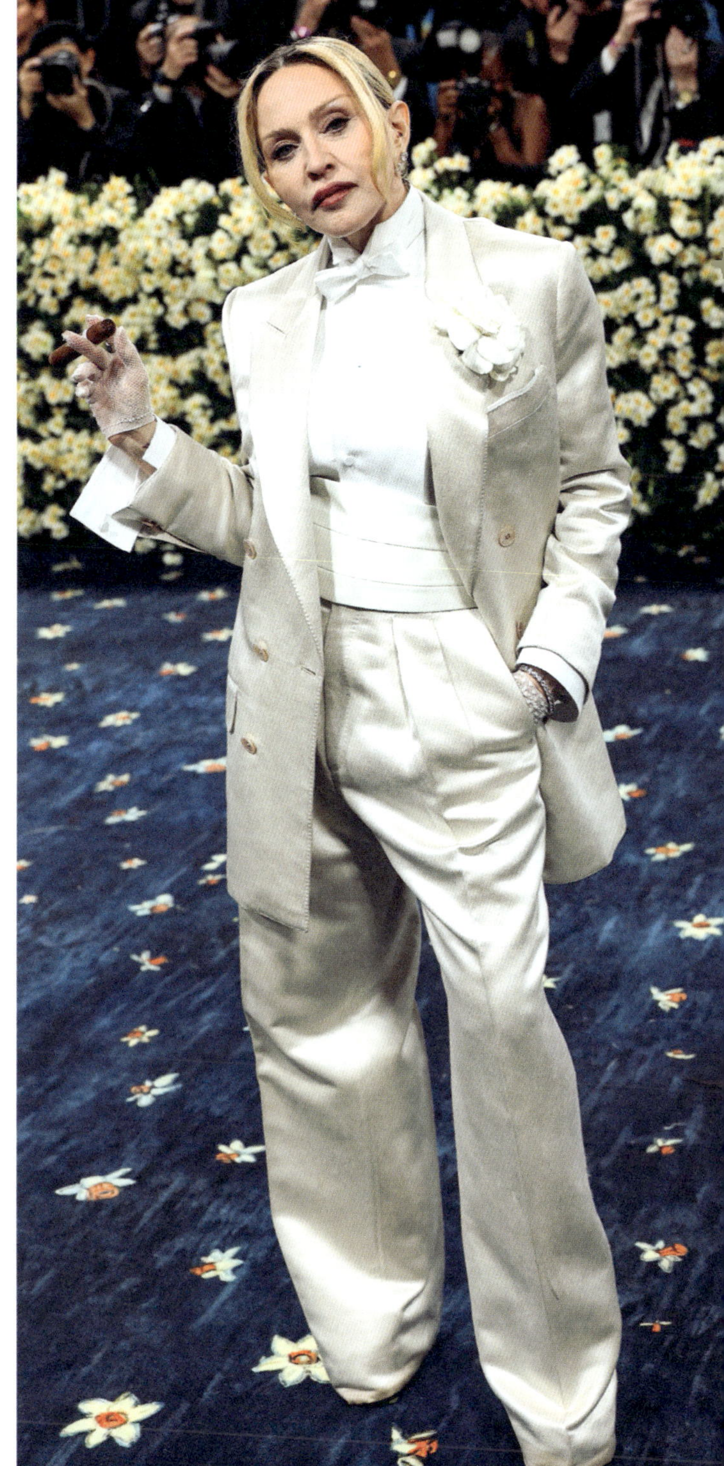

Opposite: In the 1980s, when Madonna was solidifying her style, she wore lots of denim, bold neon colours and plenty of jewellery all piled on.

Right: Madonna continues to break boundaries in New York and elsewhere. For the 2025 Met Gala, she wore a tailored Tom Ford suit, which was designed by Haider Ackermann.

REAL LIFE TO SCREEN ICONS

MARILYN MONROE AS THE GIRL

Perhaps one of the most defining New York style moments of all time involves Marilyn Monroe. Though she was born in California and mostly resided in Los Angeles, she came to New York in 1955 and lived there on and off for the rest of her life until her passing in 1962.

In *The Seven Year Itch* (1955), directed by Billy Wilder, her character, The Girl, stands above a subway grate as her white pleated dress by costume designer William Travilla blows up above her knees. The scene is so iconic that it's been referenced time and time again. The dress sold at auction in 2011, for $5.6 million (including a $1 million fee to the auction house). It's one of the most valuable dresses ever sold and also proves the immense significance of Monroe's fashion legacy. Decades later, the fascination is still there – with Kim Kardashian wearing a different dress from Monroe's historical archive to one of New York's most important nights in fashion, the Met Gala, in 2022. The light-nude silk, crystal-covered dress by Jean Louis that Monroe wore while singing happy birthday to JFK sold for $4.8 million at auction in 2016. Off-screen, Monroe often wore figure-skimming dresses, tight knits and tastefully sensual clothing that emphasized her figure. The aforementioned white pleated dress was the epitome of her most-remembered aesthetic, which many would categorize as a glamorous sex symbol.

The famed scene was originally filmed on the corner of 52nd and Lexington, and also served as an early example of aggressive paparazzi and fan culture. Approximately 1,500 New Yorkers (mostly men) gathered to watch Monroe's skirt flutter in the breeze.

Opposite: Even though Marilyn Monroe was most associated with Los Angeles, one of her most iconic fashion moments occurred in New York in 1955, during the filming of *The Seven Year Itch.*

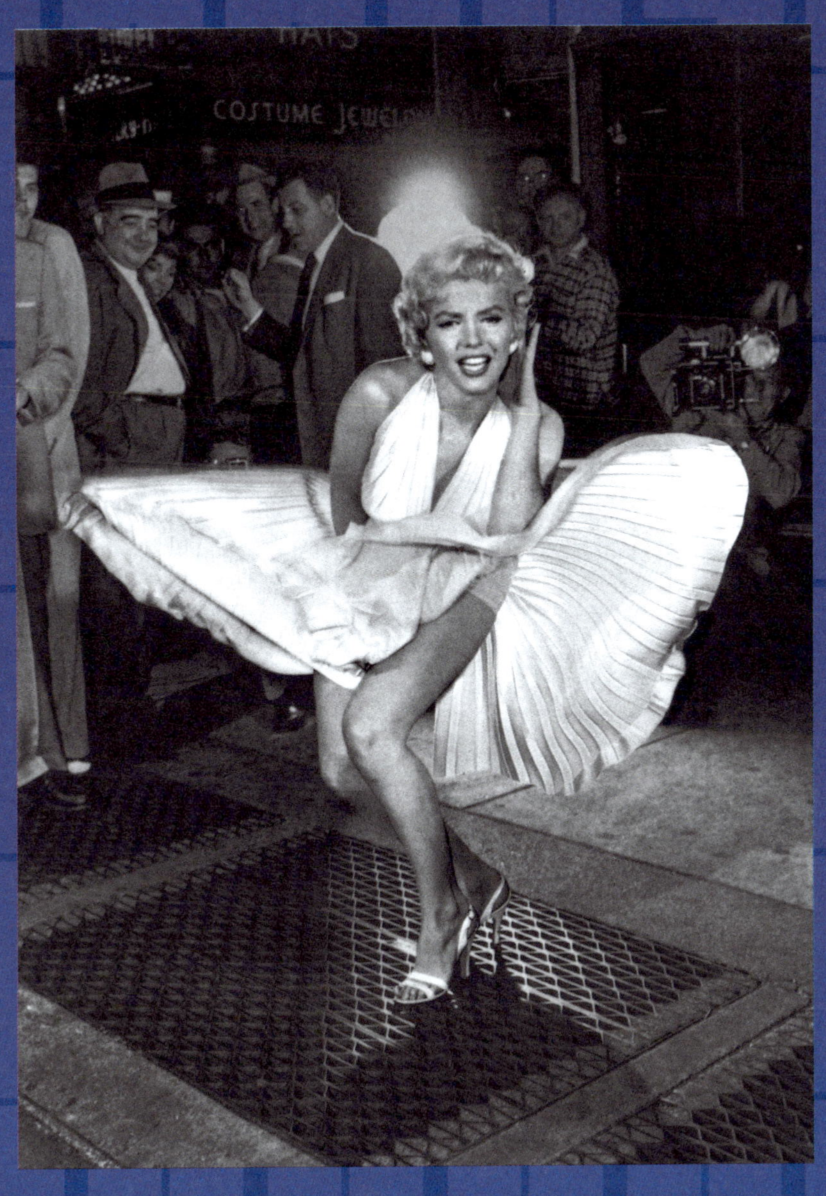
COSTUME

Capturing an Era

Some films have locked-in visual moments that define an entire era of New York fashion icons in one glance, while also representing the real rawness of style outside of central Manhattan.

Like John Travolta (Tony) walking in Bensonhurst, Brooklyn, in his burgundy heeled loafers, flared pants, wide-collared shirt, tight black leather jacket and gold necklace in the opening credits of *Saturday Night Fever* (1977). Or Spike Lee's *Do The Right Thing* (1989), which didn't just showcase a singular New York icon but rather the collective style of the Brooklyn neighbourhood of Bed-Stuy at the time: Air Jordans, sports jerseys, bright colours, jewellery and more by costume designer Ruth E. Carter. *Working Girl* (1988) follows Staten Island secretary Melanie Griffith (Tess) who impersonates her boss, Katharine (Sigourney Weaver), in the big city. The vision and heavy dose of 1980s working women's power suiting she wore has remained an influence on fashion lovers and designers alike, especially in New York, decades later. In *Uptown Girls* (2003), Brittany Murphy and Dakota Fanning epitomize early 2000s style in New York as heiress-forced-to-nanny Molly and serious young schoolgirl Ray. Runway Blumarine, denim overalls with fun patches and a Moschino dress covered in dolls dominate.

And who could forget *Party Girl*? The 1995 flick stars Mary (Parker Posey) as a downtown New York club kid who is on her way to becoming a librarian. The movie has thus become an unconventional camp icon, full of fun, high-low fashion that looks exactly like what an It-girl of today might wear. Cue the vintage Vivienne Westwood.

Opposite: Decades later, Melanie Griffith still serves as a point of reference in the film *Working Girl*. She stood for the power-dressing office worker and exemplified the concept of dressing for the job you want.

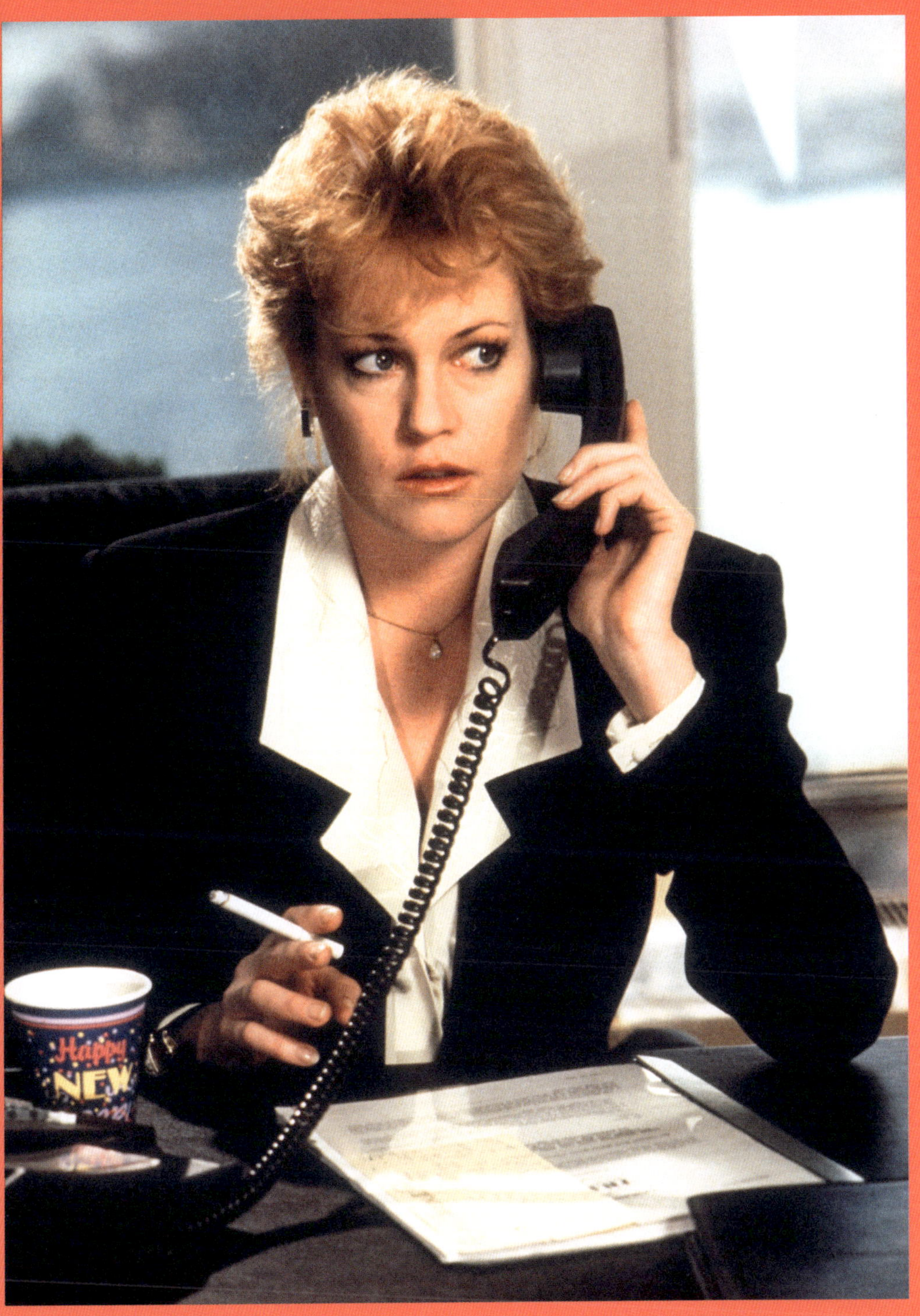
Happy
NEW

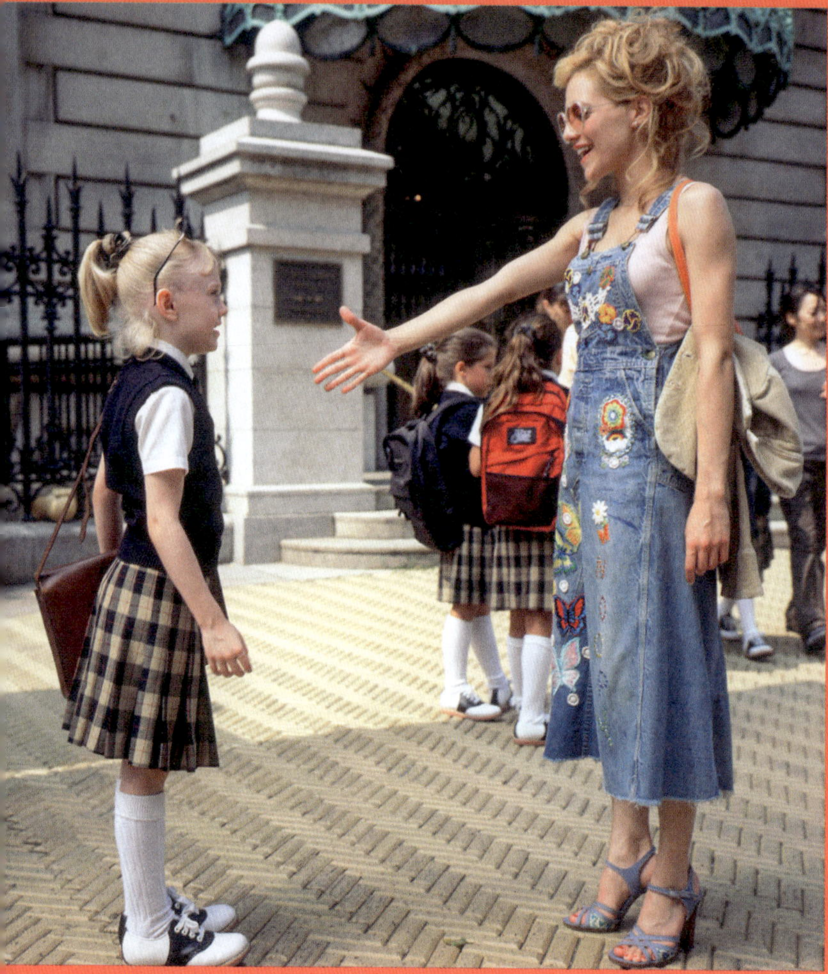

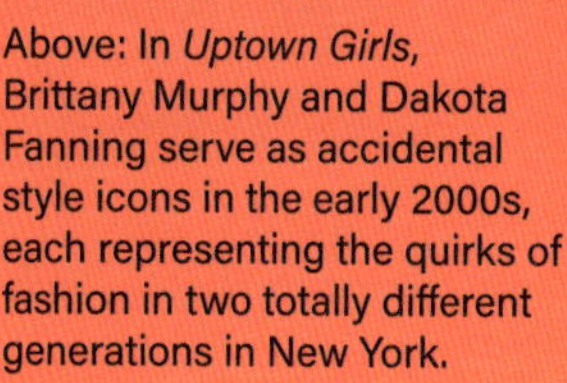

Above: In *Uptown Girls*, Brittany Murphy and Dakota Fanning serve as accidental style icons in the early 2000s, each representing the quirks of fashion in two totally different generations in New York.

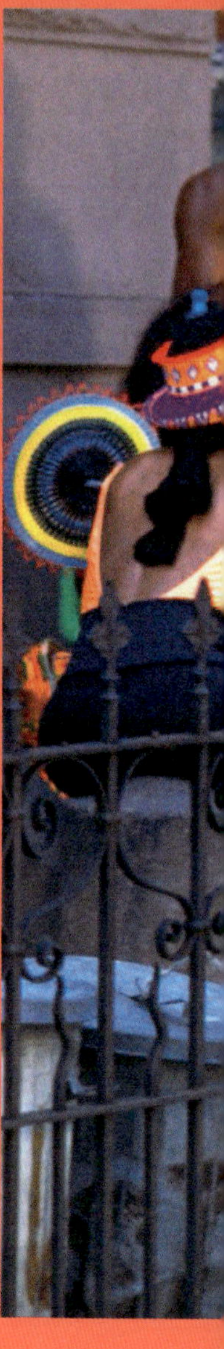

Opposite: Spike Lee's *Do the Right Thing* introduced the Bed-Stuy neighbourhood – and all the style that surrounds it – to the big screen in 1989.

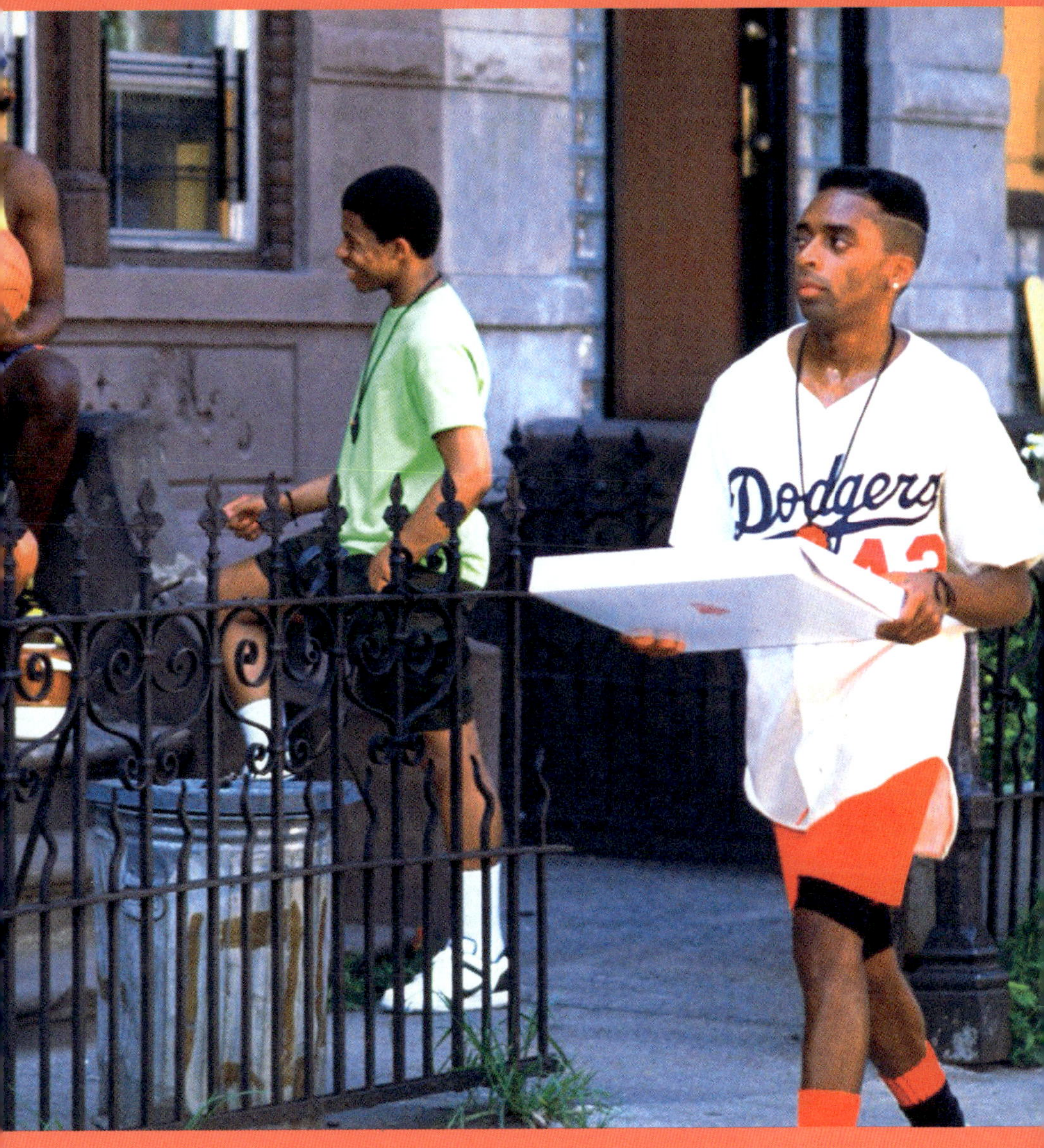
Dodgers

CHAPTER 2:

ONE-OF-A-KIND ICONS

New York City is the centre of the universe for undying individuality. It's no wonder so many people have come here from other places to reinvent themselves or create something entirely new when it comes to style. These are the ones who didn't just wear their personal style – they lived it.

IRIS APFEL

Known as one of the most important maximalists of all time, the late Iris Apfel lived her life in New York but scoured the world's flea markets, haute couture salons and local shops to find the most interesting textiles, jewellery and outfits.

As soon as she could, Apfel learned how to shop like an advanced New Yorker, finding the best discounts at places like flea markets or Loehmann's, a department store that offered designer fashion at steep discounts – which was once an iconic beacon of New York City retail. She dressed fearlessly and layered with passion: signature oversize glasses, massive numbers of necklaces, hulking stacks of bangles and copious prints. More, more, more.

Apfel travelled the world for her work, and thus was able to build her own very distinct style. The result was a mix of combining multiple cultures with her own personality and the distinct boldness of New York. Under her company, Old World Weavers, she worked in interior design and textiles, with a contract at the White House that spanned nine presidencies. She achieved mainstream notoriety in 2005 when The Costume Institute at The Metropolitan Museum of Art staged an exhibition about her personal style, called *Rara Avis: Selections from the Iris Apfel Collection*. She was 84, and at the time, it was widely reported that she was the first living person to have their clothing displayed by the museum.

Iris Apfel represents the concept of high-low – mixing inexpensive finds from anywhere and everywhere with high-end designer fashion. She collected rare pieces, such as rooster feather coats, from French brands, including Jean-Louis Scherrer and Nina Ricci. She was friends with New York designers

Opposite: The late Iris Apfel was one of New York's foremost maximalist muses, gaining recognition later in life for her eccentric outfits.

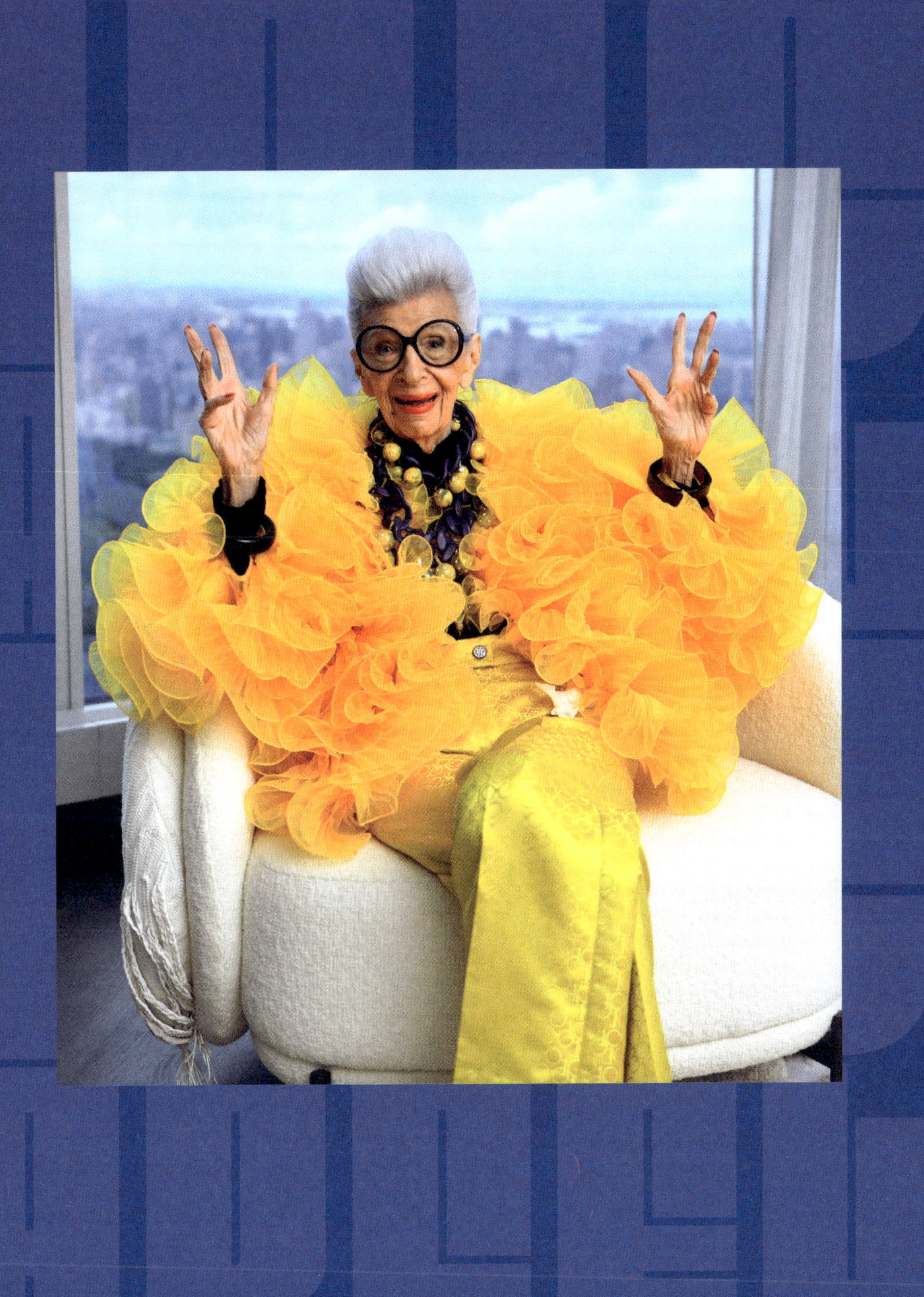

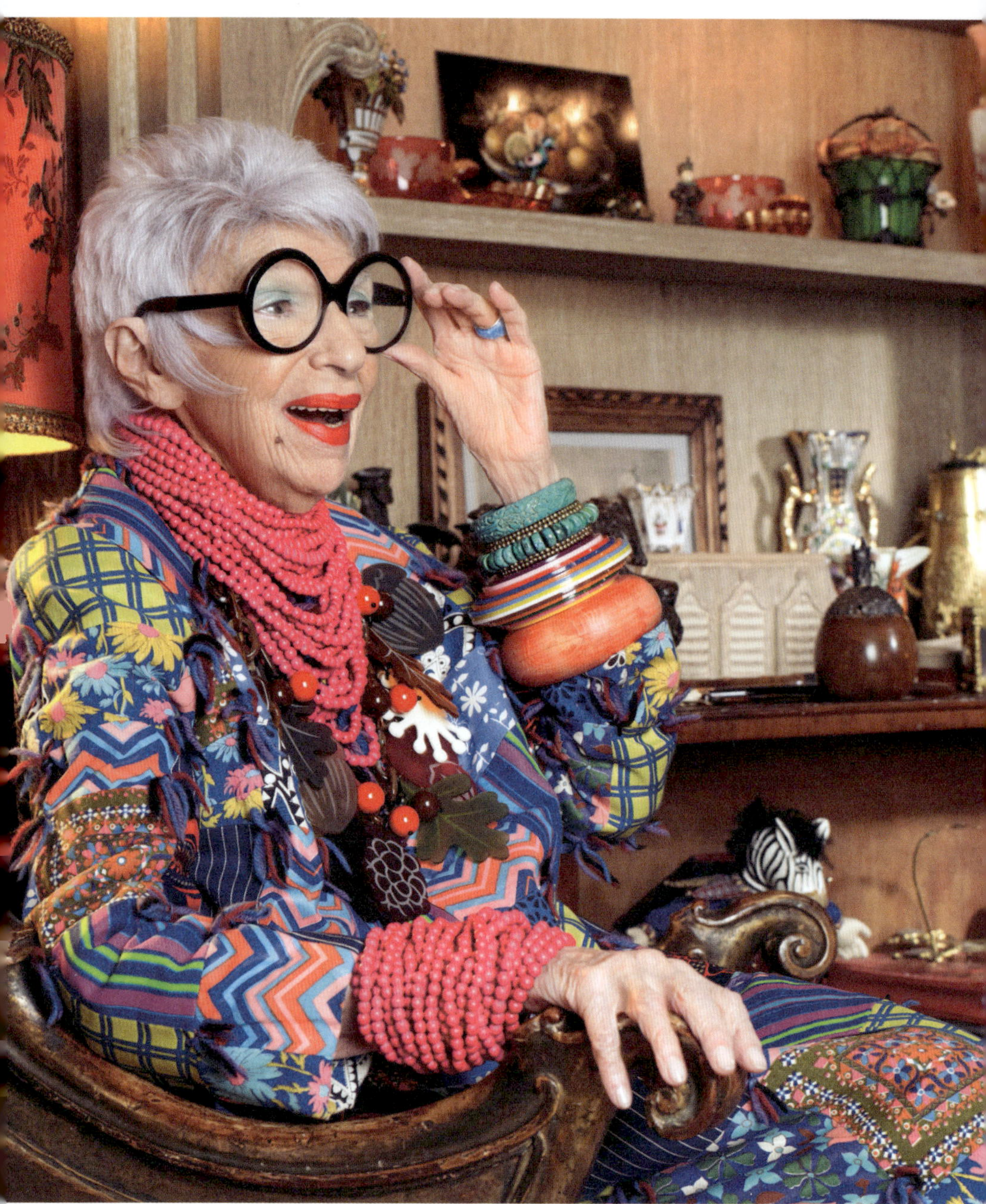

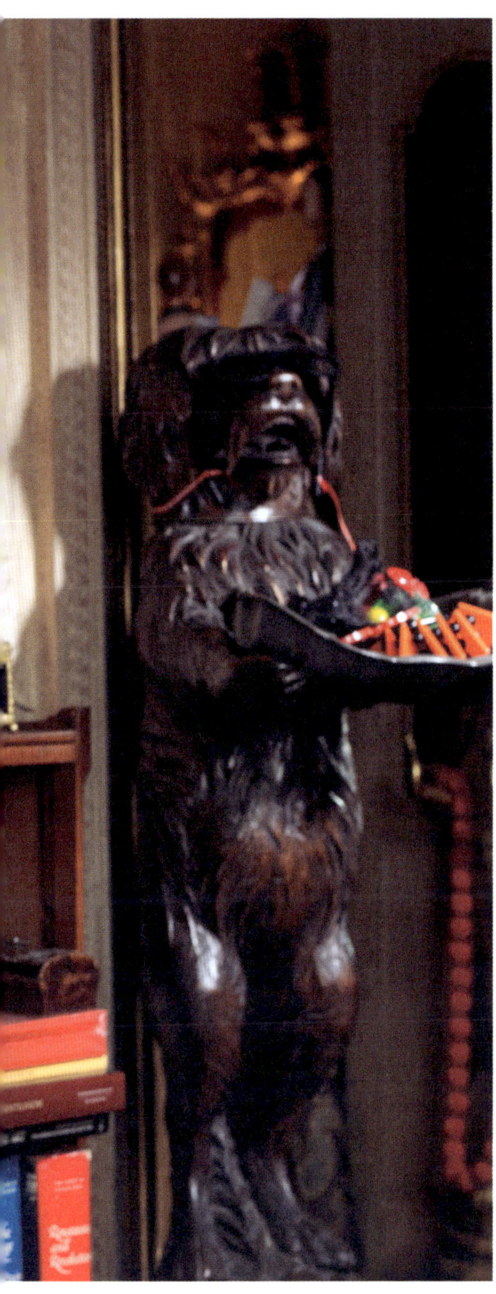

Ralph Rucci, Naeem Khan and Alexis Bittar, the latter of whom designed her large, carved Lucite bangles covered in crystals. Later in life, she launched her own jewellery brand, Rara Avis, with the Home Shopping Network. She created maximalist eccentric jewellery inspired by her own unique vintage and antique finds from around the world and she also collaborated with H&M. Apfel is also one of the few fashion icons who is well known for her eyewear. In her later years, she was never seen without a large pair of colourful, crystal-covered glasses. "More is more and less is a bore," she always said.

Apfel often said that her own mother, who "[worshipped] at the altar of the accessory", was her biggest style influence. She also cited Millicent Rogers, who collected lots of Native American jewellery, as being impactful to her own personal style. Apfel once told *Vogue*, "You must know who you are and stick to it – no flip-flopping and changing around every three seconds. You'll find it's hard work at the beginning, but it pays off. People should celebrate their originality and not want to be part of a herd."

Left: Iris Apfel was the co-founder of Old World Weavers and had a background in interiors and textile design, which inspired her global, colourful method of dressing.

DIANA VREELAND

Diana Vreeland was a notorious editor and curator who lived a life of boldness. She was so influential that she's credited with coining the term "youthquake". She served as an editor at *Harper's Bazaar* and, later, editor-in-chief at *Vogue*, before becoming a special consultant to The Costume Institute of The Metropolitan Museum of Art.

Vreeland created the "Why don't you..." column at *Harper's Bazaar*, which challenged readers with outlandish and grandiose proposals that dared them to dream or travel in their own minds. "Why don't you... Rinse your blond child's hair in dead champagne to keep it gold, as they do in France?" she once wrote.

Above all, Vreeland stood for originality and living what she preached in her work. She didn't conform to trends or conventional beauty aesthetics of the time. She had striking, black, short hair, a beautifully pronounced nose and wore scarlet-red lipstick; she piled on exceptionally large, maximalist costume jewellery. She created an incredibly memorable presence by having an iconic beauty look and jewellery on top of structured, tailored, luxurious basics like black cashmere sweaters and wool pants. "I do think jewels, not jewellery, are very wonderful and extraordinary. I also wouldn't want only one jewel. I'd want a number... the biggest and the best quality," she once said. She is also credited with discovering another New York fashion icon, model and later actress, Lauren Bacall. Vreeland put her on the *Harper's Bazaar* March 1943 cover, posing against a Red Cross office. Bacall's look can be categorized as tomboyish with an Old Hollywood flair.

Opposite: Famed editor and creative Diana Vreeland understood the power of a strong silhouette, iconic accessories, and a standout signature hair and make-up look.

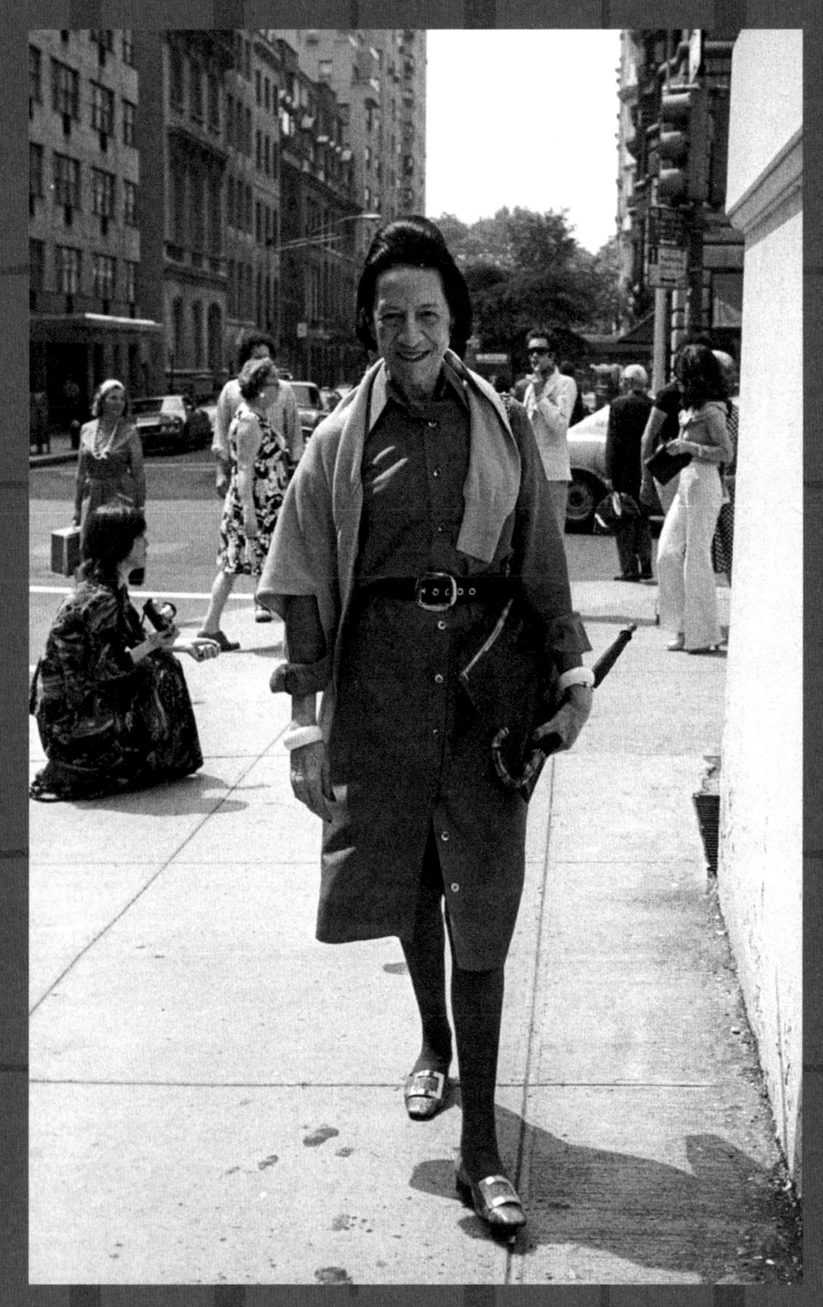

Diana Vreeland loved the colour red and wore it often – she even had her own living room made entirely red, designed by the famous interior designer Billy Baldwin. She called it a "garden in hell" and dressed to match it in a famous photograph. "Red," she once said, "is the great clarifier: bright, cleansing and revealing. It makes all colours beautiful. I can't imagine becoming bored with red – it would be like becoming bored with the person you love."

She once said: "You gotta have style. It helps you get down the stairs. It helps you get up in the morning. It's a way of life. Without it, you're nobody. I'm not talking about lots of clothes." Vreeland devoted herself to making her persona as entirely fabulous as possible. She lived for fantasy. And she also had some of the most iconic quotes of any fashion editor throughout history. "A little bad taste is like a nice splash of paprika," she once said. "We all need a splash of bad taste – it's hearty, it's healthy, it's physical. I think we could use more of it. No taste is what I'm against."

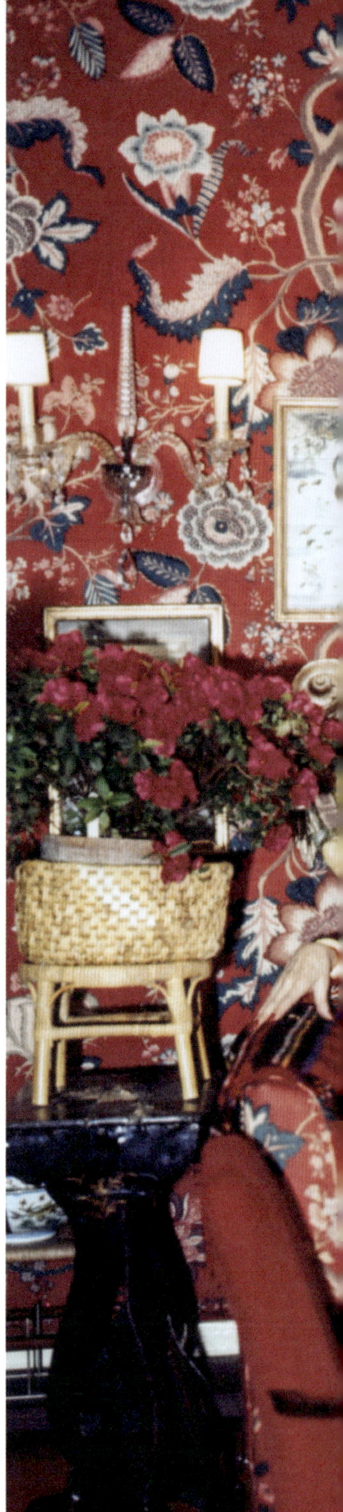

Right: Shown in her famous red room, which Diana Vreeland commissioned the famous interior designer Billy Baldwin to create.

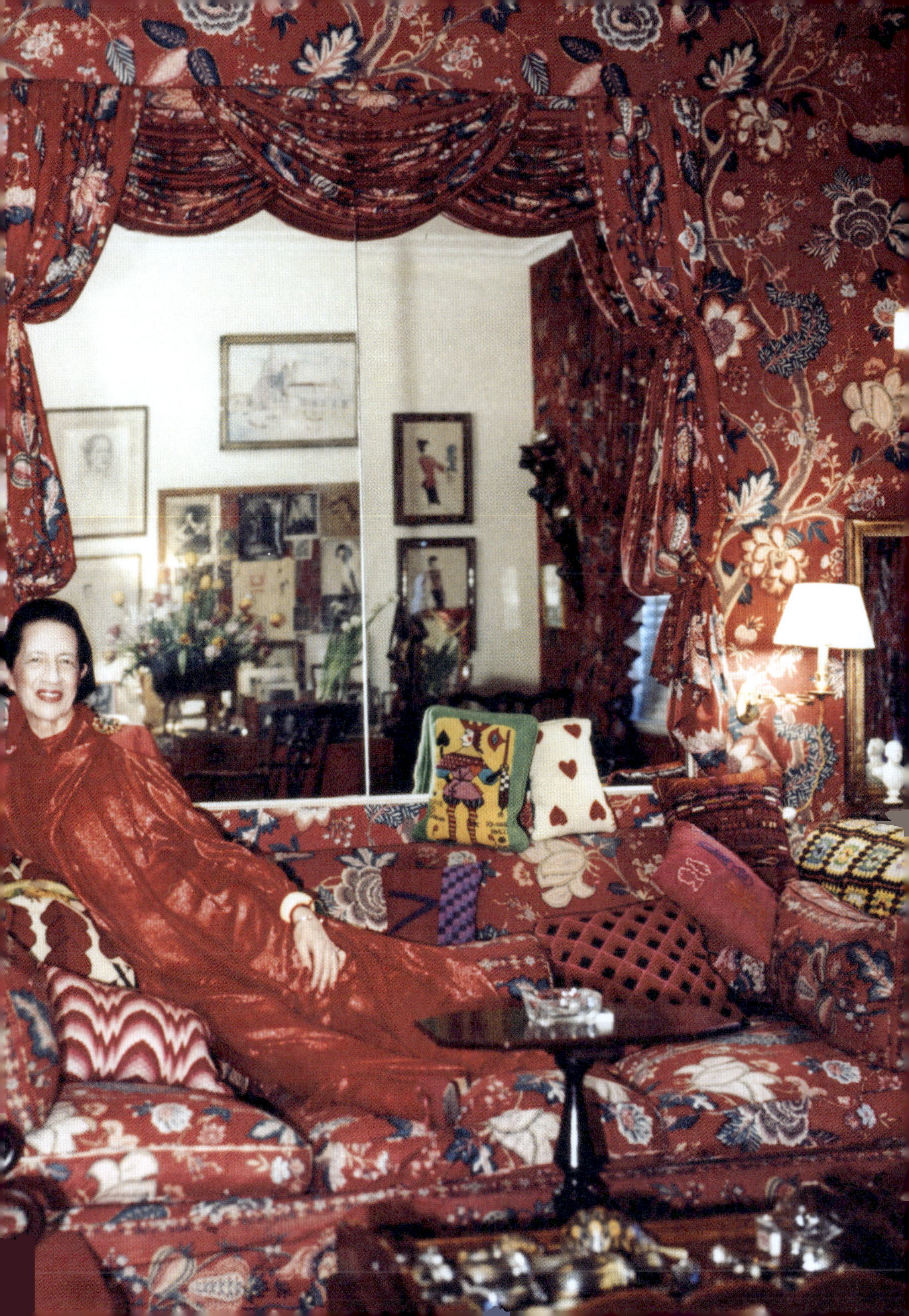

DAPPER DAN

Dapper Dan (Daniel R. Day) single-handedly changed fashion's approach to the logo. The Harlem native opened his Harlem boutique on 125th Street in 1982, and it became so popular that, at one point, it stayed open 24 hours a day. Inspired by his own personal style and the items that he actually wore, he started out by offering furs, eventually branching into casual sportswear printed with logos from the likes of Gucci, Louis Vuitton and Fendi. His influence is so powerful that in 2018 he did a design collaboration with Gucci and, later, Gap.

Dapper Dan represents his own very unique point of view in fashion; in particular, mixing casual athleisure pieces with high elements of style and designer logos. For instance, his signature piece is the hoodie. But he styles it in a very unusual way, mixing it up with fedoras, ascots, and white shirts underneath, always with his collar popped. "The journey started for me by trying to understand my spiritual self, and that's how I stumbled across logomania. When I studied all the religions in the world, I noticed that everything went back to a symbol and it made me realize the power of a symbol," he once told me, in an interview for *Vogue*.

Logomania is a term often loosely thrown around in fashion, but Dapper Dan's effect on the concept is overwhelmingly influential – especially as it relates to the wider fashion industry taking inspiration from Harlem, Black culture and hip-hop. He dressed LL Cool J, Mike Tyson, Salt-N-Pepa and Run-DMC, and icons like Missy Elliott have spoken about his influence at length.

Opposite: Dapper Dan changed fashion history with his own personal style and vision, introducing logomania and sharp tailoring to everything he did.

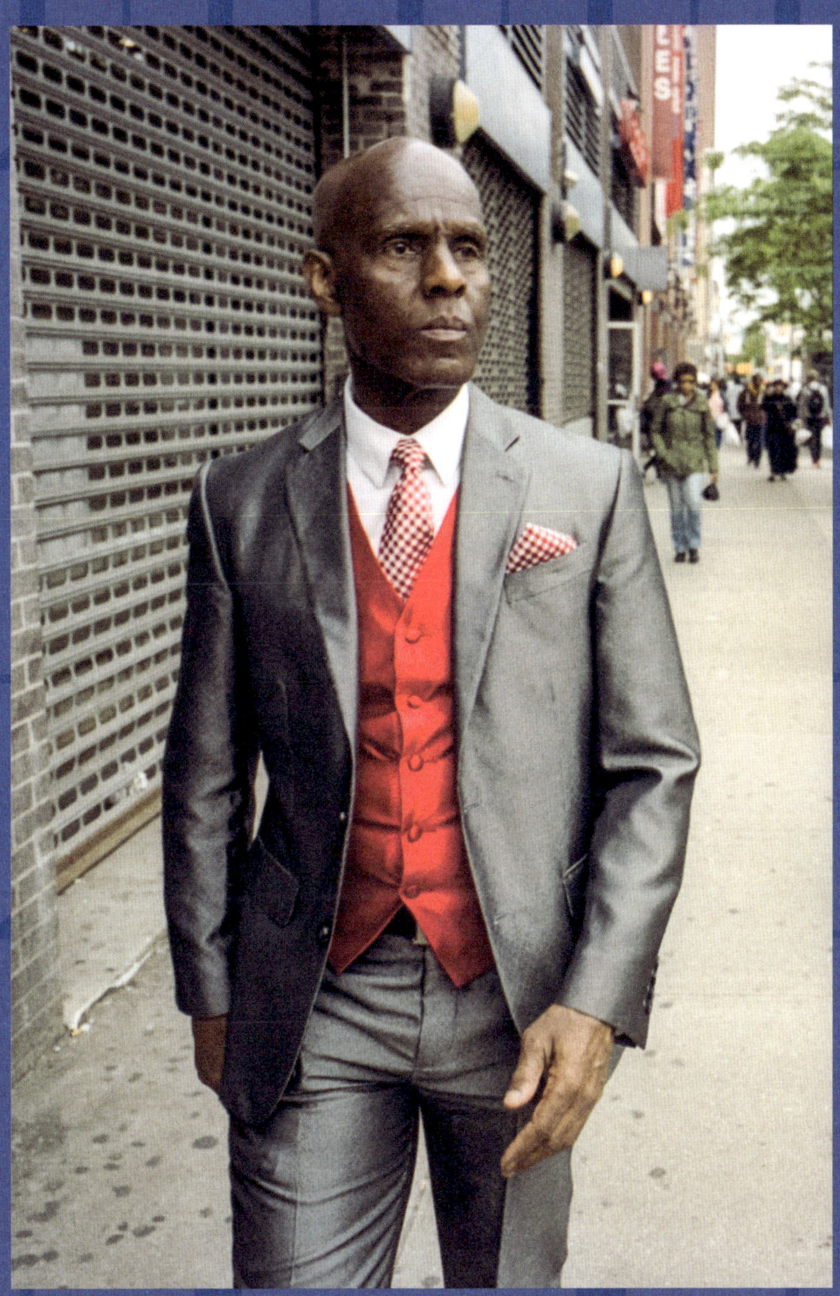

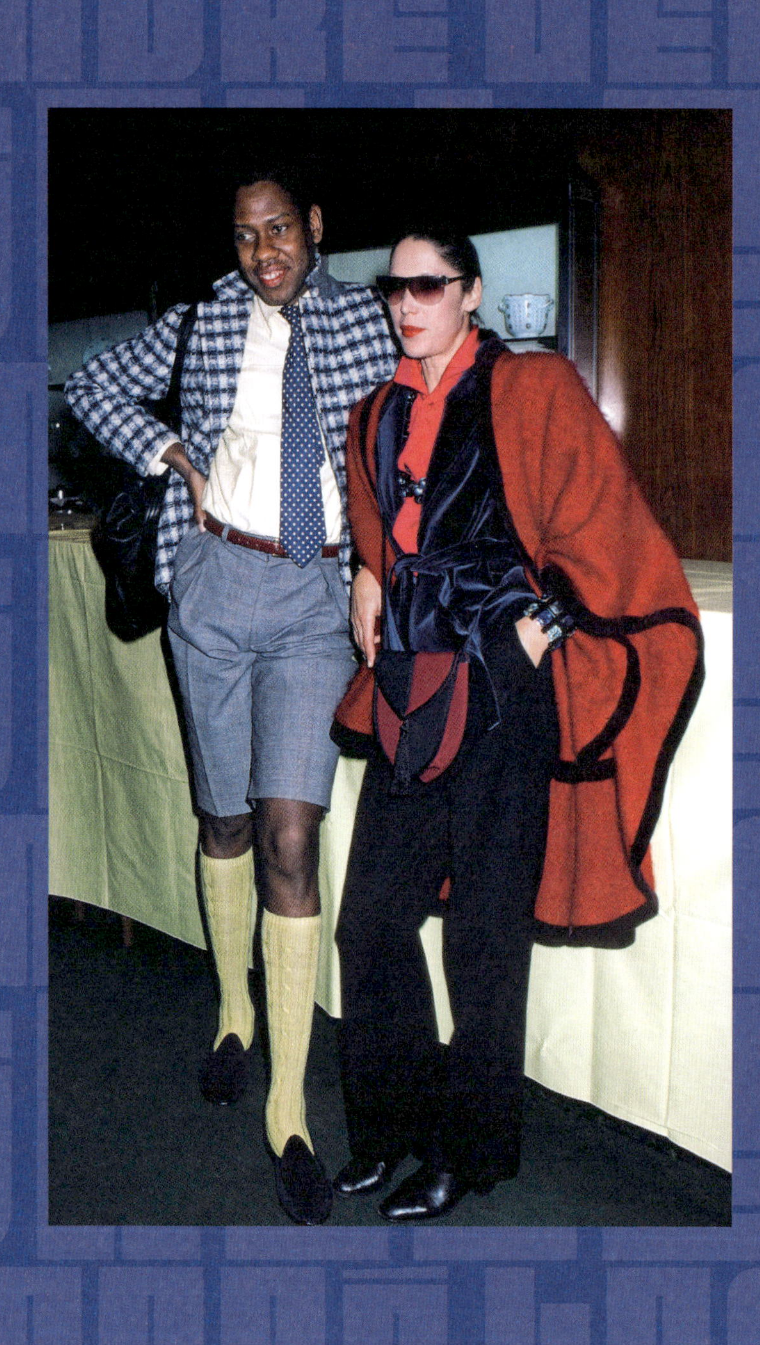

PERSONAL STYLE HEROES

ANDRÉ LEON TALLEY

When it comes to building one's own powerful presence with personal style, the late André Leon Talley is the undisputed champion. Though he grew up in North Carolina, he made his career in New York as the first Black creative director at *Vogue*, and also spent a lot of time in Paris. He wrote for *Vanity Fair*, *Interview* magazine and *Women's Wear Daily*, among others, and was close to some of the fashion industry's most notable designers, including Karl Lagerfeld, Manolo Blahnik, Diane von Furstenberg, Oscar de la Renta and Yves Saint Laurent.

Talley advocated for diversity and never compromised. He took up space with his ideas and his own wardrobe, opting for capes and kaftans that dominated and trailed behind him on the red carpet. Apprenticing under Diana Vreeland at The Metropolitan Museum of Art's Costume Institute likely had an impact on his own perception of personal style and originality. For him, fashion was pure personal expression. He loved luxury, covering himself in luscious furs, even when fashion turned away from it. He favoured Louis Vuitton luggage, and he had a penchant for comfort, wearing Ugg boots instead of formal footwear. He often donned huge, aviator shield sunglasses. Brocades, gold crosses and diamond brooches were key to his collection.

Talley often wore the work of his aforementioned designer friends, but it was all customized for him, such as Diane von Furstenberg's psychedelic printed kaftans or a bespoke red and gold embroidered kaftan designed by Dapper Dan. Nigerian designer Patience Torlowei also created custom kaftans for Talley. He was further immortalized

Opposite: A young André Leon Talley (pictured with model Marina Schiano) showcases his early predilection for prepster style.

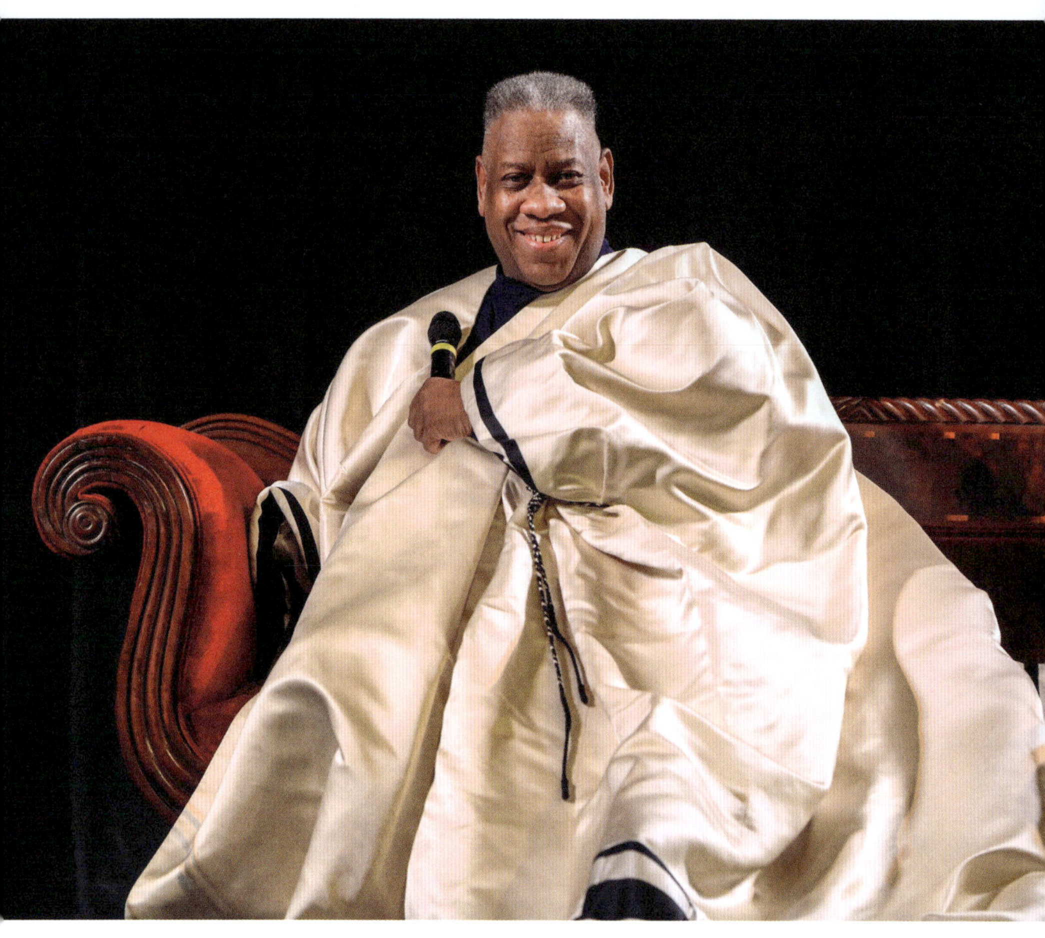

for his iconic style and larger-than-life personality in the 2009 documentary *The September Issue*. "It's a famine of beauty. The famine of beauty, honey! My eyes are starving for beauty!" he famously exclaimed.

Above: André Leon Talley became incredibly well known for his kaftans, often designed by some of the fashion industry's most prominent designers, such as Karl Lagerfeld or Diane von Furstenberg.

Opposite: In the 1990s, André Leon Talley and Anna Wintour attended the Met Gala, both dressed in an opulent, lush rococo style composed of eye-catching silks, furs and sequins.

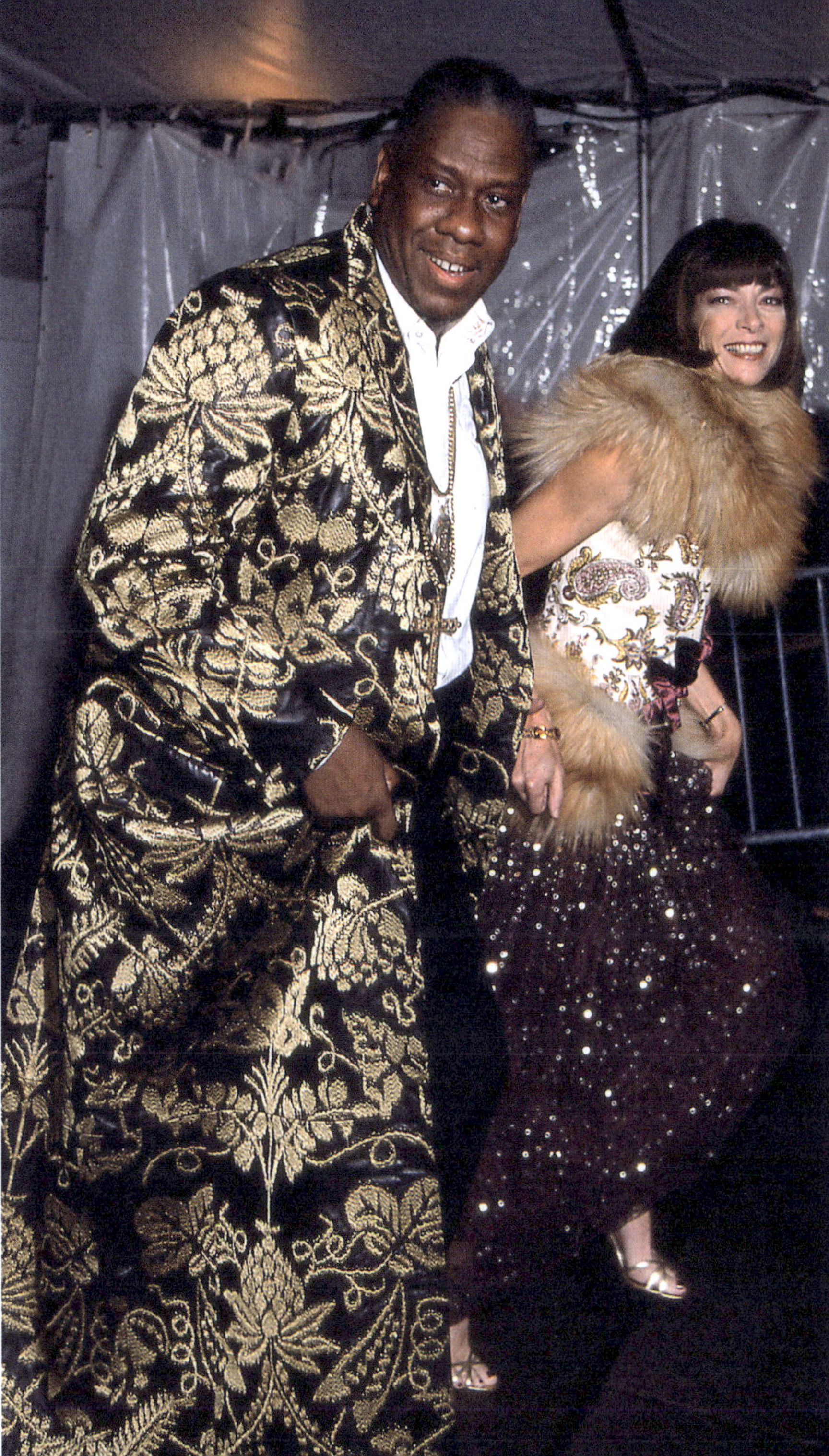

FRAN LEBOWITZ

Fran Lebowitz personifies New York uniform dressing to a T. One of the most iconic writers of New York City, she can be spotted in the streets wearing her signature combination that never changes: she almost always wears a white Oxford shirt, a blazer, Levi's 501 jeans, pristine pocket squares, brown cowboy boots and her trademark tortoiseshell glasses. She mixes in pieces like gold vintage Alexander Calder cufflinks.

Her hair is worn in a bob, untamed, and without make-up, she is instantly recognizable. Lebowitz's personal style is underscored by the fact that she avoids trends. She is also an avid supporter of tailoring clothes to fit perfectly. Her jackets are mostly from Anderson & Sheppard in London. Her favourite shirts were from Brooks Brothers, until one day they stopped making her preferred style. She now gets her shirts from Hilditch & Key, opting for a men's style which she then has shortened. Her glasses and cowboy boots are custom-made and she remains tight-lipped about her go-tos for those. She has been outspoken about taking care of her clothes – getting them dry-cleaned by the most expensive cleaner, never wearing them inside her home, and starching her shirts.

"What people don't know is: Clothes don't really fit you unless they're made for you," she once told *Elle*. "Especially when you wear men's clothes, like I do. American women think that clothes fit them if they can fit into them. But that's not at all what fit means."

Opposite: Writer Fran Lebowitz is the ultimate example of creating one's own personal uniform in New York.

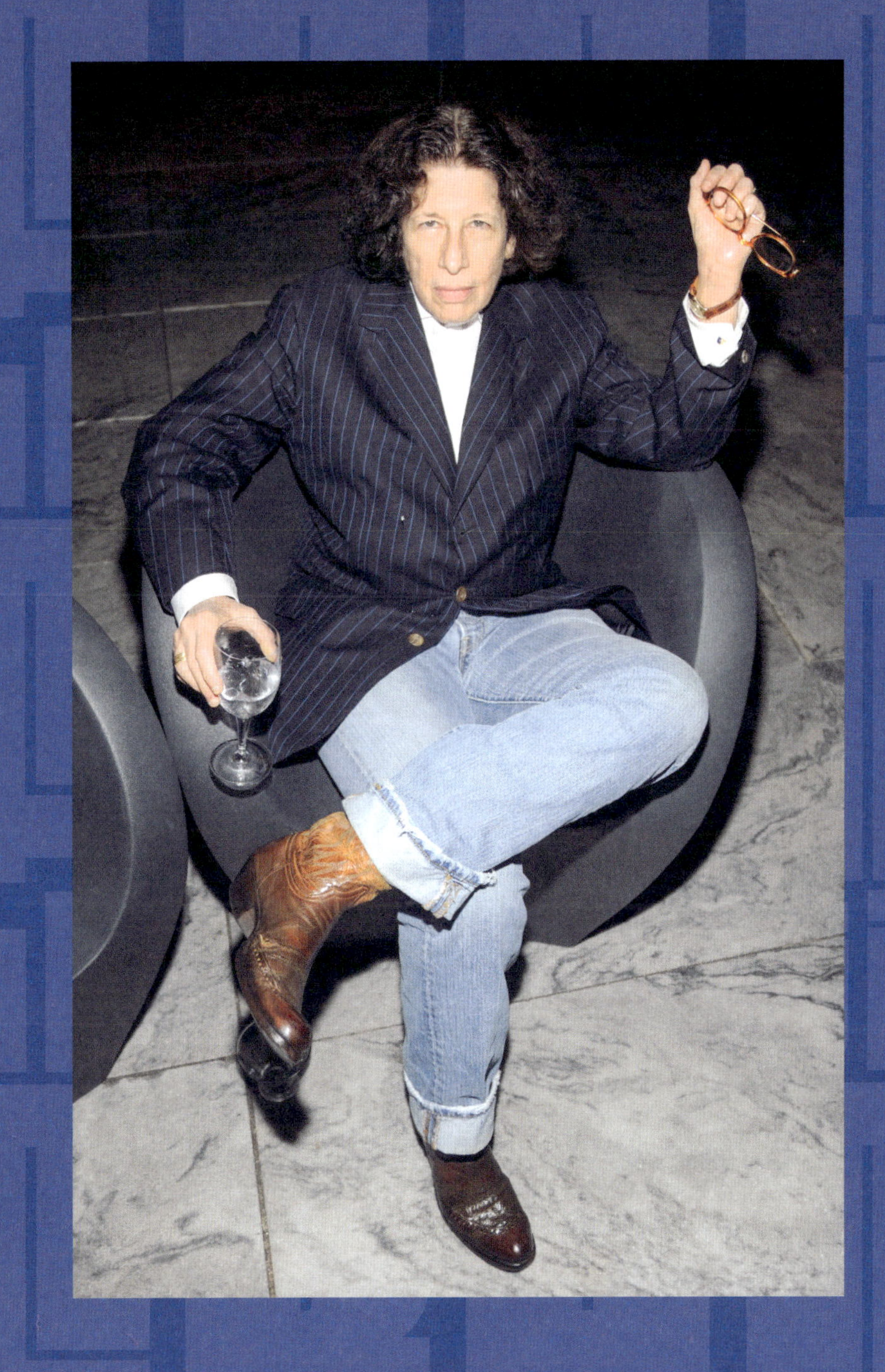

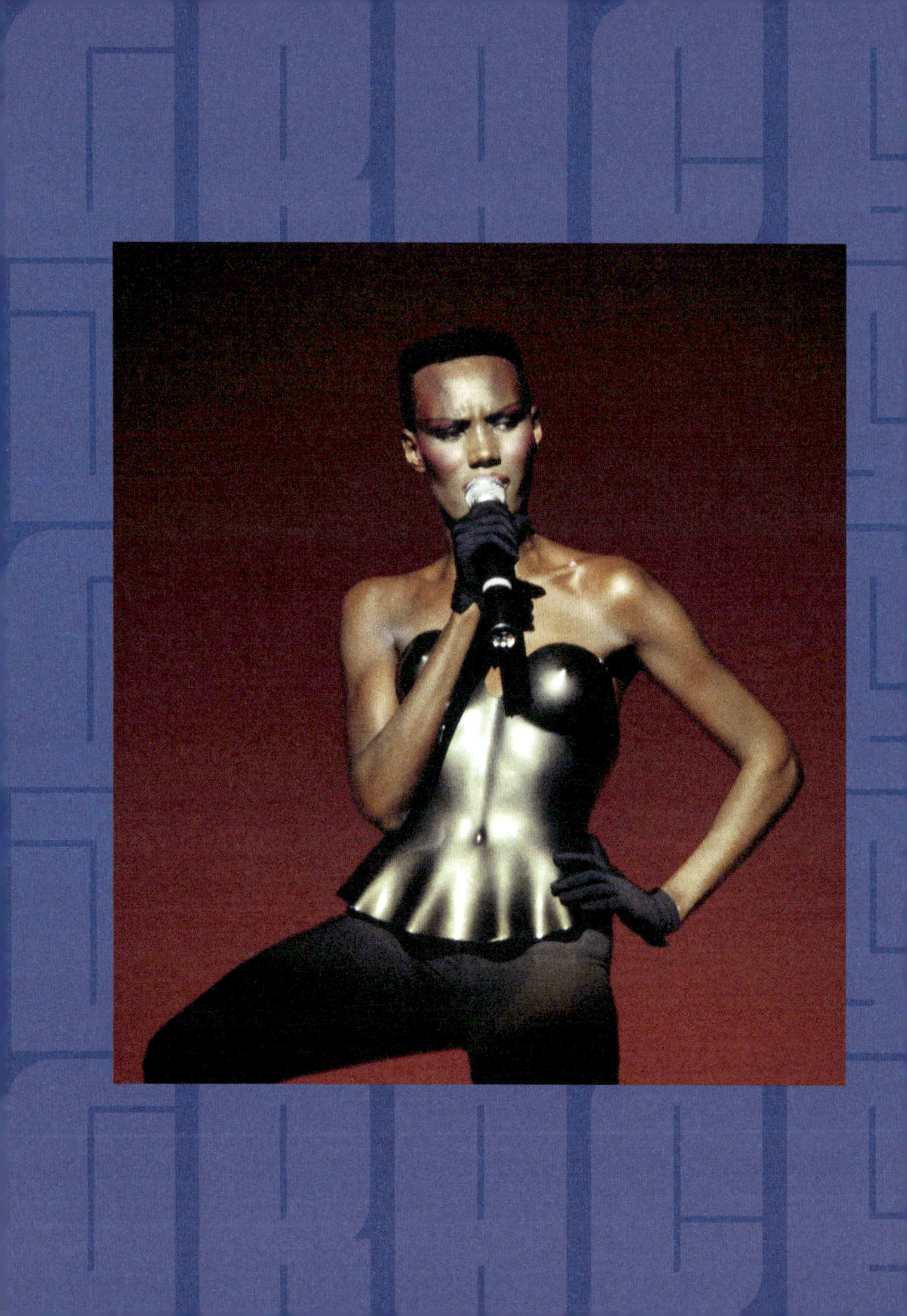

GRACE JONES

Grace Jones ruled the music and fashion scene by doing her own thing. The Jamaican-born star exploded onto the scene in 1970s New York City, taking nightlife spots Palladium, 12 West and Studio 54 by storm. Brazenly beautiful with her razor-sharp hair and pop art geometric make-up, she was always incredibly influential and recognizable. When Jones dressed up, she chose the most boundary-breaking editorial pieces from Issey Miyake, Thierry Mugler and Kenzo Takada.

Jones didn't just wear high-end runway fashion – she opted for the museum-quality pieces that literally changed fashion history. Take, for example, the time she wore the iconic Issey Miyake sculpted plastic bustier from his autumn/winter 1980–81 collection. Her experience as a model walking the runway for some of the top brands in the world only aided her experimentation and appreciation of experimental high fashion.

Elsewhere, she created recognizable wardrobe codes that could go on to serve as a reference point for major designers and other contemporary New York City icons. A good example are her swooping Alaïa hooded outfits, which Lady Gaga replicated early on in her career. From bold geometric leather jackets and striking gold cuffs to African prints and tailored oversized blazers worn open with nothing underneath, she challenged gender stereotypes and fashion norms. "I'm not fashion, I'm style," she once said.

Opposite: Performer and icon Grace Jones often wore rare runway Issey Miyake, as seen here.

Right: Grace Jones defined her own sense of personal style with strong accessories and a groundbreaking hair and make-up statement.

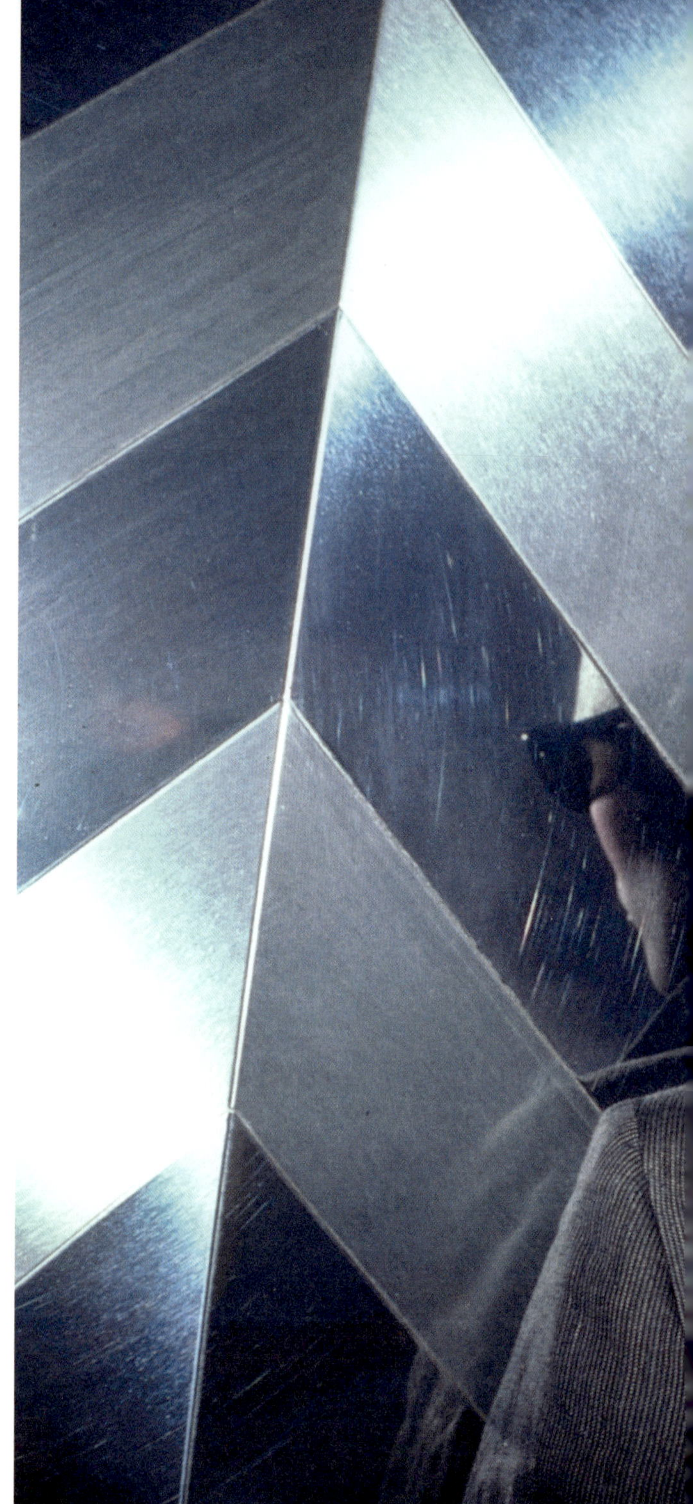

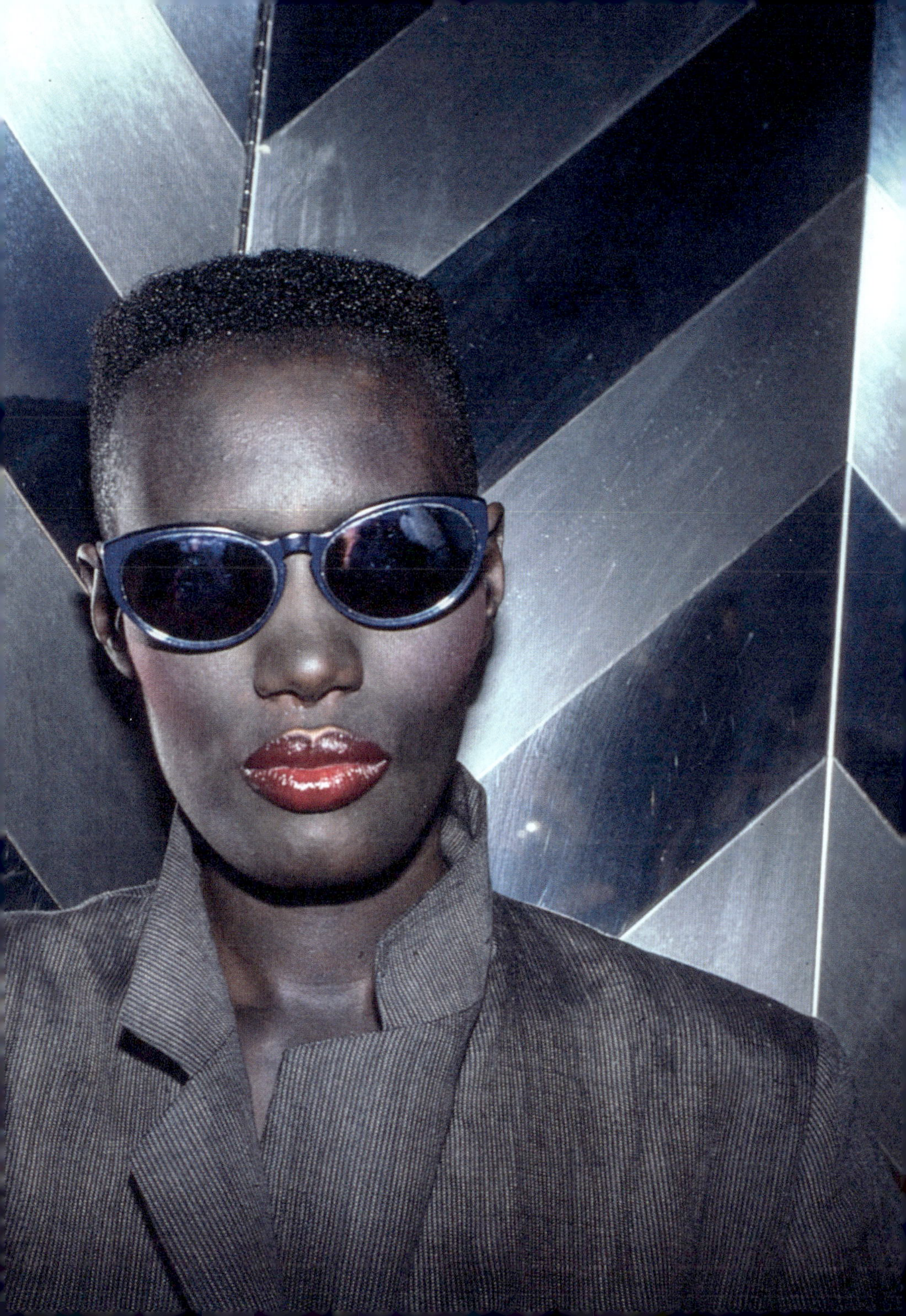

CHLOË SEVIGNY

In 1994, the *New Yorker* solidified Chloë Sevigny as one of New York's perpetually cool It-girls with a profile all about the up-and-coming actress and her personal style, penned by Jay McInerny. She has done it all: opened a Miu Miu show, starred in a Sonic Youth music video, acted in Larry Clark's movie *Kids* and hosted one of the most legendary public closet sales of all time – all in New York.

She's frequently spotted out and about in her oddball mix of ingenious styling: a mash-up of printed tights, sparkling dresses, Margiela Tabis, band T-shirts, polos and chunky black boots – a style staple almost any New Yorker could agree on.

Whether she's wearing a little floral print dress with a leather jacket, matcha in hand, or denim cut-offs with pointed black pumps, she adds items that give her look that signature It-girl twist. Think loafers with visible white socks, or a utilitarian Gap windbreaker with a black- and-white gingham skirt and sporty ballerina flats. Even at her most visible public events, she pushes conventions. A case in point is when she chose to wear emerging designer Dilara Findikoglu to the 2024 Met Gala. Her Victorian-style, puff-sleeve gown with embroidered flowers stood out as one of the most exciting looks.

Like most New Yorkers Sevigny understands the power that outerwear holds during winter. After all, when it's cold out, it's the only thing you see. She's been spotted wearing instantly iconic, over-the-top Prada coats as well as standouts from Gucci, like one baby-blue, ecclesiastical-coded coat dripping with a large collar, made in collaboration

Opposite: Chloë Sevigny is New York's most iconic It-girl. Here, she wears a rare, limited-edition coat from creative director Alessandro Michele's Gucci x New York Yankees collaboration.

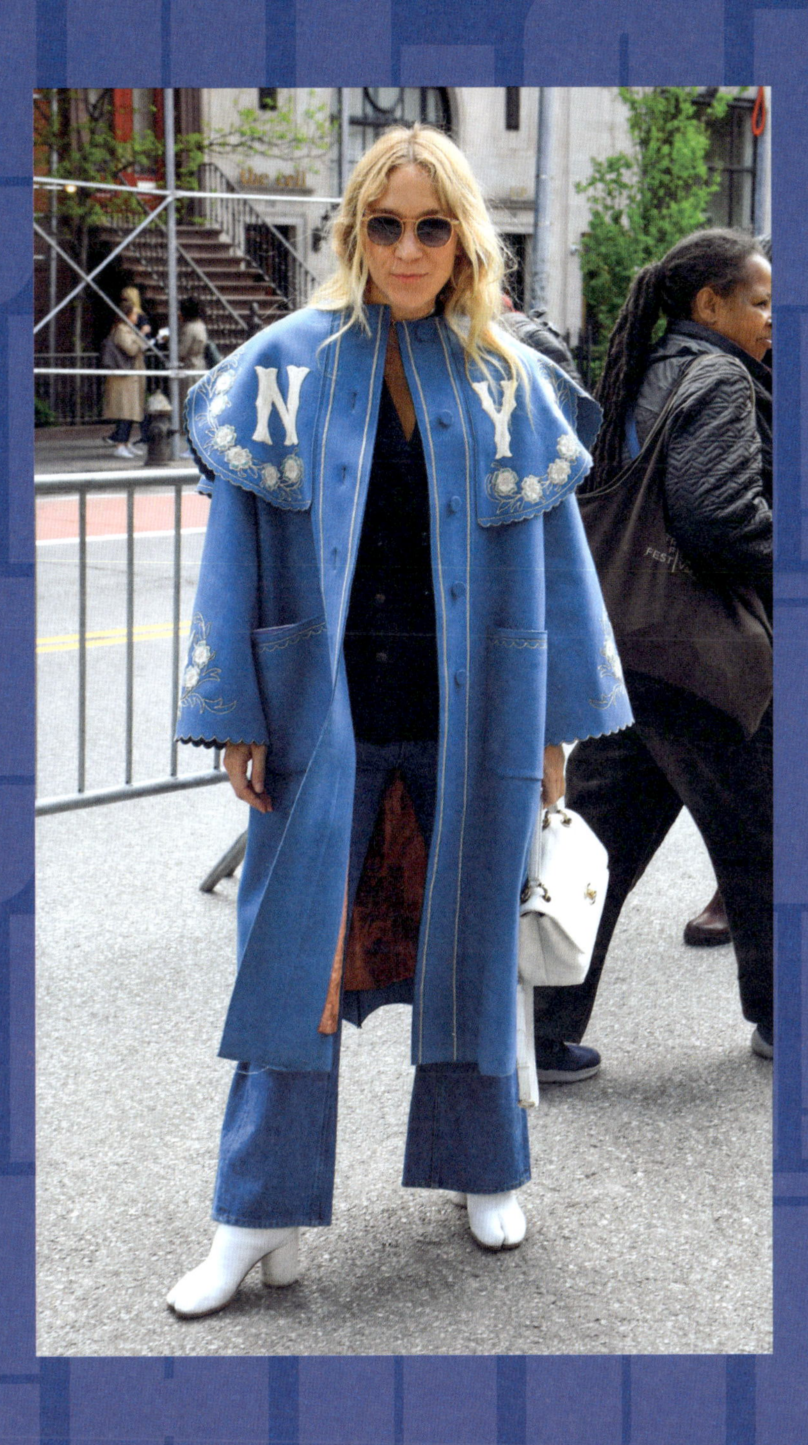

N Y

with the New York Yankees. She's also not afraid to experiment with menswear staples, such as tailored shorts and jackets. And, of course, she also supports designers like Simone Rocha and Christopher John Rogers, both of whom have incredibly unique points of view and instantly recognizable aesthetics. Though she was born in Massachusetts, Sevigny's style screams New York.

She told *Vogue* of her forever style staples: "Always a clunky black shoe. Denim, obviously. Oxford shirts, fisherman's sweaters, a good blue blazer. Band T-shirts. Some incredible denim pieces thrown in. That preppy-with-a-twist vibe is kind of an overarching theme in my style."

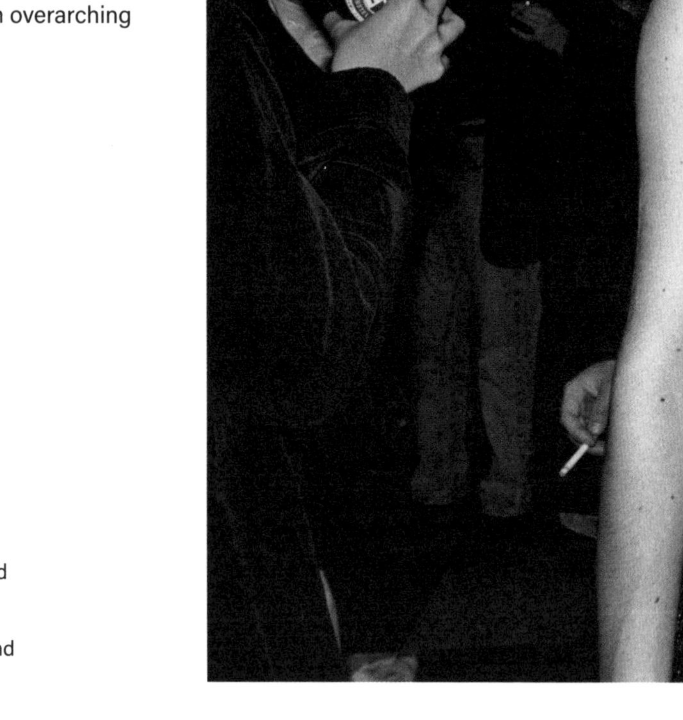

Right: Chloë Sevigny is known to mix and match casual and formal, high and low, typical and atypical, as seen here where she is wearing a beaded dress and quirky brooch.

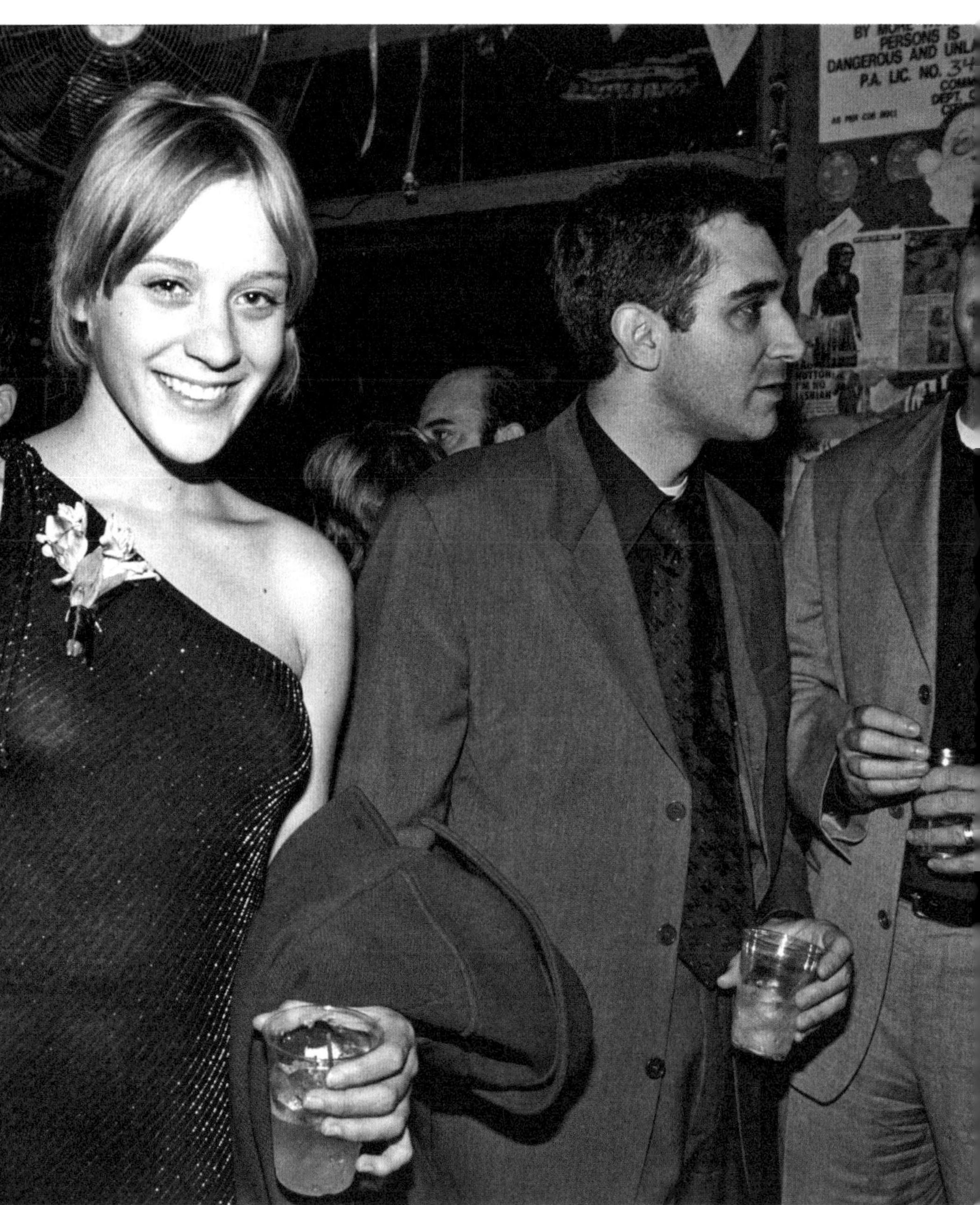
PERSONS IS
DANGEROUS AND
P.A. LIC. NO.

KATHARINE HEPBURN

Even though she was at the height of her fame in Hollywood, Katharine Hepburn will forever be associated with New York City, especially by fashion history's most devoted followers. Raised in Connecticut, she began acting as a student at Bryn Mawr College before heading to New York to perform on Broadway. She owned a Turtle Bay Gardens townhouse from 1931 until her death in 2003, and she starred in 13 Broadway theatre productions from 1928 to 1982, with her biggest success being *The Philadelphia Story* (1939–40) at the Shubert Theatre.

On screen and in the streets, Hepburn was known for gender-defying personal style and her refusal to conform to Hollywood's beauty perceptions. When journalist Barbara Walters asked if she owned a dress, her response was: "Yes, Mrs. Walters. I have one, which I'll wear to your funeral."

She wore trousers when it was considered controversial for women to do so, and adored menswear. During her career in the Golden Age of Hollywood, instead of conforming to ultra-feminine stereotypes, A-line dresses and little kitten heels, she led with power suits, wide-leg trousers, sharply tailored shirts and loafers. "Every time a man tells me he prefers a woman dressed with a skirt, I tell him to try it on. Try wearing one," she reportedly told fashion designer Calvin Klein. In her films, she dabbles in equestrian wear, work-inspired shirts and menswear-inspired staples – practical, stylish things that are everyday items in New York City wardrobes today, but back then, Hepburn broke barriers.

Opposite: New Yorker Katharine Hepburn changed fashion history with her approach to androgynous style.

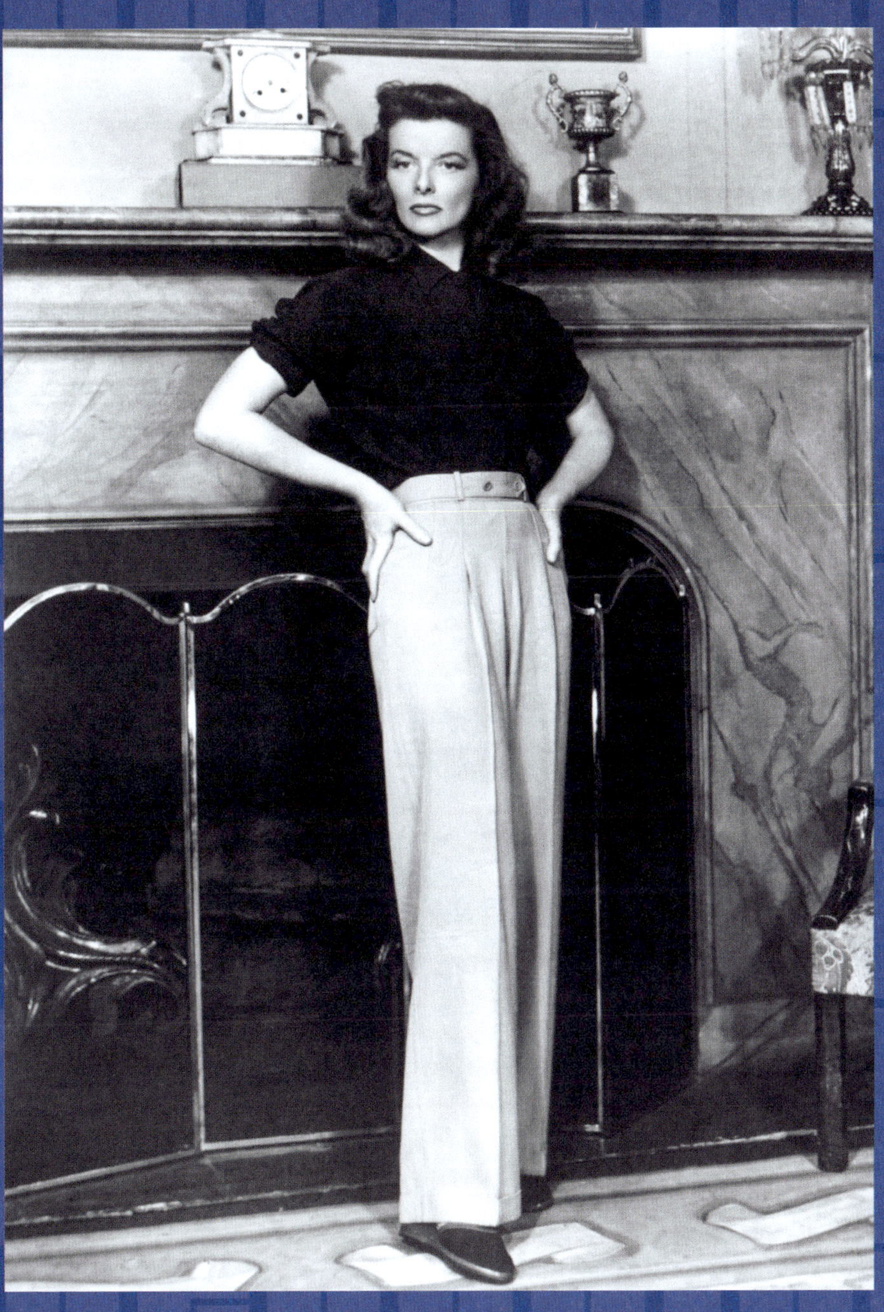

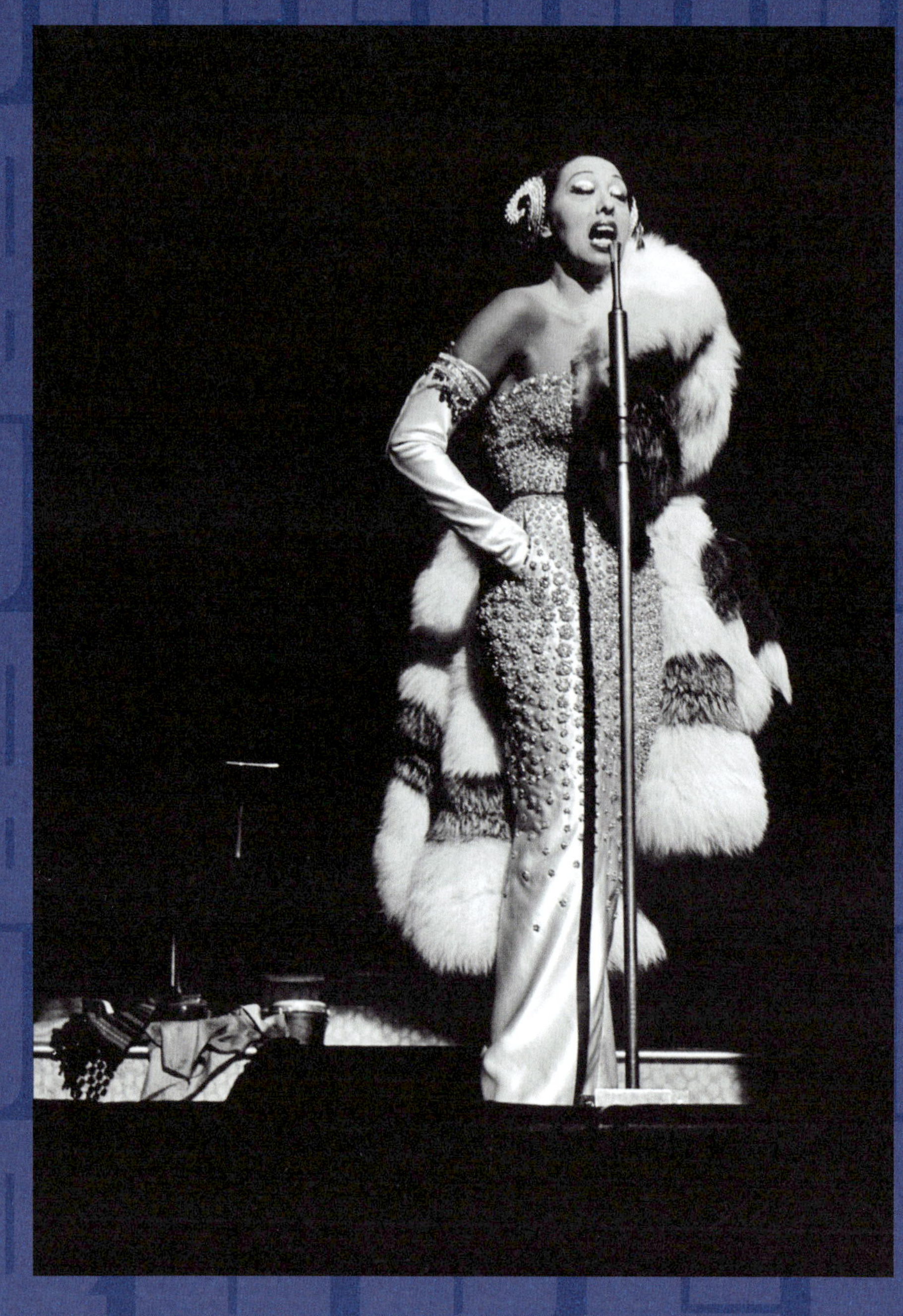

JOSEPHINE BAKER

Performer Josephine Baker is renowned as a star of the Parisian scene, but she also had a significant influence during the Harlem Renaissance in New York, when she arrived in 1922. She was born in Missouri and came from nothing. She started her career in the south by touring with a trio of instrumentalists called the Jones Family Band and later a vaudeville troupe known as the Dixie Steppers. In New York, she performed at the Plantation Club, and joined the chorus line of a highly successful Broadway show called *Shuffle Along.*

While on stage, Baker epitomized the look of the classic showgirl: glorious eyelashes, sequins, feathers and crystal jewels. Offstage, she had her own personal style, consisting of beautiful straw hats, draped dresses and armfuls of stacked chunky bangles. Alongside becoming an international American sensation in Paris, she was also a civil rights activist and a spy during the Second World War, passing vital information to allied agents.

As an honorary New Yorker in France during the 1920s and beyond, Baker certainly made a splash. Her most iconic look was her 1926 banana skirt, paired with a bra and copious amounts of necklaces, worn at the Folies Bergère in Paris for her *La Revue Nègre* musical. Dolls wearing replicas of the skirts were sold all over Europe at the time. Fellow influential New York fashion icon Marc Jacobs, as well as Miuccia Prada, Rihanna and Beyoncé, have all cited her aesthetic as a reference. Offstage, she wore the finest fashions by Paul Poiret and Madeleine Vionnet, leading couture designers of the 1920s, often while walking the streets of Paris with her pet cheetah, Chiquita.

Opposite: Josephine Baker is typically associated with Paris, but she got her style start in New York, wearing showgirl-style get-ups on stages in Harlem.

JOAN RIVERS

An unforgettable personality who was full of life, Joan Rivers had a rare passion for fashion, and even more so for jewellery, which she voraciously collected. The New York native with an accent to match was famously blunt and funny, known as much for her talk shows (she was the first woman to host a late-night network television talk show) as she was for being a co-host on *Fashion Police*.

Her celebrity interviews and commentary were legendary. She also knew how to dress and did so without fear, seamlessly experimenting and often seen hand in hand with her daughter, Melissa, right by her side. On the red carpet, Rivers was always over the top. Think crystal-covered gowns, piles of jewellery that could have been in the world's top museums (she collected rare, antique fine jewellery) and, above all else, glamour.

Later in her life, she created an extremely popular affordable costume jewellery brand under her own name in partnership with QVC. She was an advocate of taste and style at every price point, and she created stunning, quality replicas-with-a-twist of her rare, fine jewellery collection – many of which are still collectible today.

Opposite: Joan Rivers ruled the red carpet and commentary, doling out humorous quips and wearing stunning, maximalist, glam gowns and accessories.

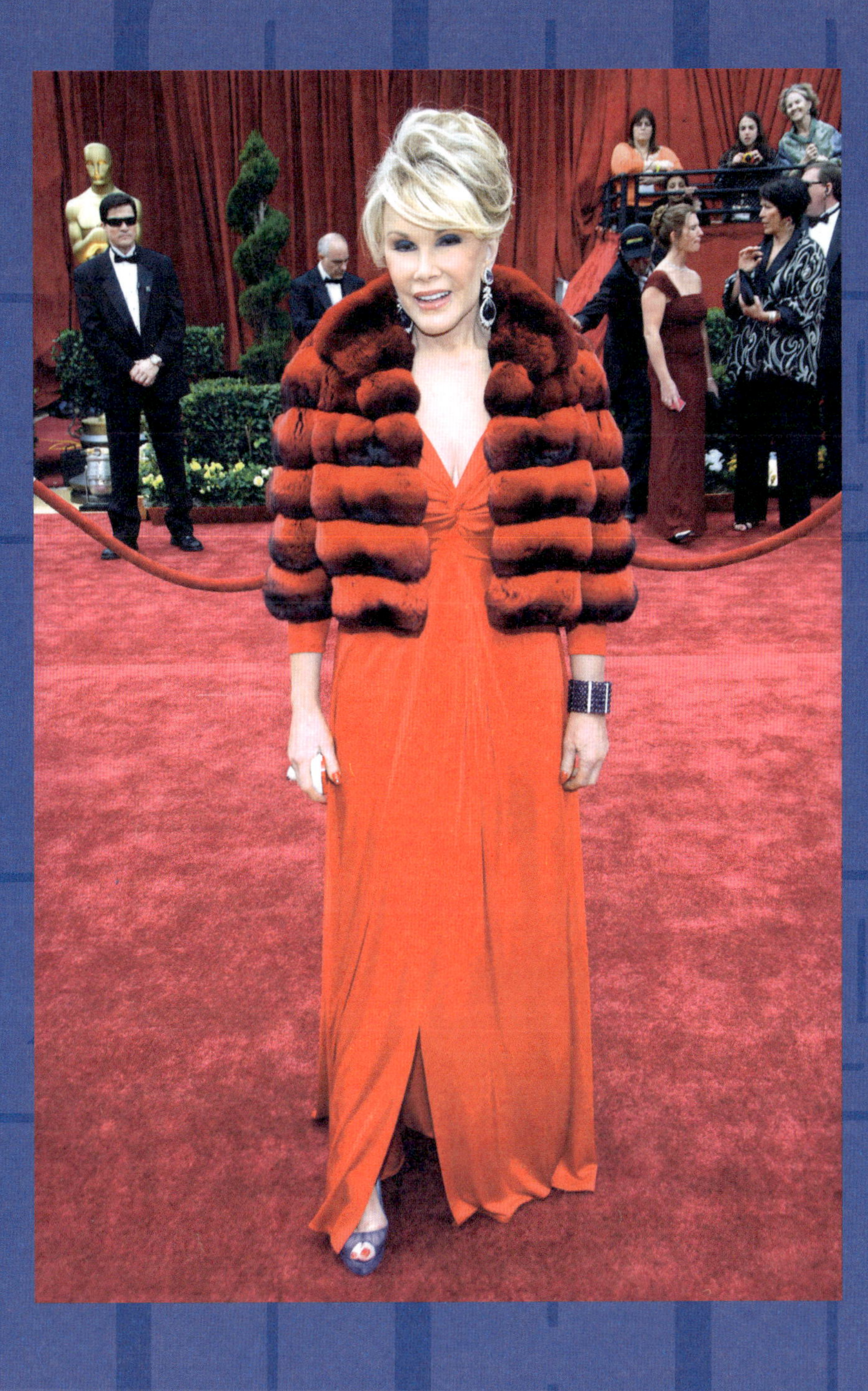

CHAPTER 3:

NIGHTLIFE ROYALTY

The kings and queens of the night take New York personality and bring it to bold, new extremes. These are the performers, visionaries and club kids who are now forever fashion icons.

AMANDA LEPORE

She might just be the single most iconic face of New York nightlife of all time – and an everlasting influence on the very New York idea of being yourself in your own way. Amanda Lepore grew up in suburban New Jersey in the 1970s and 1980s before moving to New York City and dominating the underground club scene.

The ultra-glammed-up trans model would go on to become one of the most famous club kids of the New York network, but even today, she can be seen wearing next to nothing – or decked in rare designer finds at events or in magazines. She's taken aesthetic cues and visuals from some of the most iconic femme fatales in history, like Marilyn Monroe and Jessica Rabbit, and merged them into something new that verges on performance art, with her expertly drawn make-up, blown-up lips, big blonde hair, nipple pasties and huge collection of Christian Louboutin heels. She's modelled for Jean Paul Gaultier, Balenciaga and bygone iconic New York brand Heatherette, and the likes of Lady Gaga and Pamela Anderson have all expressed admiration for her. Lepore is also the muse of art photographer David LaChapelle. She takes the male gaze to a new, subverted level with incredibly tight corsets and cartoonish proportions that become art. Tiaras, crystals, leopard print, big jewellery, pink furs, latex: Lepore takes the drag queen aesthetic and makes it her own, bringing it to a wide audience like never before, with her social media audience of over half a million captivated.

Opposite: Amanda Lepore is the undisputed queen of the nightlife scene, often wearing revealing, skintight gowns in bright colours.

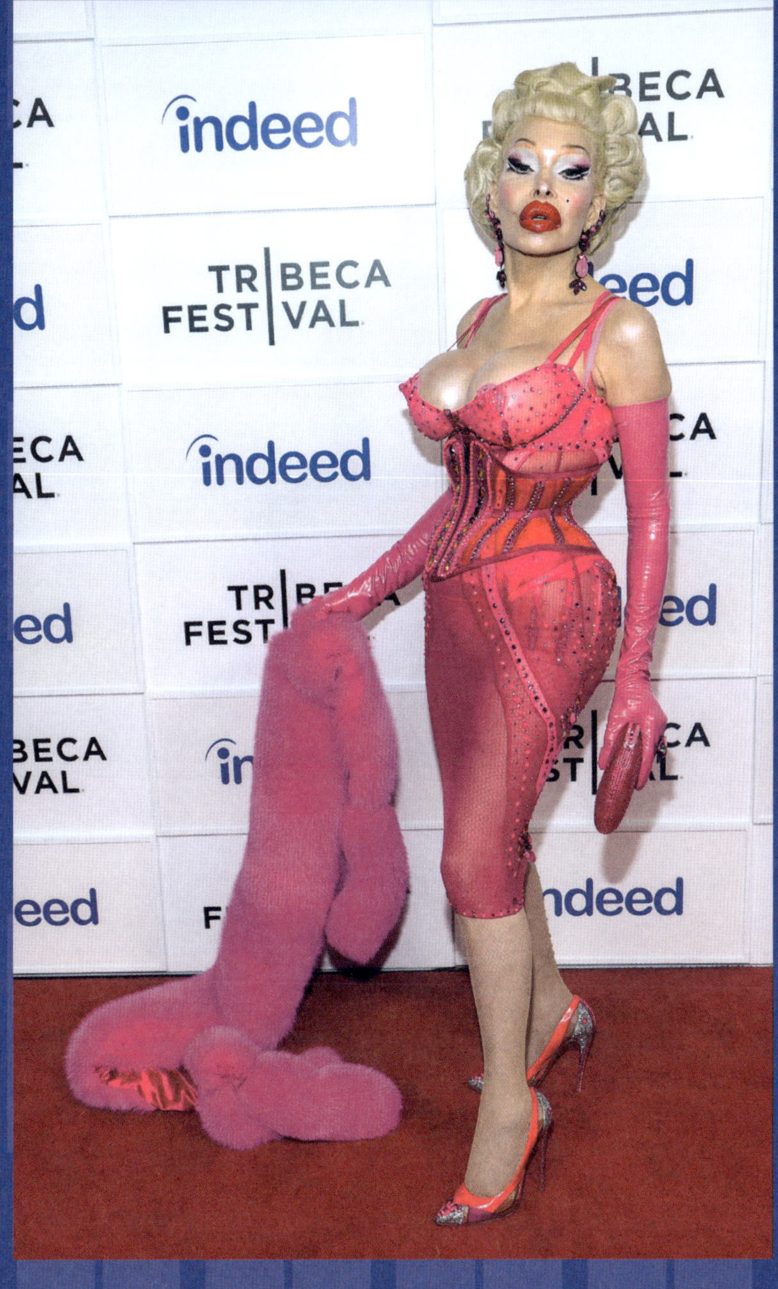
indeed
TRIBECA
FESTIVAL

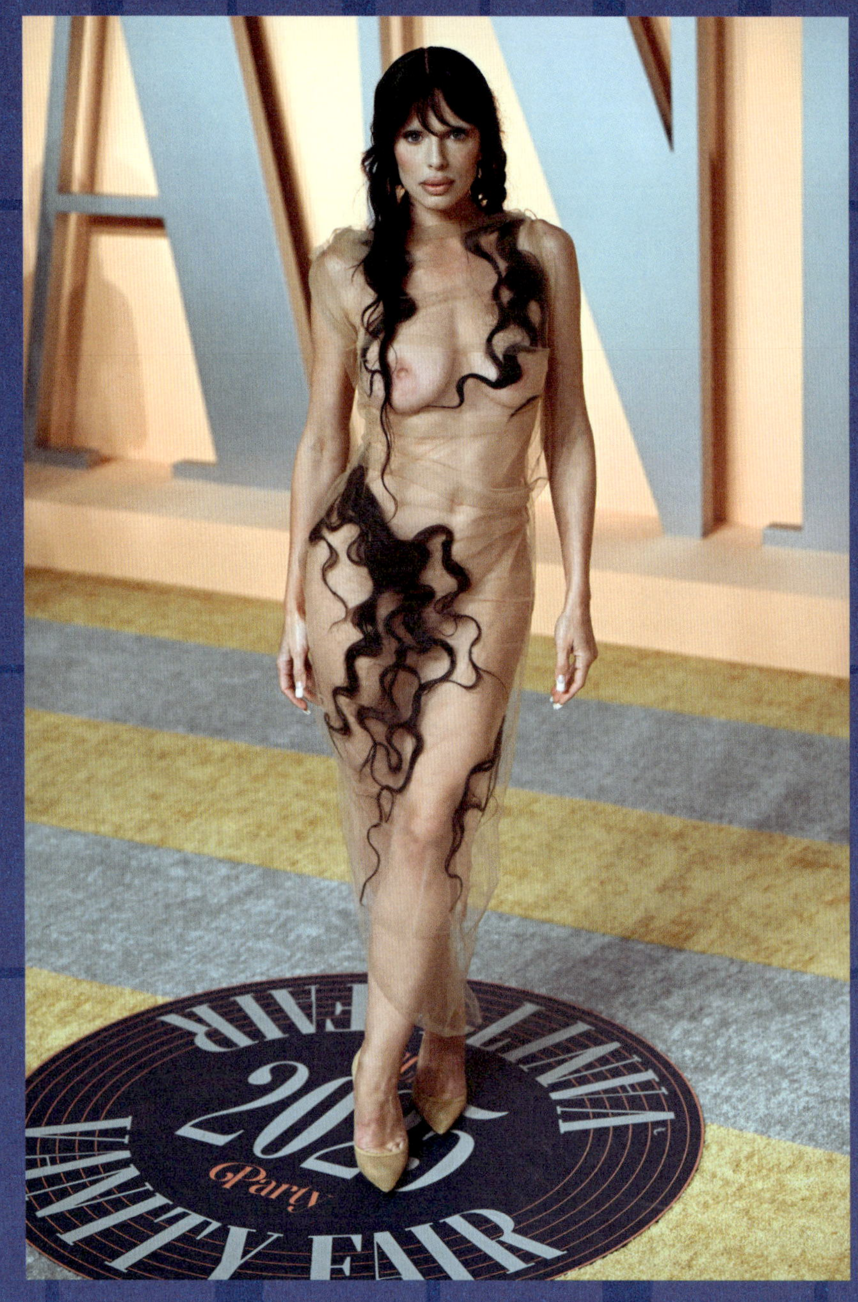
VANITY FAIR
Party

JULIA FOX

One of the most exciting dressers in recent New York history is, without a doubt, Julia Fox. The Italian native moved to the city at the age of six. Fox rose to fame after starring as Adam Sandler's girlfriend in 2019's *Uncut Gems*, and a brief relationship with Kanye West. She quickly became a forever presence in the front row.

Seemingly overnight, she went from New York City underground nightlife icon to all-round fashion fan favourite with a predilection for provocation – shocking, make-you-look-twice, unexpected pieces from emerging designers. For Fox, nothing is off-limits, and she blends her interesting personal past with experimentation. She was an underground icon for years and also worked as a dominatrix, resulting in a unique life that contributes to her bold, unafraid personal style.

New York native Briana Andalore is Fox's stylist, and together they create looks that tell stories and blur the lines between shock value and walking art. Fox has worn entire looks made out of condoms, or watches...she's worn a wedding dress and veil to a fashion show. She decidedly bares it all but does so in a way that's often considered camp, and more central to the female and queer gaze than the usual male-centric, naked dress. A good example is the time she wore a sheer Dilara Findikoglu dress accented only with swirls of brunette hair (her own extensions!) to the 2025 Vanity Fair Oscars Party. "I dress for the girls and the gays for sure, and me a little bit," Fox said in 2024. "I'm the artist but I'm also the canvas."

Opposite: Julia Fox changed the landscape of New York nightlife in the early 2020s by stunning the world with high fashion through the female gaze.

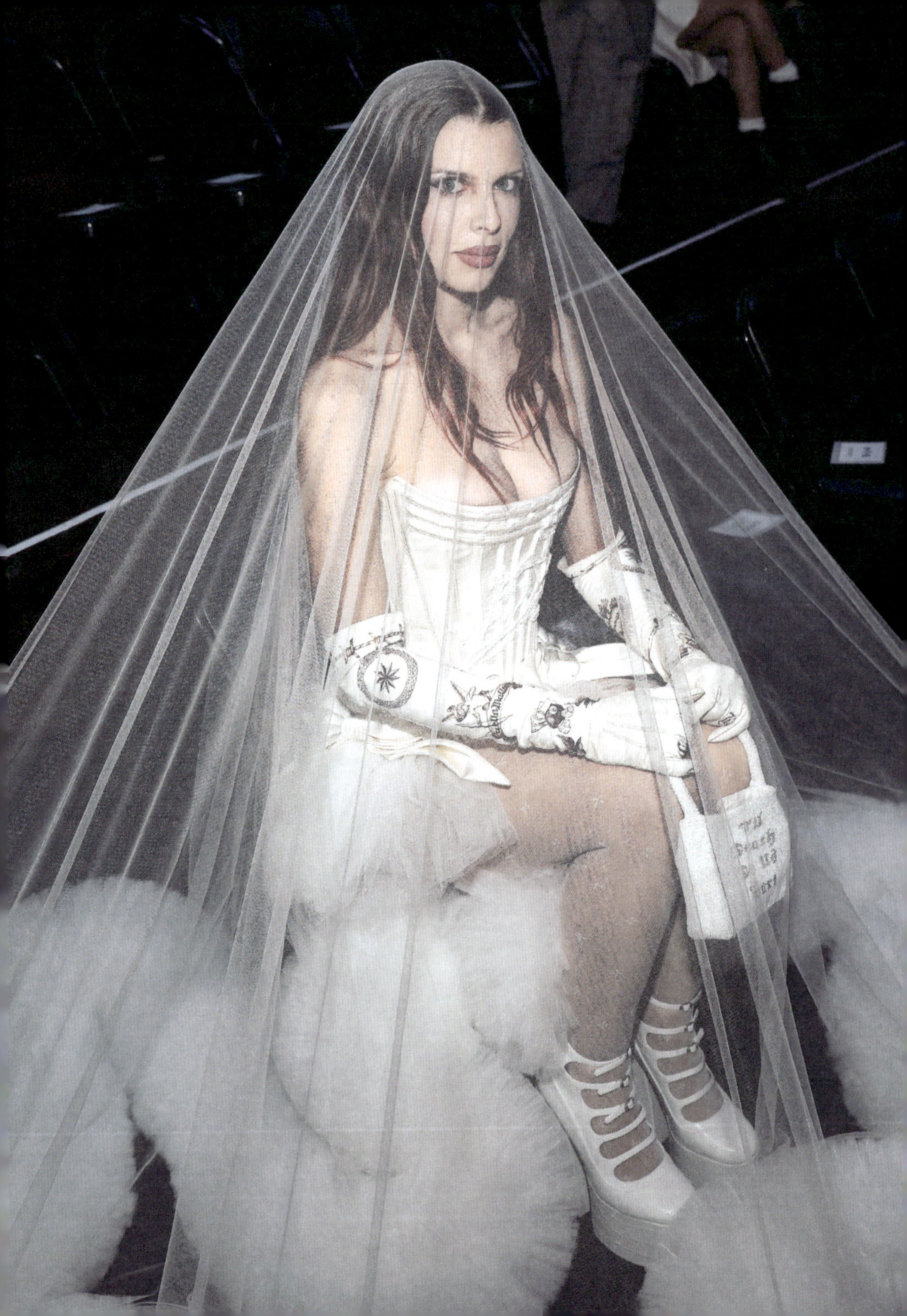

“I dress for the girls and the gays for sure, and me a little bit. I’m the artist but I’m also the canvas.”

THE CLUB CULTURE SCENE

New York's most legendary venue, Studio 54, wasn't just a club – it was a place where one came to *dress*. Consider the times style icon Bianca Jagger was photographed inside the venue: on a white horse in one of her signature slinky jersey outfits, or holding a dove in each hand in a lace dress. New York's clubs – especially Studio 54 – gave eccentric, expressive city dwellers their moments to transcend to forever fashion icons.

The rock music scene in New York, born in clubs, also birthed many icons.

Below: Bianca Jagger loved a dramatic entrance and ruled Studio 54, as shown here with her live white doves in 1977.

Opposite: In 1977, for her birthday at Studio 54, Bianca Jagger posed atop a horse in a casual glam jersey outfit.

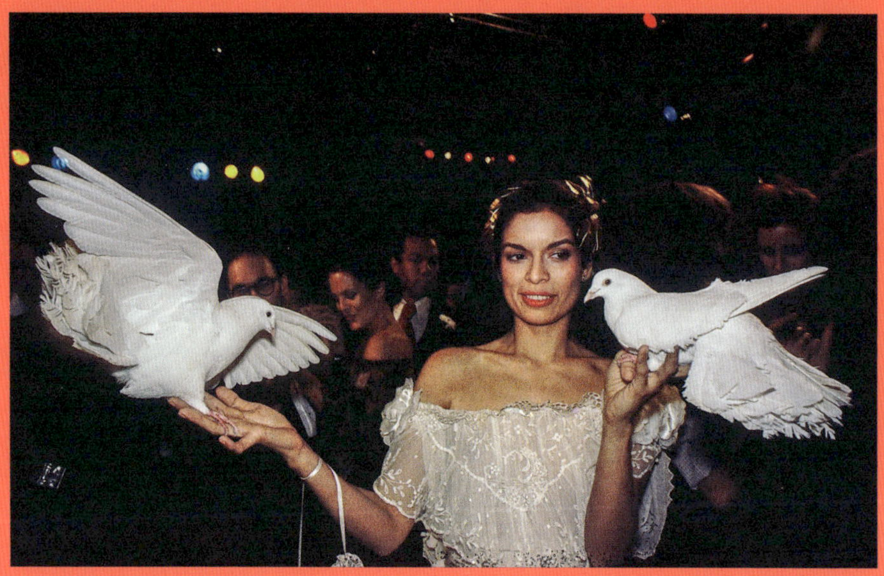

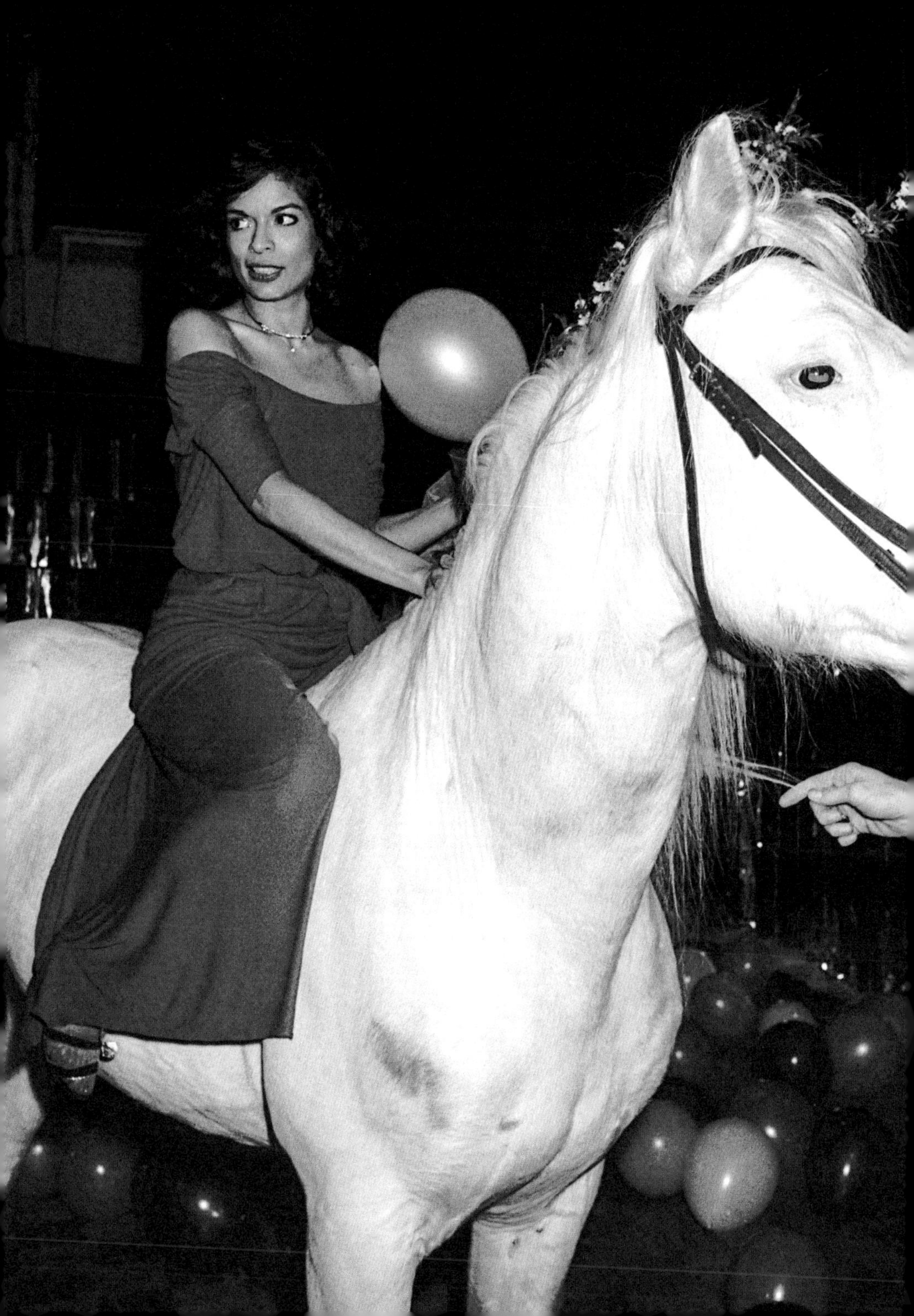

PATTI SMITH

Punk legend, singer and author Patti Smith dressed in her own expressive oversized tops, military shirts, field jackets, dungarees and down-to-earth staples when she broke into the scene in the 1970s. It's a look that would come to be replicated for decades. Smith is also legendary for her friendship with the designer Ann Demeulemeester. Early in her career, Demeulemeester saw Smith's *Horses* record (on the cover, she wears a tucked-in, white button-down and her jacket thrown over her shoulder) and was inspired to send her a package of three white shirts. "I derive great power from wearing Ann's clothes," Smith said at an event with the designer in 2014. "Since I began performing again, after that first gift, I have never gone on stage without wearing a piece by Ann. All of Ann's clothes are significant. A jacket, a vest, a shirt...they are such a part of me. They make me feel confident, they make me feel truly like myself. They are talismanic."

Patti Smith's style stands out because it's inherently practical but also heavily androgynous. It's not at all try-hard and feels fully authentic. She gravitates towards Ralph Lauren jeans. Her style echoes and celebrates music icons of the past, such as the skinny, folksy scarves of Bob Dylan. In the 1960s, she studied fashion magazines, absorbing various cultural references and storing them away to remember later. She idolized Audrey Hepburn in *Funny Face*.

Smith doesn't shy away from blending in. "My style says, 'Look at me, don't look at me'," she once told the *New York Times*. "It's, 'I don't care what you think.'" Her look is, at the end of the day, a carefully curated reflection and refraction of control and statement-making expression.

Opposite: Patti Smith will always represent the perpetually cool, downtown, rock 'n' roll soul of New York, often opting for pieces designed by Ann Demeulemeester.

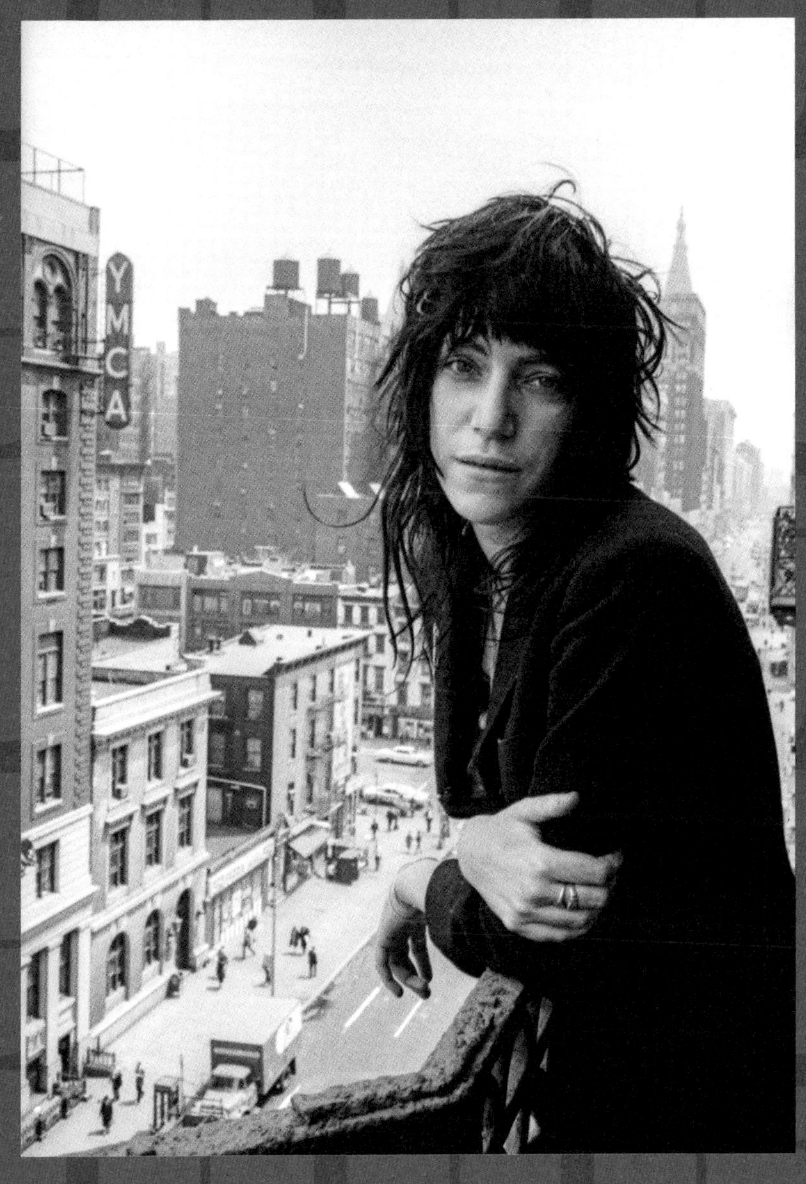
YMCA

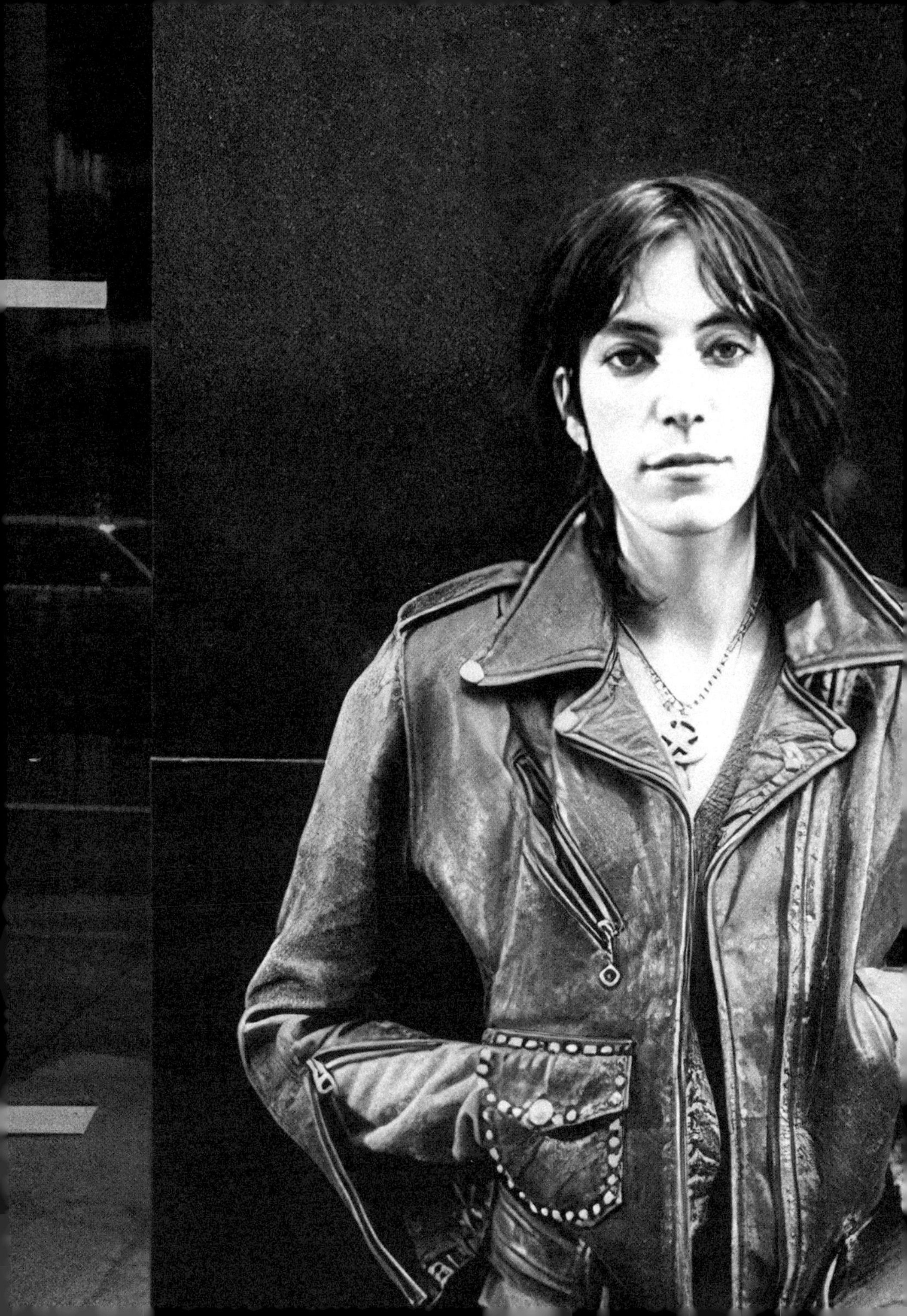

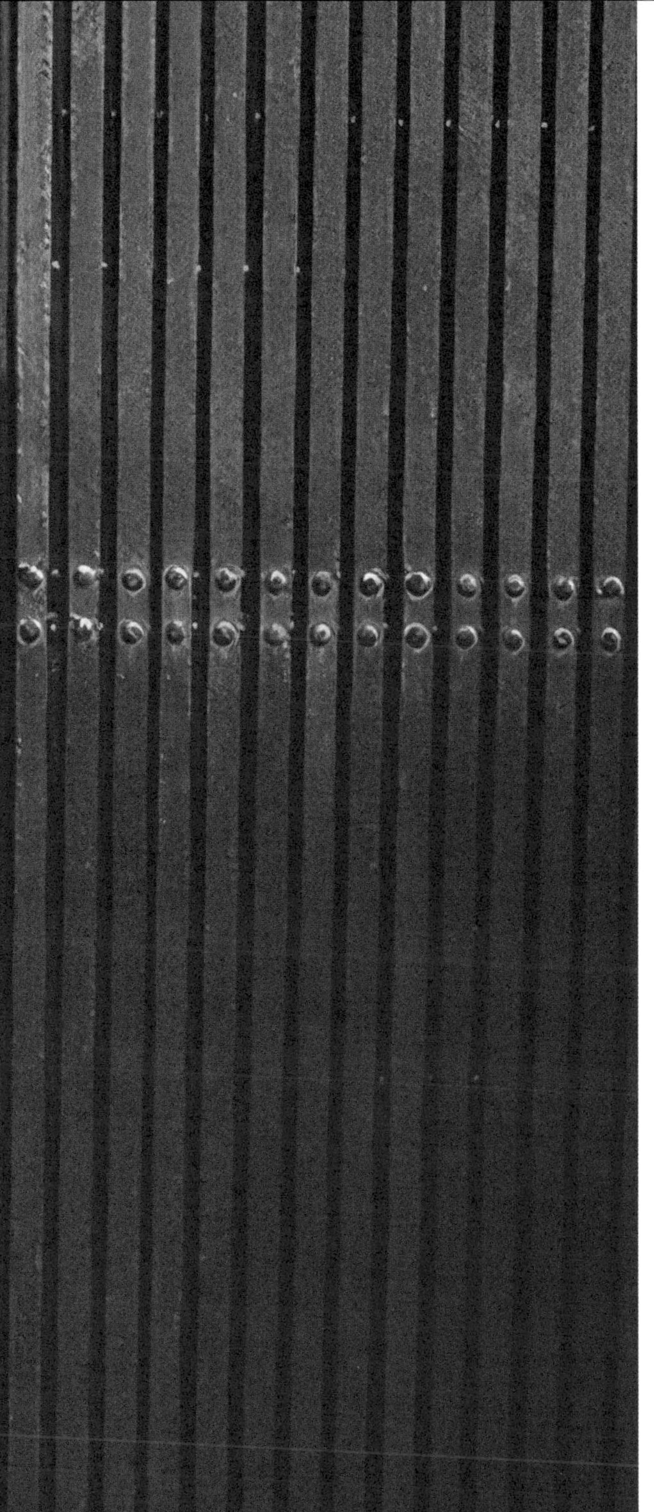

Left: The style staples of Patti Smith consist of worn-in leather jackets and cool, messy hairstyles. Button-down shirts also feature.

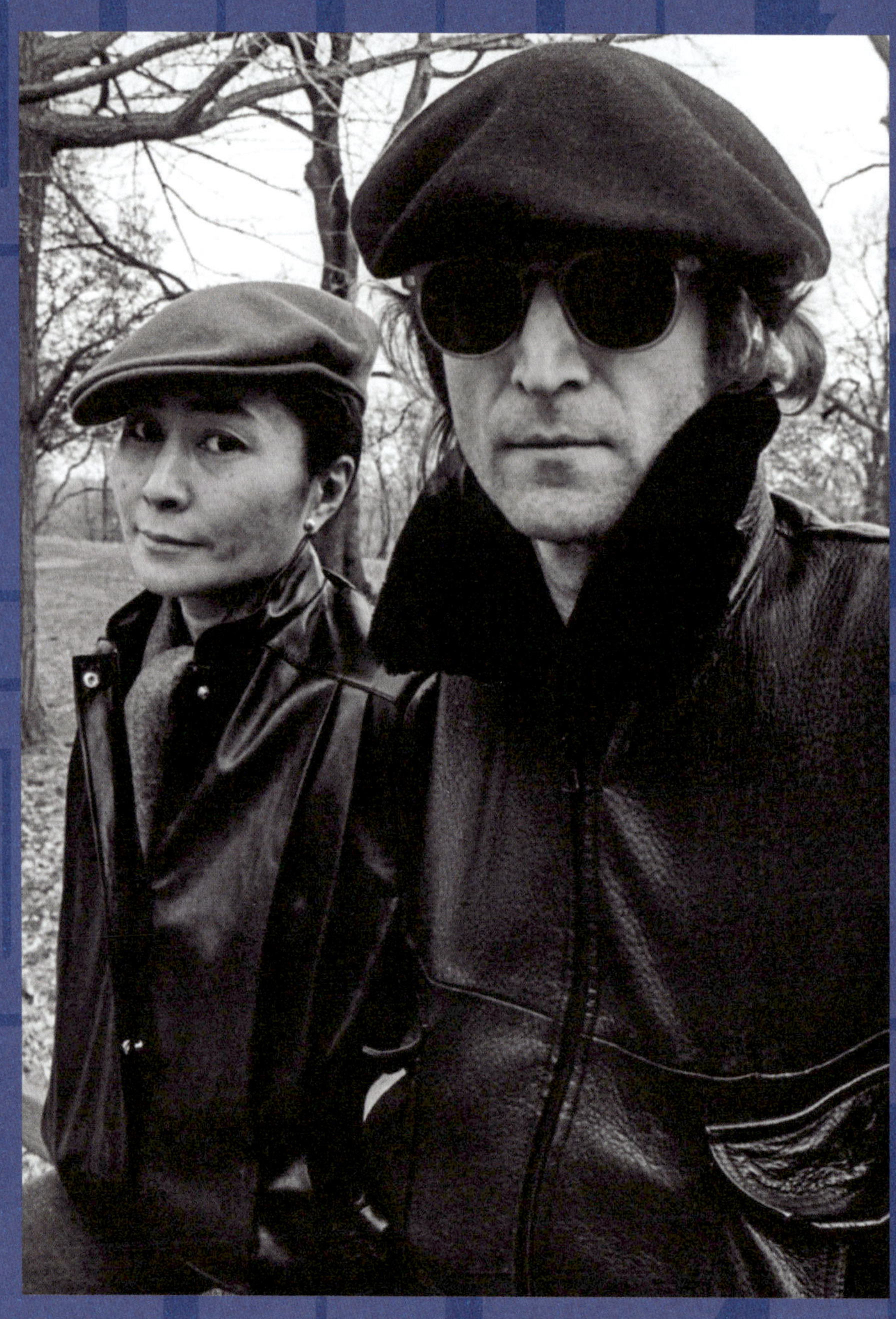

JOHN & YOKO

Yoko Ono and John Lennon each served as hippie rock fashion icons when they moved to New York in 1971, making waves with floppy hats, sunglasses, ties, turtlenecks, little scarves and leather jackets. The duo were arguably one of the most watched couples in New York at the time, standing together as a powerhouse. Lennon was well remembered for his little round glasses and bohemian blouses, without a doubt The Beatles member who had the most fashion credibility. Ono lived in little mini-dresses, satisfyingly eccentric coats and textural, hippie-coded wonders that played well with her long, luscious hair.

Ono herself had a major presence and impact on the avant-garde art scene long before she joined forces with Lennon, and with that came her influence of style. Her work tackled topics of feminism, politics and gender, even involving fashion to a varying degree. In her 1964 work titled *Cut Piece*, she invited the audience to cut her clothing from her body. Ono famously married John Lennon while wearing sneakers, a mini-dress and floppy hat. She once spent $400,000 on 70 fur coats for herself and late husband Lennon at Bergdorf Goodman. "She's me in drag," Lennon once said of Ono in a 1969 interview with British journalist David Wigg. She's the artsy minimalist, but she also plays the role of the highly expressive oddball; always with an incredibly distinct point of view.

Opposite: There may not be a musical duo as significant for their style in all of New York history as John Lennon and Yoko Ono, who each had their own artistic, counterculture-inspired style.

THE RAMONES

At the same time, the early punk band the Ramones formed in the Queens neighbourhood of Forest Hills and became known for their tight skinny jeans, shaggy mullets and tiny leather jackets – staples later to be revived by the emo and indie sleaze subcultures. Johnny Ramone, in particular, was known for performing in his leather jackets, no matter the weather. In the early days, the group was inspired by the glam rock aesthetic. "We were more glamorous when we started, almost like a glitter group," Dee Dee Ramone told *Spin* magazine in the 1990s. "A lot of times, Joey would wear rubber clothes and John would wear vinyl clothes, or silver pants. We used to look great, but then we fell into the leather-jacket-and-ripped-up-jeans thing."

Simply look at any of the brands today referencing rock 'n' roll culture, and it's impossible not to notice the Ramones' ultimate fashion influence. Their aesthetic can be seen in places as far ranging as the indie sleaze and e-boy revival on TikTok to the work of former Celine creative director Hedi Slimane. Joey Ramone famously lived and shopped in the East Village where he would often visit the original punk store on St Mark's Place, Trash and Vaudeville. His favourite item was the stretch jean, exclusively worn with sneakers and a beat-up leather jacket.

Opposite: The Ramones are one of New York's most influential bands, both in terms of influence and style: tight jeans, T-shirts, mullet shag hairstyles and all.

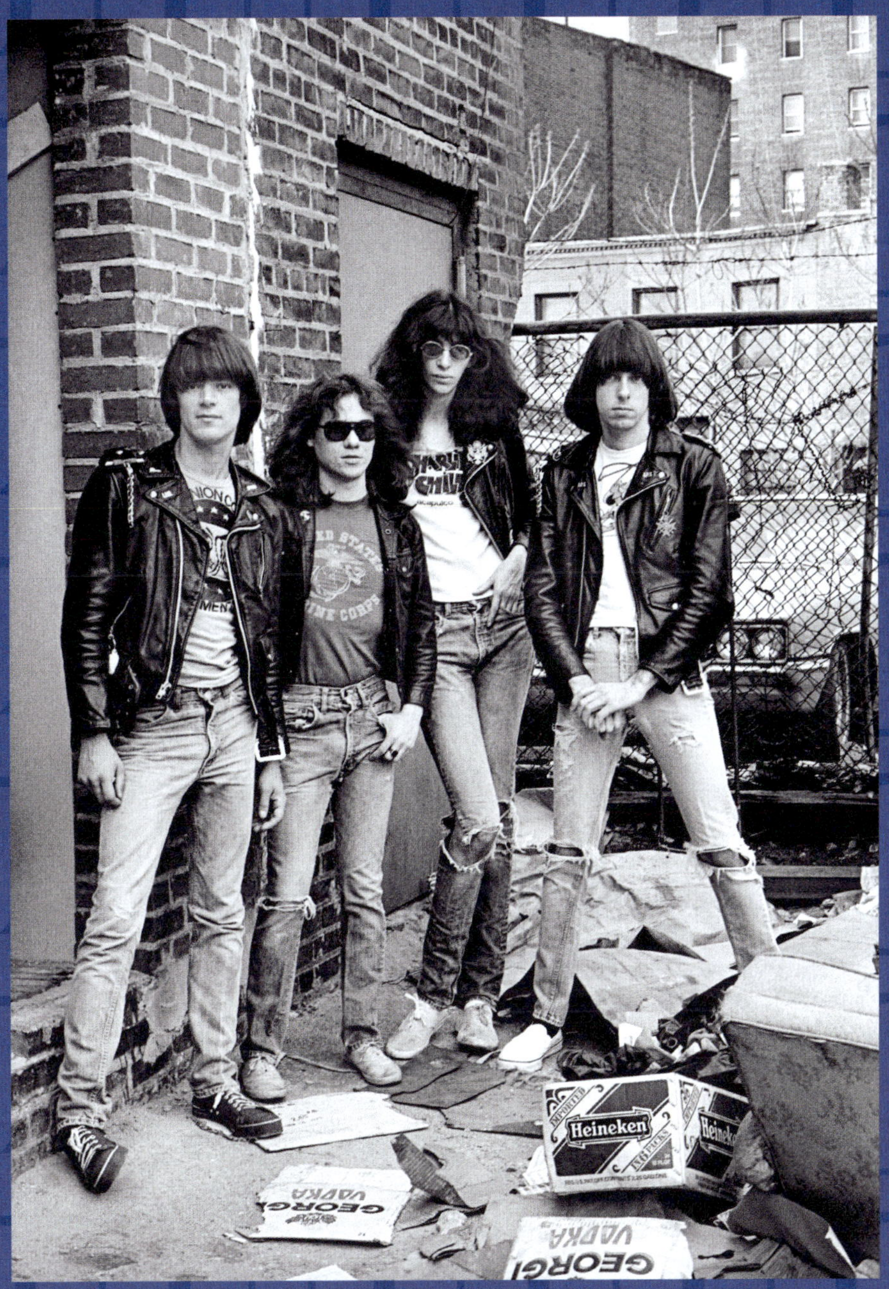
IMPORTED
Heineken
GEORGI
VADKA

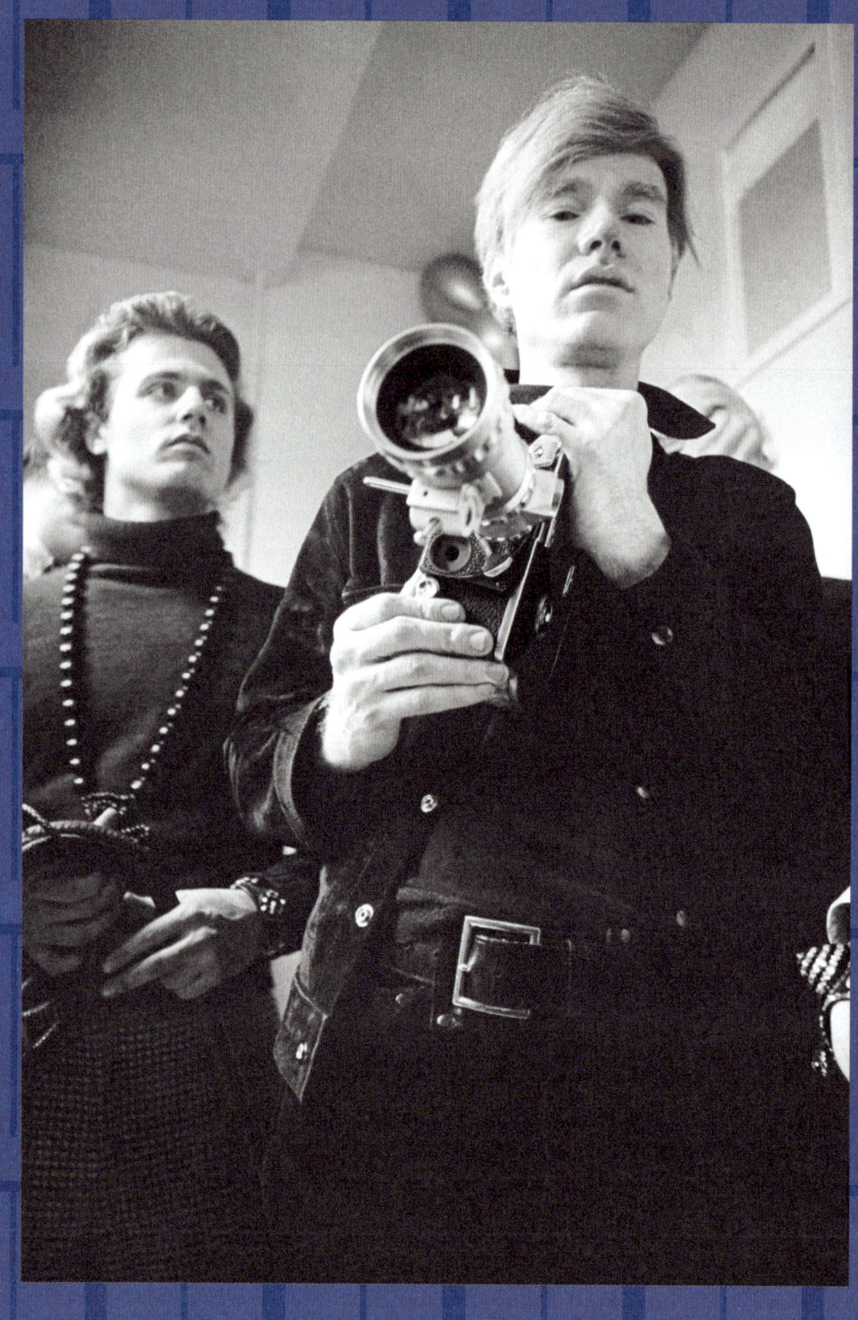

WARHOL & HIS SUPERSTARS

Andy Warhol was a regular at Studio 54, and served as his own kind of fashion icon in his never-changing, rotating outfits of black leather jacket or blazer, a tie or bow tie, black turtleneck or white button-down, black boots, jeans and his silvery wig. The famed pop artist was instantly recognizable and another great example of uniform dressing. At The Factory, Warhol's studio and cultural hub from 1963 to 1987, he collaborated with memorable style icons, including Edie Sedgwick, who starred in a number of Warhol's films and became known for her chic short haircut, big earrings, little tights, tiny leotards, capes and cool, black-and-white mod style during that time. The 1972 flick *Ciao! Manhattan* is a semi-biographical retelling of her time in New York, cementing her as one of the city's first It-girls. Elsewhere, transgender icon Candy Darling starred in Warhol's *Flesh* and *Women in Revolt*, and became known for her glamorous gowns, fringe scarves, big hats, pearls, and feathered and fur jackets, reminiscent of her own kind of Hollywood siren.

Opposite: Andy Warhol defined a generation of art and style in the city, both with his own presentation of himself as well as with his group of factory models, actresses and creatives who he called muses.

Overleaf: Andy Warhol was at the epicentre of culture in New York and was often seen with other famous style icons such as Debbie Harry, pictured here alongside Jerry Hall, Truman Capote and Paloma Picasso at Studio 54.

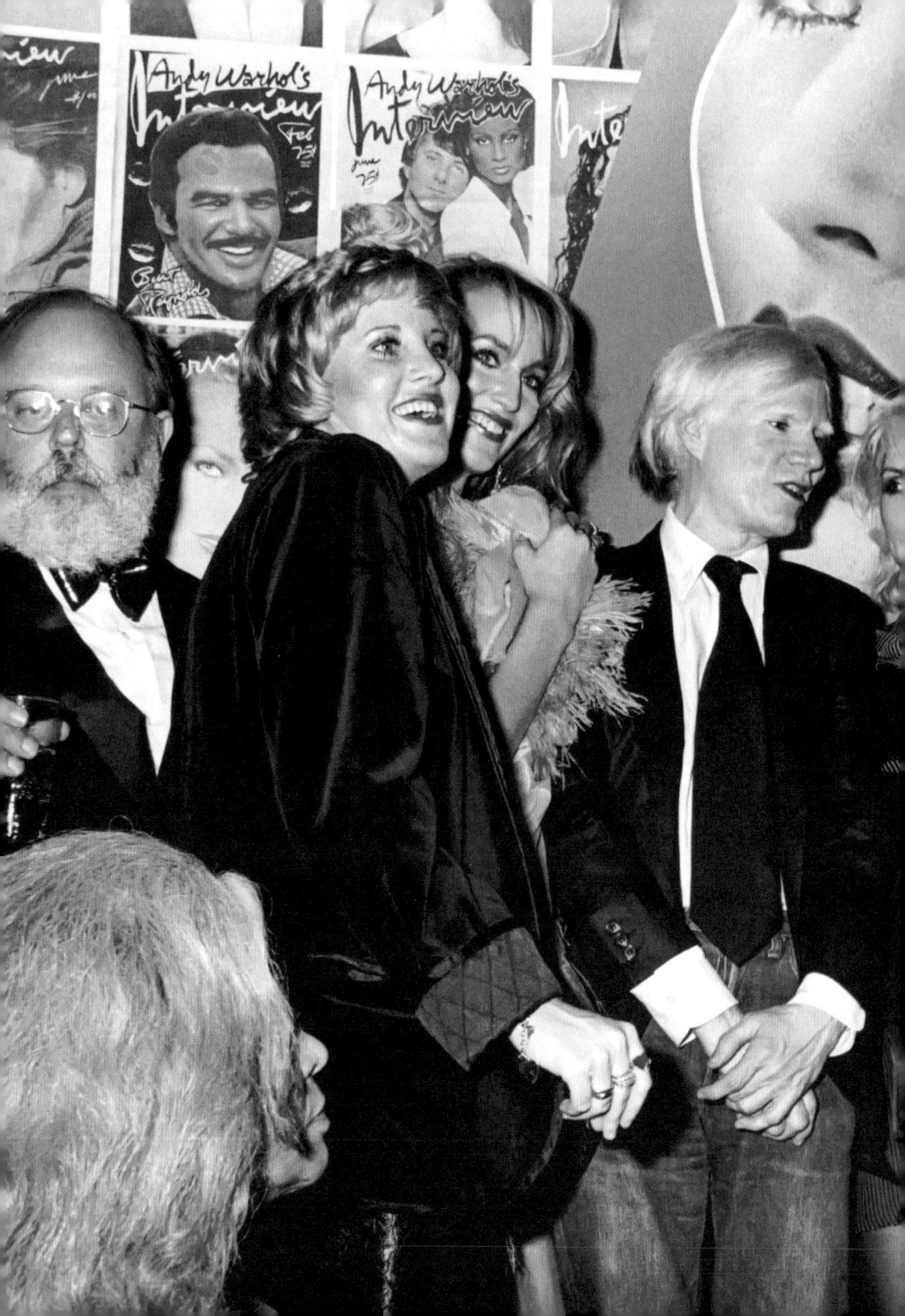

Andy Warhol's
Interview
Feb 75
Burt Reynolds
Andy Warhol's
Interview
June 75

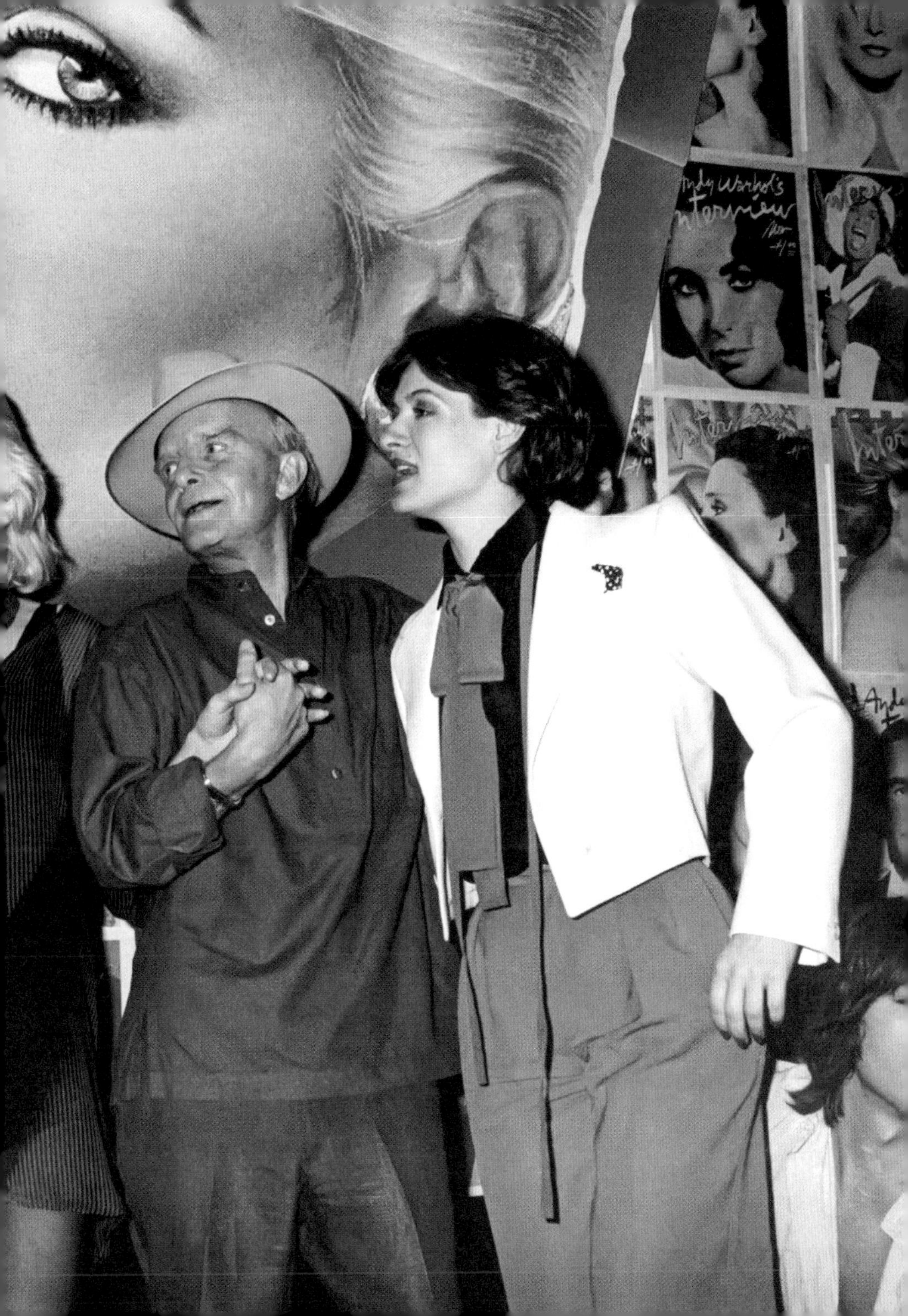
Warhol's

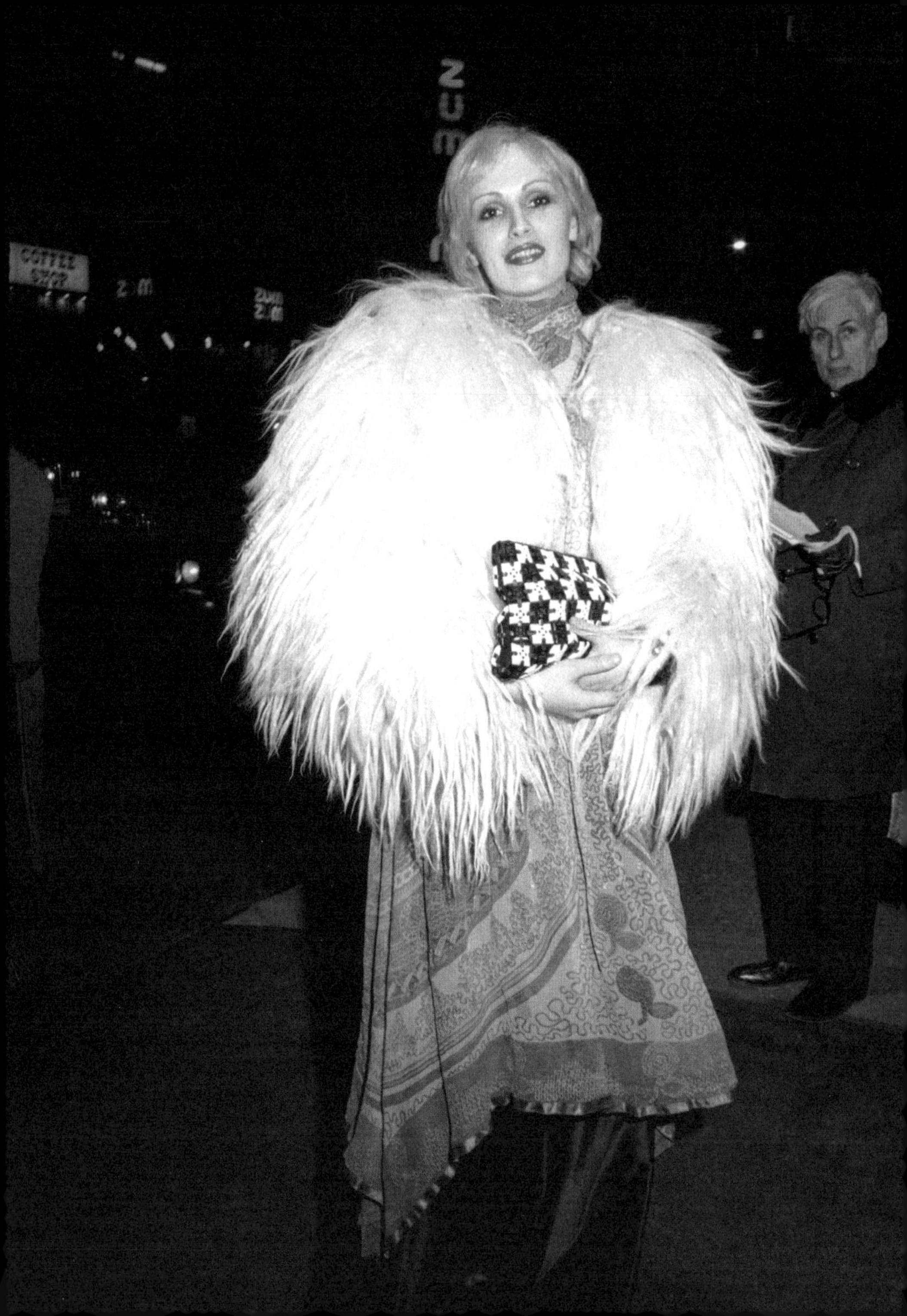

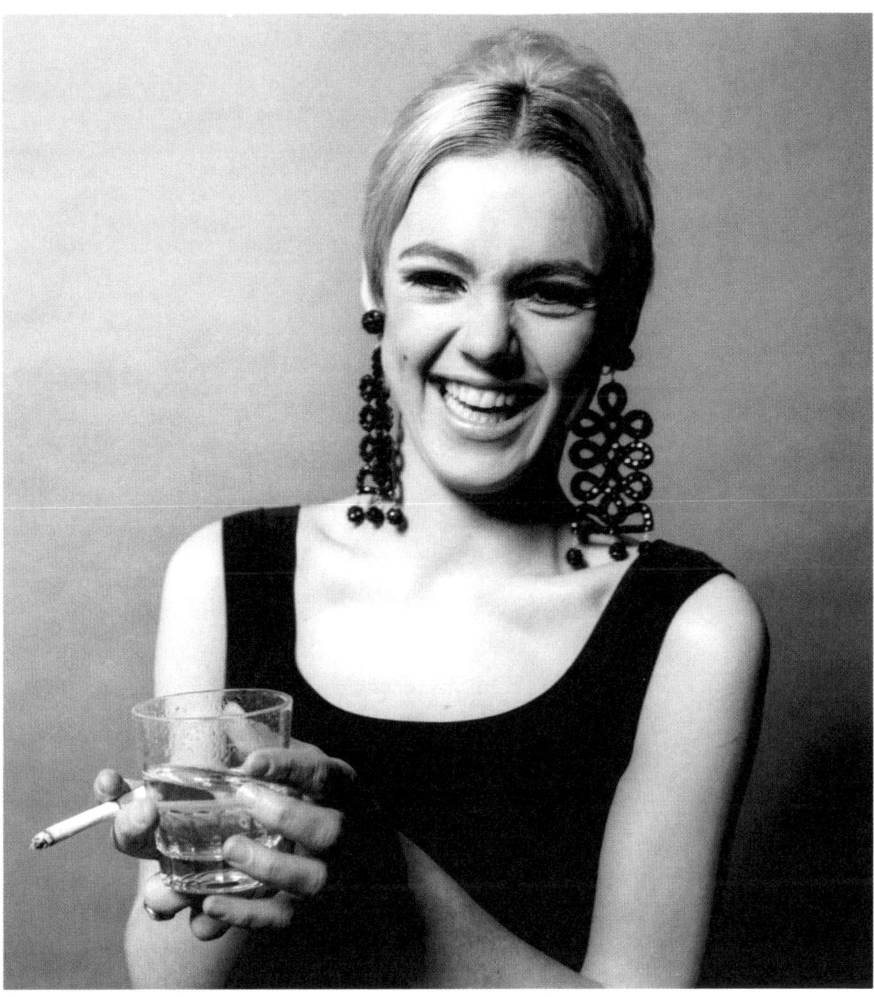

Opposite: Candy Darling, seen here, was one of the fashion icons in the circle of Andy Warhol.

Above: Edie Sedgwick was also one of Andy Warhol's muses. She defined a legacy of style with her iconic, short haircut, huge, decorative earrings, and graphic, sleek mini-dresses.

DEBBIE HARRY

As the lead vocalist of the band Blondie, Debbie Harry epitomizes the New York DIY scene in the best sense of the word. She co-formed Blondie in 1974 in New York City, after working various jobs as a waiter, dancer and Playboy Bunny. The singer created her own version of New Wave feminine punk style with her shaggy blonde hair – an ode to Marilyn Monroe. And she started it all in some of New York's most infamous punk clubs in the 1970s – CBGB and Max's Kansas City.

While on stage, Harry often wore denim on denim. She also experimented with emerging designers at the time, such as Stephen Sprouse, who would later go on to collaborate with fashion giants like Louis Vuitton. Harry wore the designer's TV scan lines dress for her 1979 "Heart of Glass" music video, which was groundbreaking at the time. She mixed prints and patterns, wore purposely distressed pieces and had a penchant for printed tees. She has always been at the forefront of DIY, attaching safety pins and other accessories to her own looks. Today, she continues to wear her own offbeat creations to public appearances.

Above all else, and through all the seismic style changes throughout the years, her hair is one of the most iconic things about her look. "The attention [from being blonde] can be very flattering," she once told *Interview*. "As a colour it's like wearing a neon sign over your head. It's like walking around with your own spotlight. It's definitely a showbiz-y kind of thing to do, even for people who aren't in showbiz. But being blonde was a great merchandizing thing for me. I never got as much promotion as I did when I was Blondie. I did a couple of films as a redhead and there just wasn't that hook in people's brains."

Opposite: Debbie Harry symbolized rock culture in the city, DIYing many of her own looks from the very beginning and leaning into slashed, deconstructed pieces, as seen here.

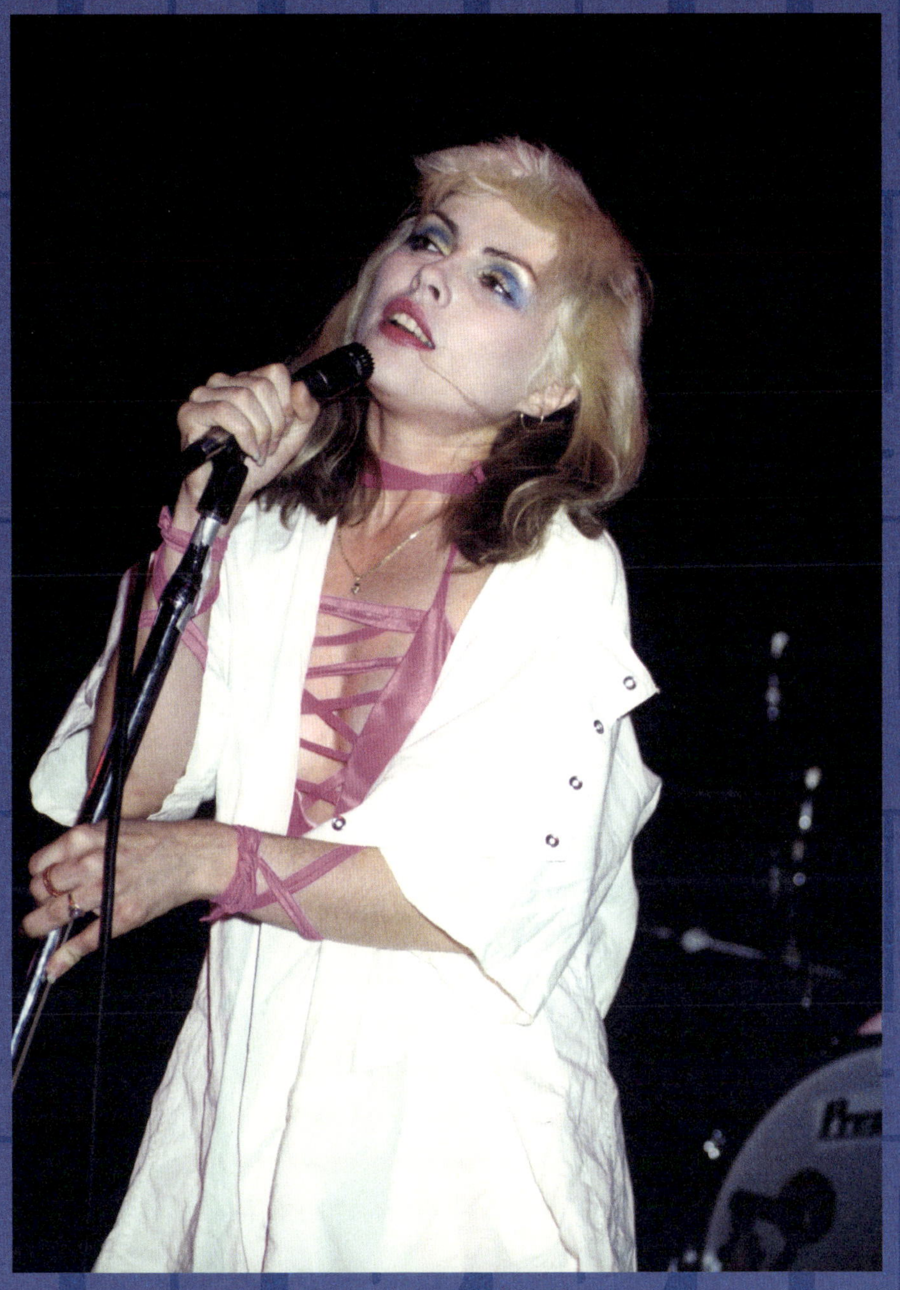

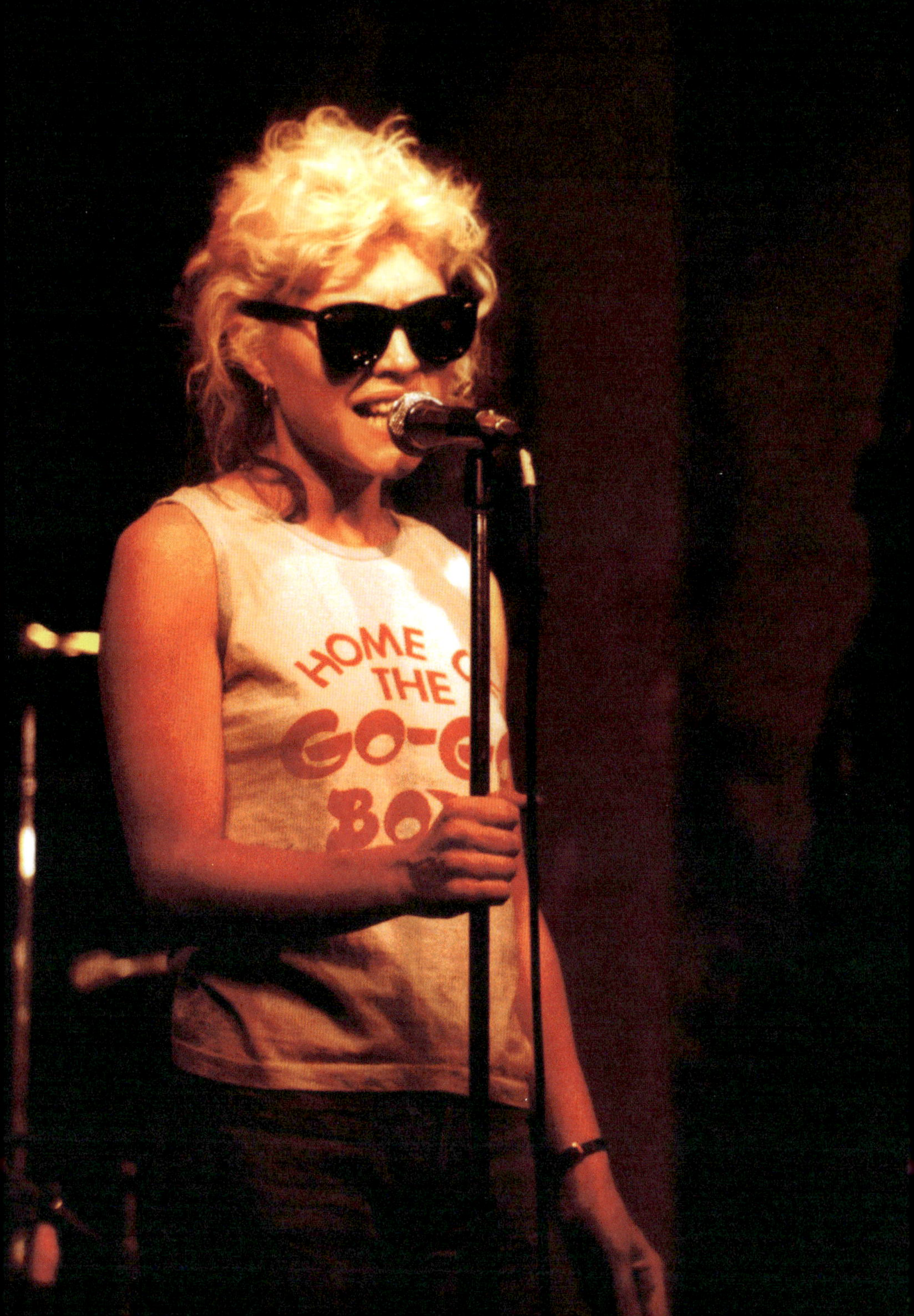
HOME
THE

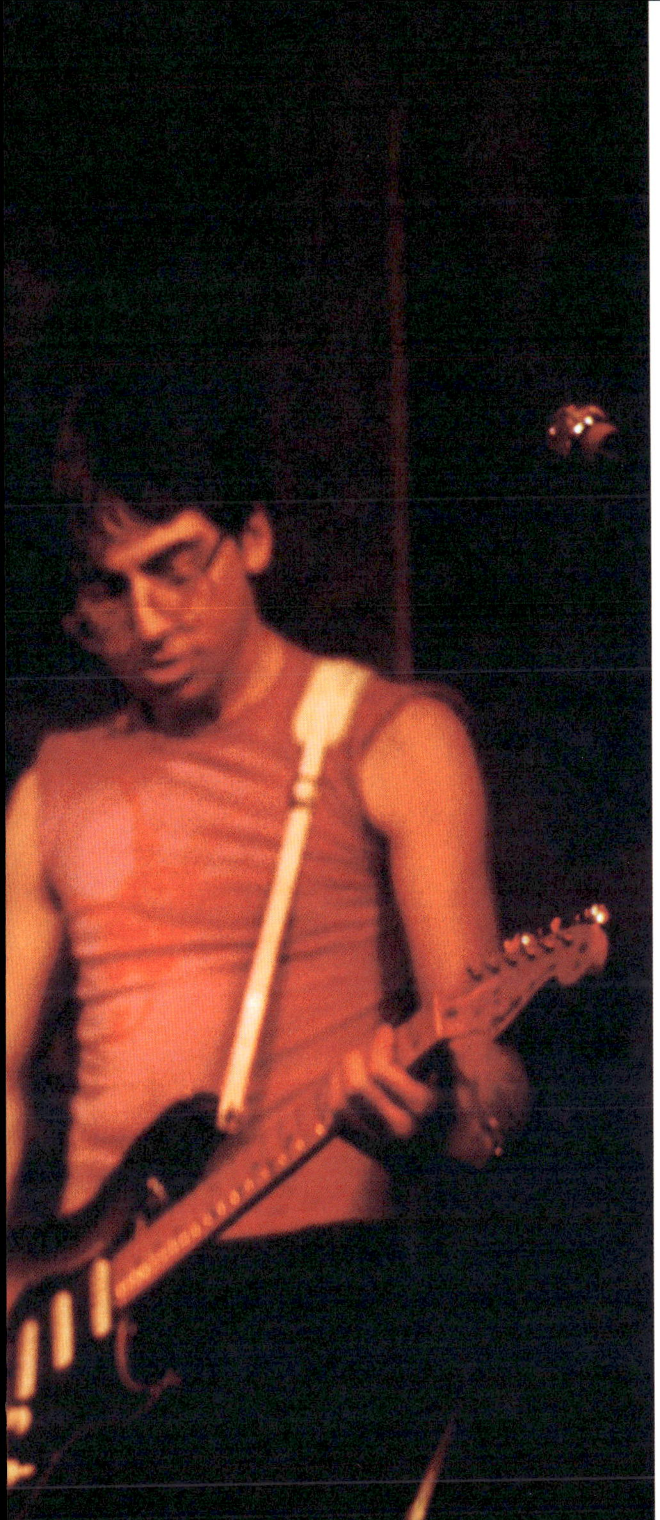

Left: Debbie Harry also had an iconic beauty look, with bright blonde hair (true to her Blondie name); she sometimes liked to perform in dark sunglasses.

CLUB KIDS

Later in the 1980s and 1990s, New York had its own club kid cultural renaissance, which introduced a slew of innovative fashion style stars.

Queen of drag RuPaul made style history in New York, with over-the-top outfits, wigs and performances in the LGBTQ scene. RuPaul's debut single, 'Supermodel (You Better Work)' (1993), and MAC Cosmetics Viva Glam campaign (1994) were both incredibly boundary-breaking at the time, and laid the footwork for the artist's eventual 14 Primetime Emmy Awards, three GLAAD Media Awards, a Critics' Choice Television Award, two *Billboard* Music Awards, and a Tony Award. Artist Susanne Bartsch also dominated the club kid resurgence, with her wildly creative outfits and parties, which would later earn her a fashion exhibition at The Museum at FIT in 2015. Others, such as Dianne Brill, Jenny Dembrow, Connie Fleming and Walt Cassidy, changed DIY fashion history with their incredibly out-there club kid looks. Actress and activist Laverne Cox was also part of the scene, and now remains one of the city's best dressed, and most serious, archival fashion collectors. Along with acting as an activist for fellow transgender women, she owns and regularly wears some of the rarest archival vintage runway pieces by Thierry Mugler, Alexander McQueen, John Galliano and others.

Opposite: RuPaul has been incredibly influential in the New York scene, breaking boundaries for generations to come and leading with dramatic wigs, as well as highly detailed, sequined dresses and outfits, all worn with dramatic flair.

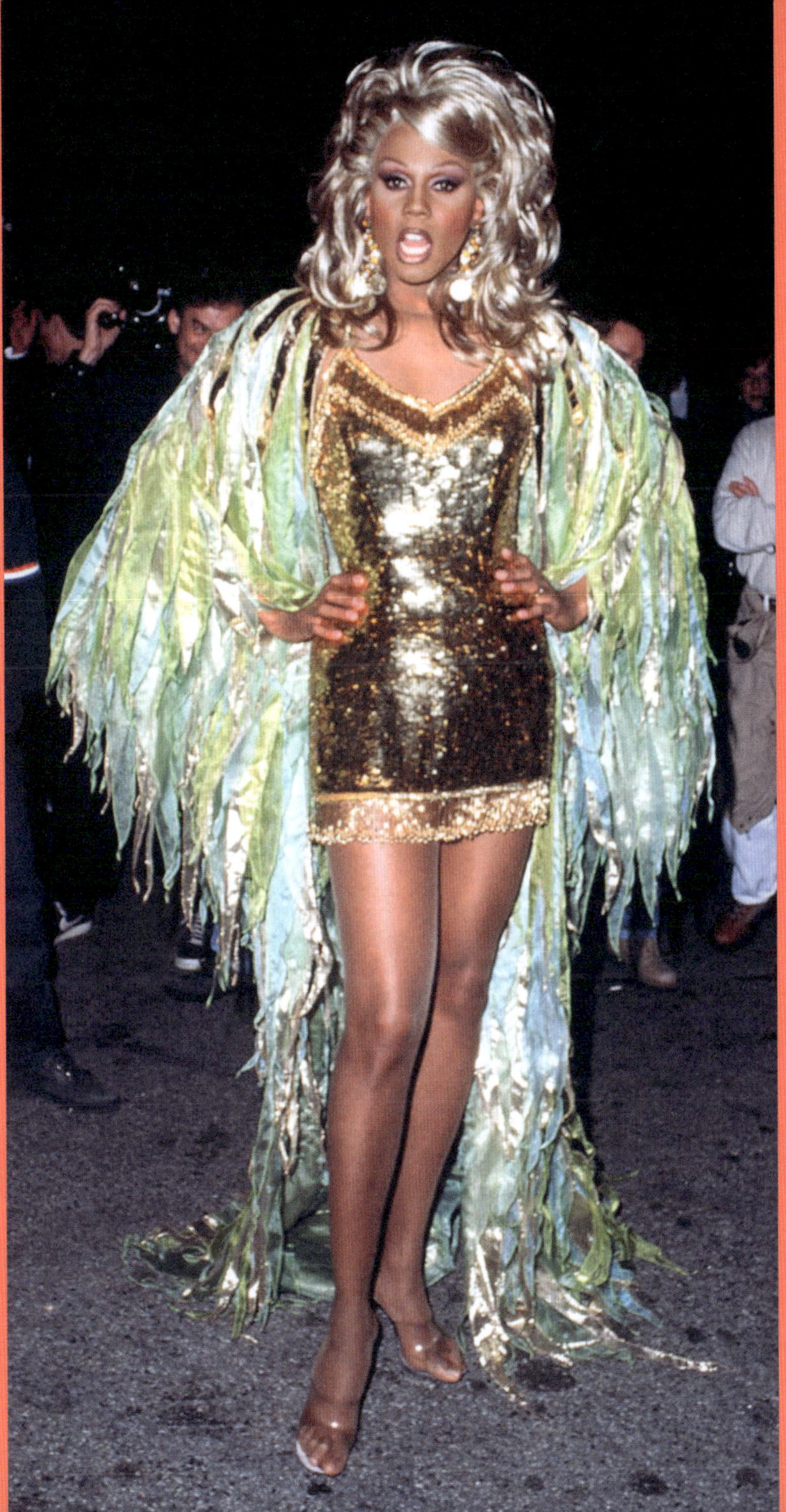

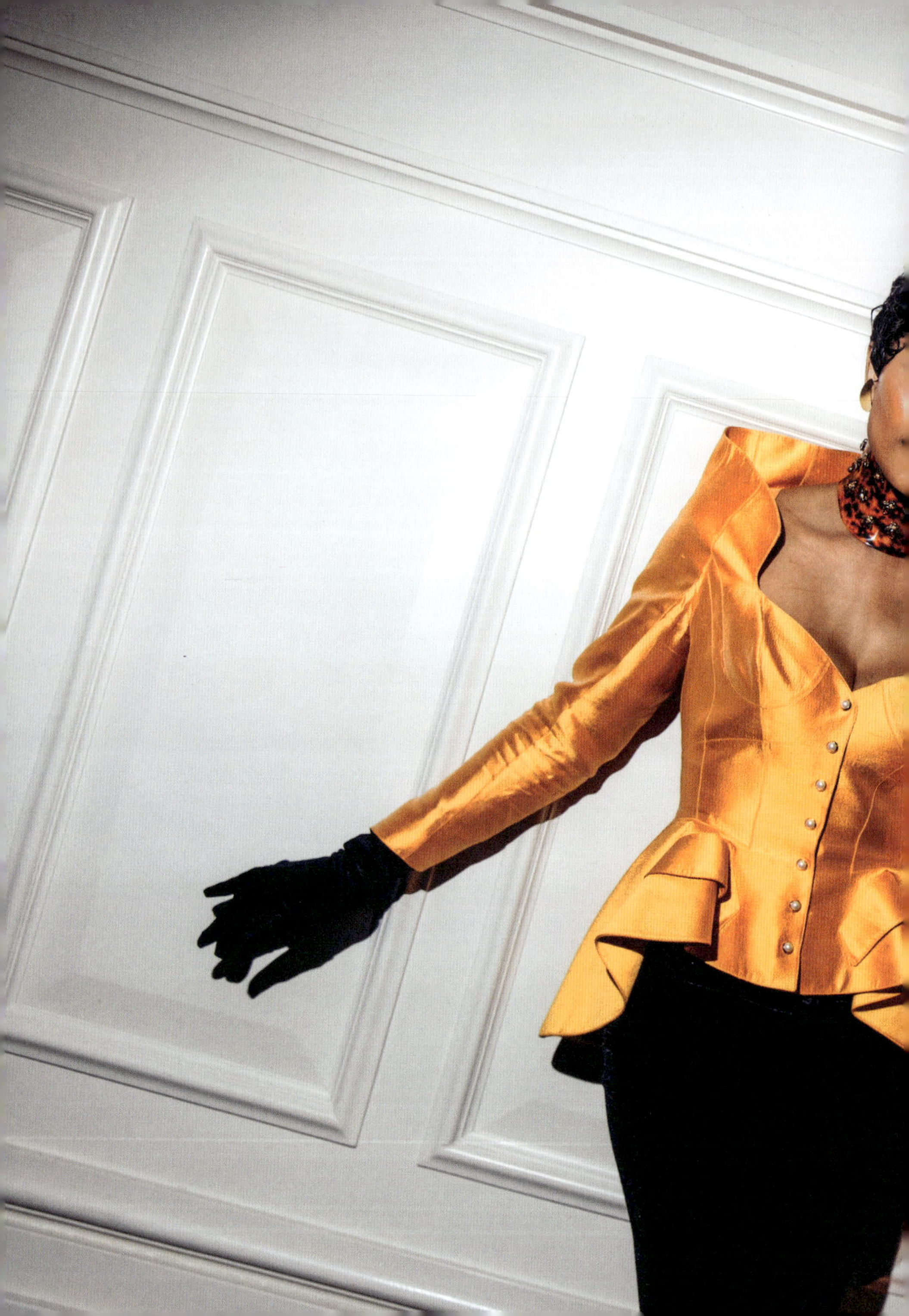

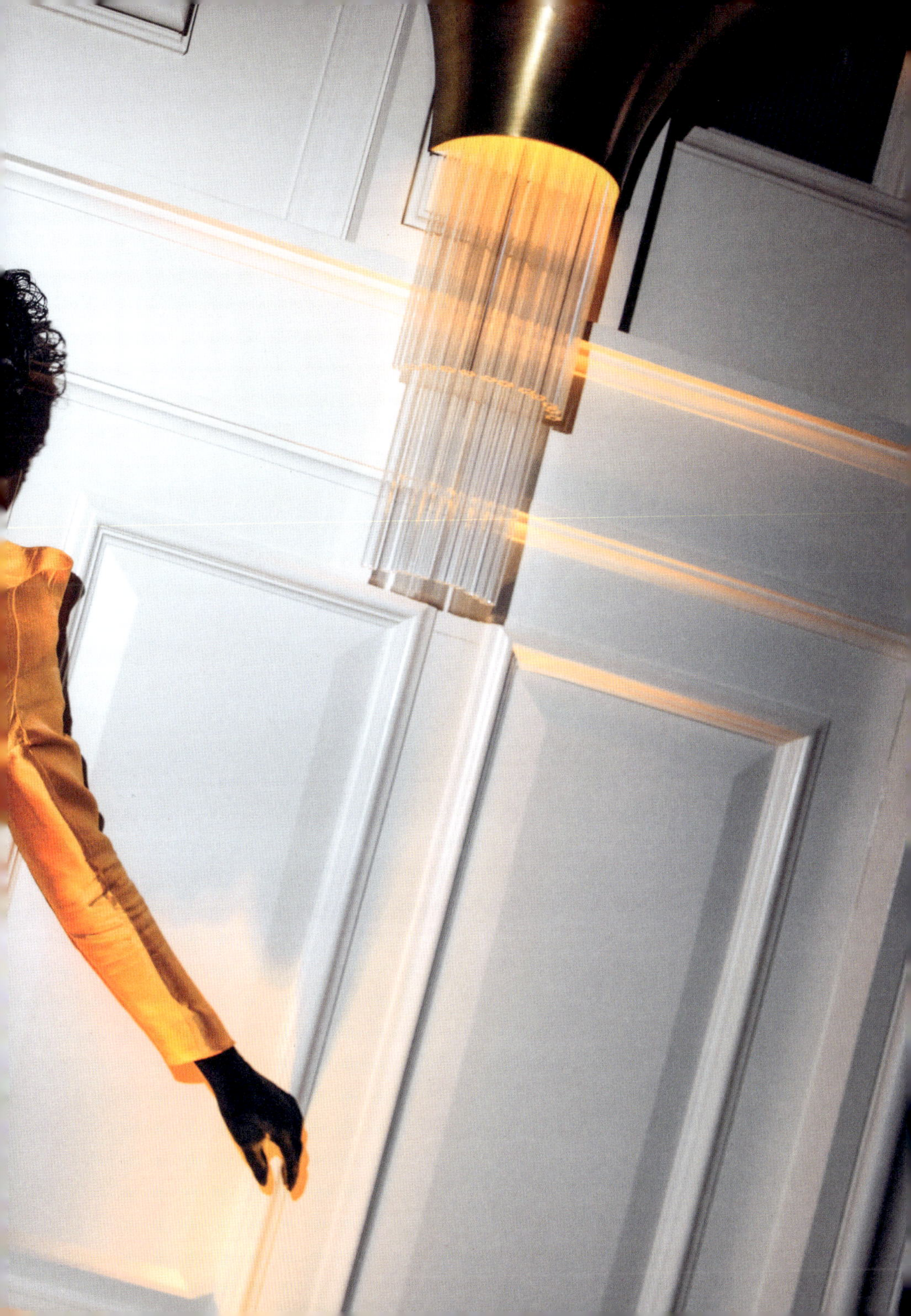

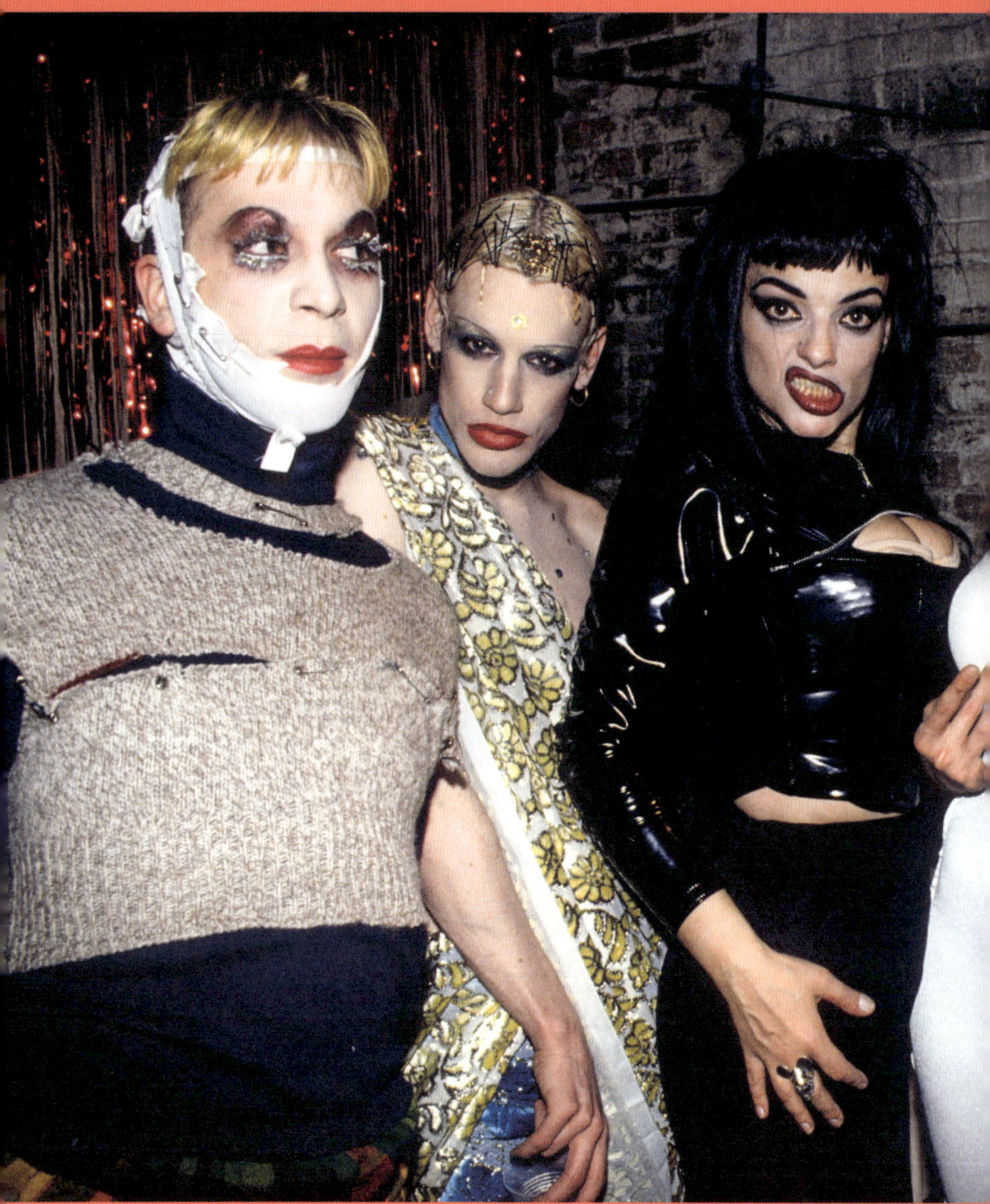

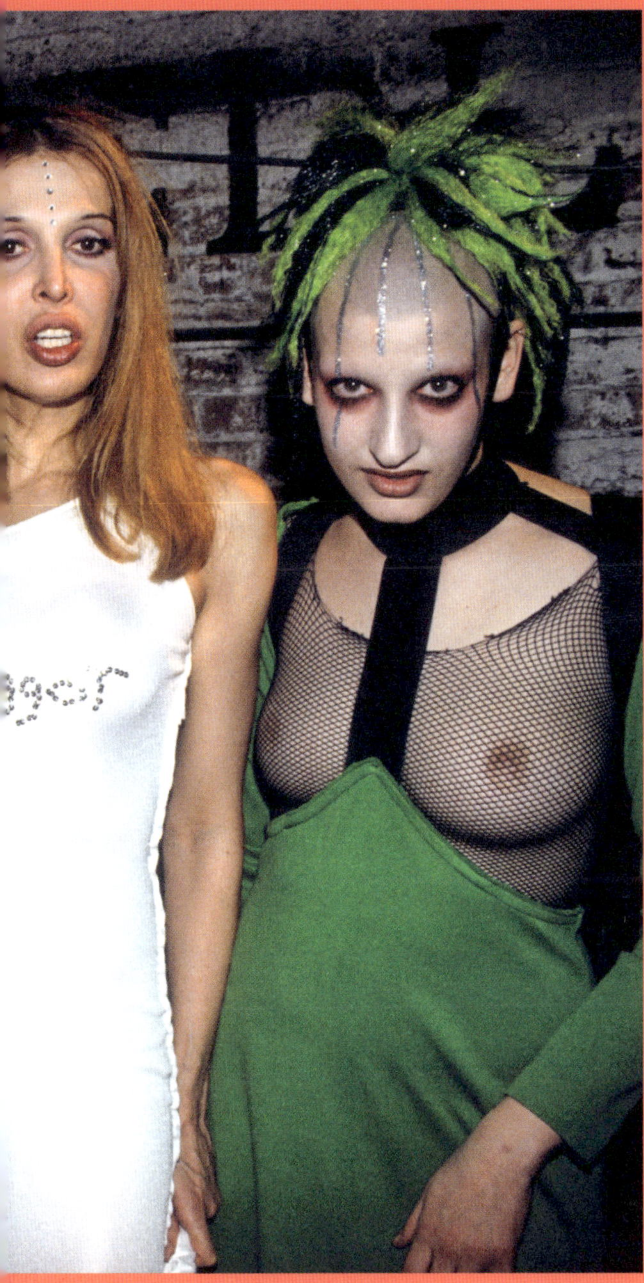

Previous: Today, Laverne Cox is one of the best-dressed New Yorkers, with a collection of rare vintage to rival a museum. She frequently wears vintage Thierry Mugler, as seen here.

Left: The OG "club kids" of 1990s New York were original style icons for their DIY looks. From left to right, Michael Alig, Richie Rich, Nina Hagen, Sophia Lamar and Genetalia at the Tunnel Club in New York City.

BARBRA STREISAND

It wouldn't be New York without its fabulous Broadway scene. With a native theatrical talent and natural love of drama, the stars and producers behind New York's iconic theatre district have a devotion to dressing. New York-born Barbra Streisand is the first performer to earn an Emmy, Grammy, Oscar and Tony award, and an early advocate for embracing one's own natural beauty, even against harsh criticism of her natural nose.

From her beginnings on the city's nightclub scene and on Broadway, to glamorous star of the silver screen, Streisand owns her individuality. Her onscreen style is as memorable as her astonishing voice – from head-to-toe leopard print in her movie debut *Funny Girl* (1968) to white suiting and that baker-boy hat in *What's Up, Doc?* (1972). She has been loved for the sequins, fringe and glamour in *A Star Is Born* (1976) and the gold and feathers in *Hello, Dolly!* (1969). She lives for drama and accessories. When she picked up the Oscar for Best Actress in 1969, she was wearing a sequinned Arnold Scaasi bell-bottomed trouser suit – always an original star.

Opposite: In her early days, Barbra Streisand shaped her style legacy by wearing chic hats and leopard prints.

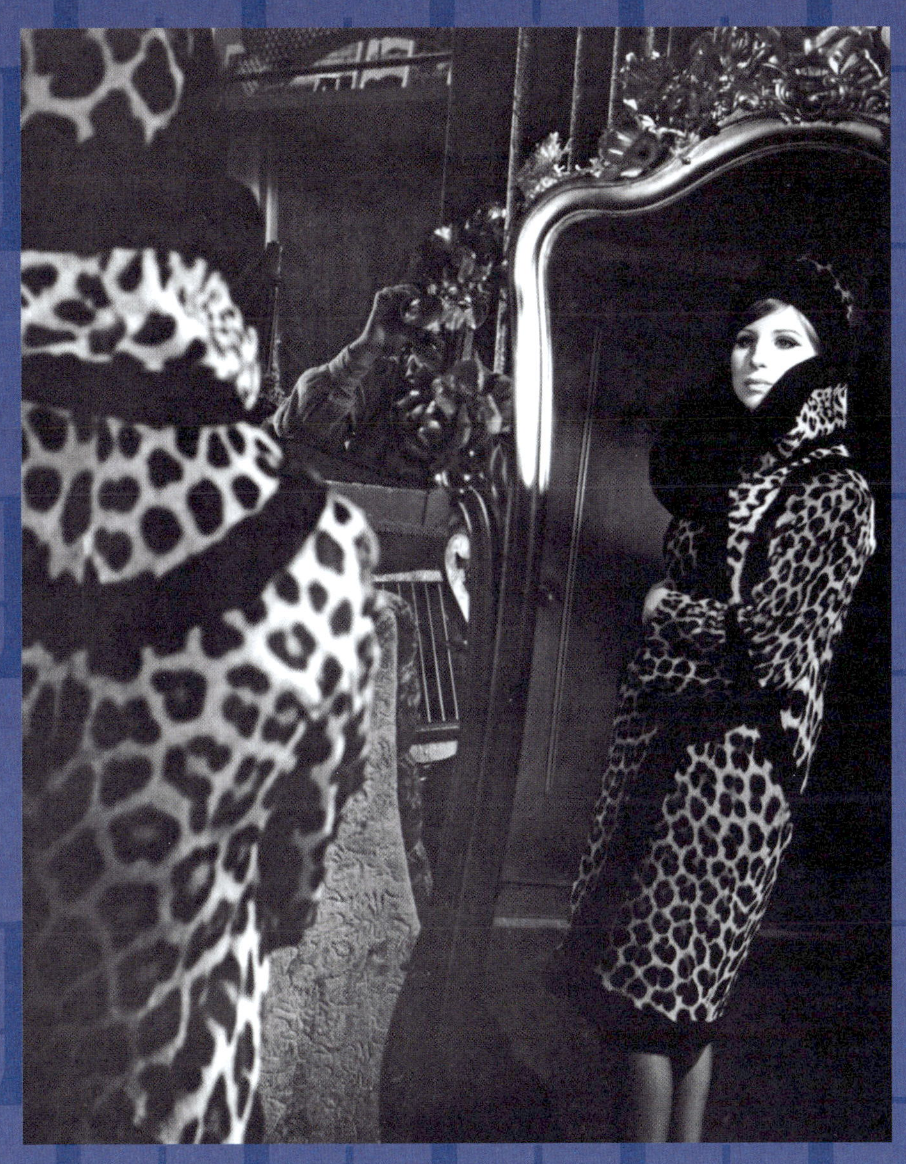

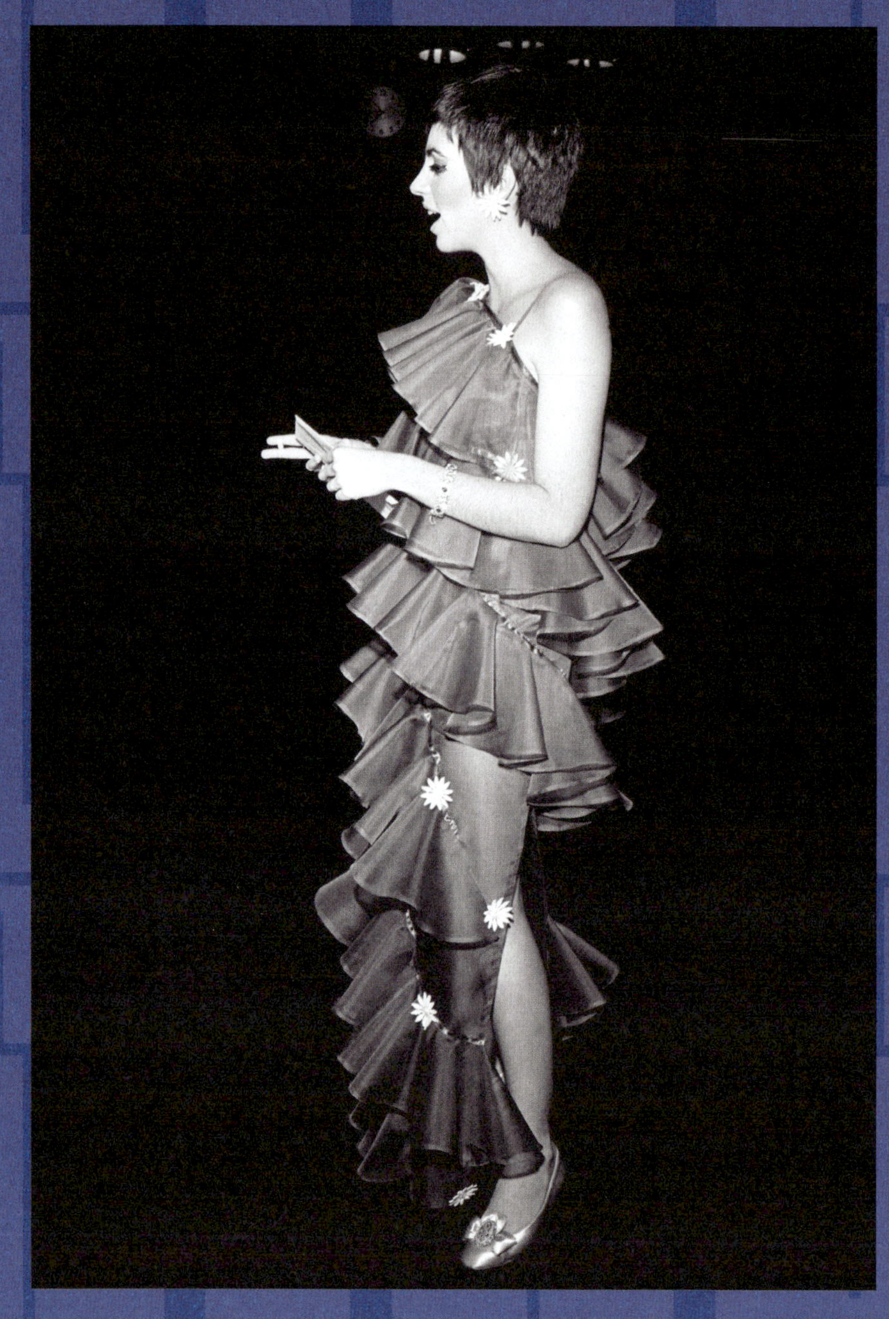

LIZA MINNELLI

Liza Minnelli moved to New York City in 1961 and kicked off her career as a musical theatre actress and club performer. Born to Hollywood royalty, Judy Garland and Vincente Minnelli, it's no wonder she had an innate love of drama. In the 1970s, she frequented Studio 54 with Andy Warhol, whom she was introduced to by way of the designer Halston. But her appearance alongside Joel Gray in *Cabaret* sealed the deal on her status as a style icon: with her short trademark pixie haircut and quirky glam look now serving as her signature. She was a muse to Halston – king of silky, sexy jersey dresses and flashy, liquid-like gowns. She was also a supporter and wearer of Elsa Peretti's designs for Tiffany & Co., especially the chic Bone Cuff bracelet.

Opposite: Legend Liza Minnelli defined her personal style through her iconic, spiky hair and her love of Halston.

In particular, the icon used fashion to enhance the storytelling in her work. She would often immerse herself in her work, and pull inspiration from the productions she was in at the time – especially in the 1970s, with *Lucky Lady* (1975) and *New York, New York* (1977). Minnelli was reportedly inseparable from Halston, who was always on hand to dress her and offer up outfit ideas for nights out on the town. His prolific use of jersey allowed her to be comfortable and move when she was dancing and on-stage. It was comfortable, chic and sexy. But she also never steered away from the dramatic. Red sequins by Halston were another forever wardrobe staple for her. "Once I started doing more one-woman shows and concerts, I saw how fashion could be part of the stories that I would tell in the songs," she once explained. "I knew I needed a new look that I could call my own, one that would reflect me and connect with the audience."

THE NEW FACES OF BROADWAY

A new and exciting generation of stylish showmanship is on display in New York's theatre district, starring Cole Escola in their play *Oh, Mary!*, which won the Tony Award for "Best Actor in a Play" in 2025. The non-binary star is a thoroughly eccentric maximalist who has worn everything from a corseted Wiederhoeft dress to honour Bernadette Peters at the Tony Awards to a Christopher John Rogers suit covered in an explosion of flowers to the Met Gala. In 2025, the star posed for *New York* magazine dressed up as one of the most legendary New York fashion style muses of all time: Little Edie (more on her later).

Jordan Roth is another international street-style star favourite who brings the drama of Broadway to fashion week. Roth is a seven-time Tony Award-winning producer and couture collector who documents everything about his fashion escapades online, from attending Schiaparelli couture shows to getting into his wild, art-worthy fashion pieces, which rival some of the work in the world's greatest fashion museums, complete with accessories, make-up and hair to match.

Opposite: Cole Escola wore the emerging brand Wiederhoeft to the 2025 Tony Awards – an homage to Bernadette Peters's 1999 Tony Awards gown.

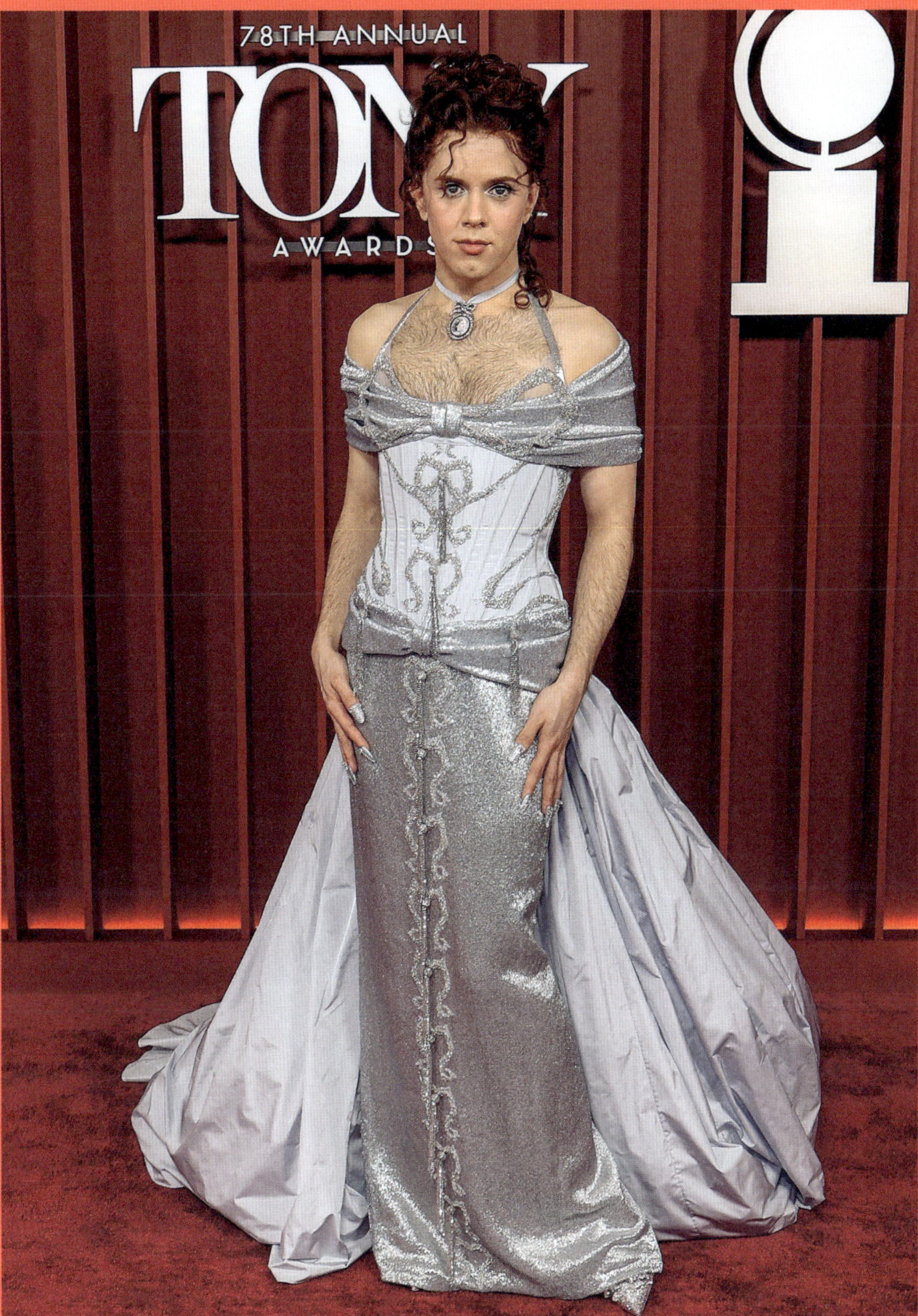
78TH ANNUAL
AWARDS

CHAPTER 4: THE MEGAWATTS

A-listers, pop stars and socialites have one thing in common: they're constantly in the public eye. Which naturally lends itself to a certain style of dressing. Oftentimes it's boldness, and sometimes it's the exact opposite: highly curated restraint.

JENNIFER LOPEZ

Fashion's flashiest dressers are often from the city of New York. It's an obvious frame of mind. Here, there are no rules and the more one pushes the boundaries, the more exciting things get. New York fashion icons have been breaking rules for decades. Take Jennifer Lopez as one example. Born in the Bronx, the singer, songwriter and actress rose to fame through acting before launching her debut album – when she literally changed fashion history, but also shaped modern technology, with a single dress.

During her day-to-day life or when she's photographed by paparazzi in the streets, Lopez keeps things low-key with casual glam looks that involve nice tailoring and subtle statement accessories like hats. During performances or events, she takes her signature style to the next level with more glammed-up versions of her understated look. "I think the key is to always authentically be yourself and [do] what feels good to you in the moment, whether that's something that's older that you've done before, and classic, or something that's totally new," Lopez has said on her personal style. "It just has to feel right for me right now."

But back to the single dress that changed history. The year was 2000, and for the 42nd Grammy Awards ceremony Lopez wore a vivid green, tropical-looking dress, designed by Versace, which plunged below her navel. Former Google CEO and executive chairman Eric Schmidt said on Project Syndicate in 2015, "People wanted more than just text. This first became apparent after the 2000 Grammy Awards, where Jennifer Lopez wore a green dress that, well, caught the world's attention. At the time,

Opposite: In 2000, Jennifer Lopez changed fashion and internet history by wearing her iconic, green Versace dress at the 42nd Grammy Awards ceremony.

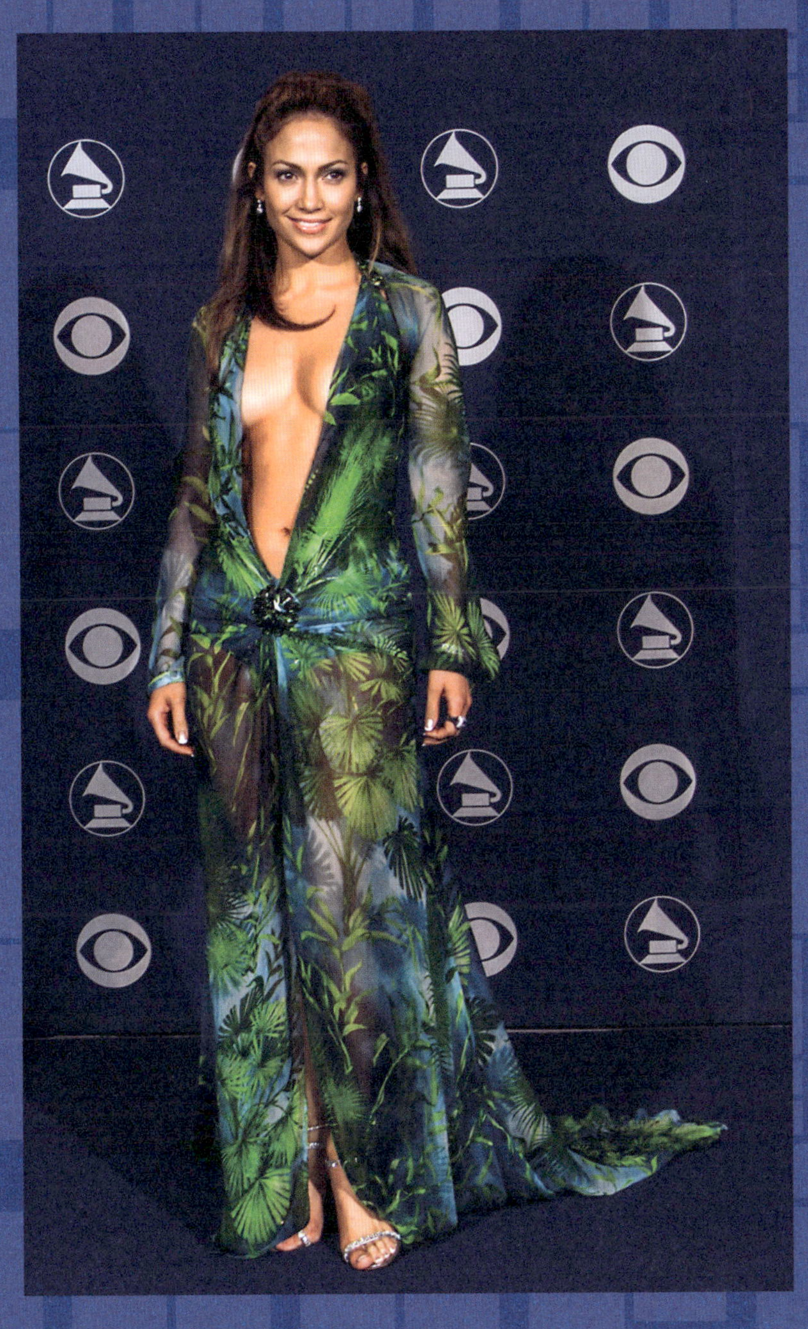

it was the most popular search query we had ever seen. But we had no surefire way of getting users exactly what they wanted: J.Lo wearing that dress. Google Image search was born." The moment was also celebrated during Versace's Spring 2020 runway show in Milan, where Lopez walked the runway in the same dress. Like many of the women who came before her, Lopez took the kind of fashion risk that a famous New Yorker wouldn't even think twice about.

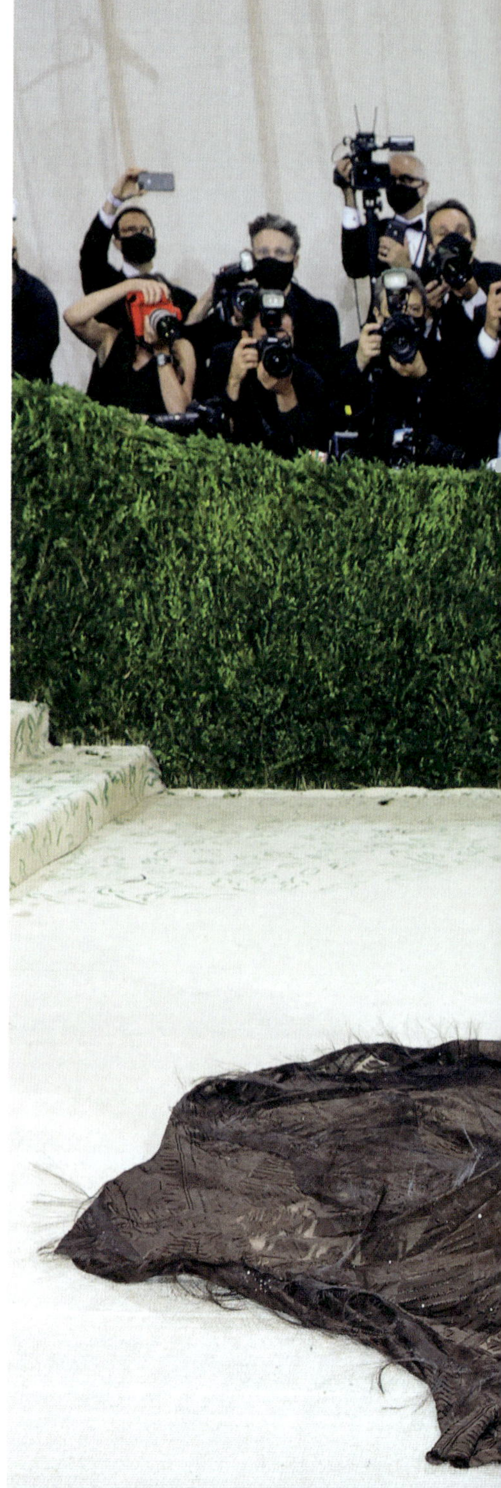

Right: Jennifer Lopez is always bold on the red carpet, opting for boho Western looks in recent years, as with this Ralph Lauren outfit at the 2021 Met Gala.

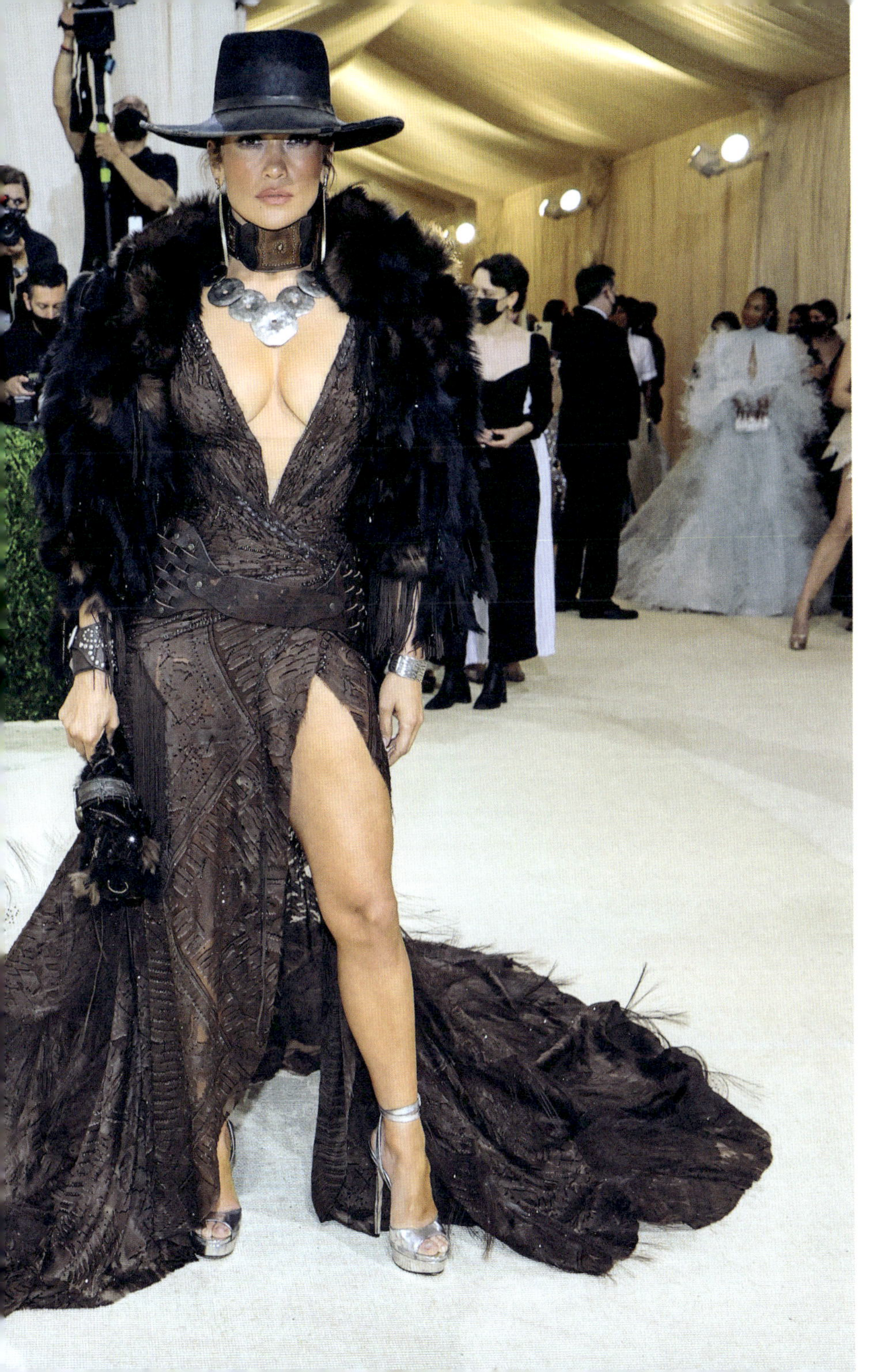

CHER

Even locals or transplants are inspired by the boldness of certain icons who walked the streets before them. Take, for example, Cher, a California native who had a residence in New York City in the Silk Building in the 1980s until she sold her apartment in 1990.

Cher is a bona-fide style influencer, and her most iconic moment of all time took place in New York, when she walked the Met Gala red carpet in 1974 wearing the famous see-through, crystal-covered, so-called naked dress, which was designed by Bob Mackie. That dress would go on to define generations of red-carpet dressing, and was later emulated by Kim Kardashian, Beyoncé, Kate Moss, and so many other celebrities it's impossible to keep track. Cher is the ultimate icon of glamour. She pushed boundaries with sequins, fur, fringe and revealing, skin-baring get-ups. Think glittering pant sets, full fluffy feathers and floor-length printed gowns. In the 1970s, Bob Mackie would reportedly design up to 20 different outfits per episode of her variety series, *The Sonny and Cher Show*. Today, top-tier style icons like Zendaya cite Cher as a huge influence on how they dress for the red carpet.

These days, Cher is also a major fan of the dark, minimalist fashion of Ann Demeulemeester and has been seen attending the label's shows. She reportedly collects pieces from the brand. One thing she'll never wear: "Something that looks like *Little House on the Prairie*," she once told me in an interview for *W* magazine. "That's never going to happen. Unless I do a movie, because there's nothing about that kind of clothing that's me."

Opposite: Cher changed fashion history with a single look, and it happened in New York. She wore the infamous Bob Mackie naked dress at the 1974 Met Gala.

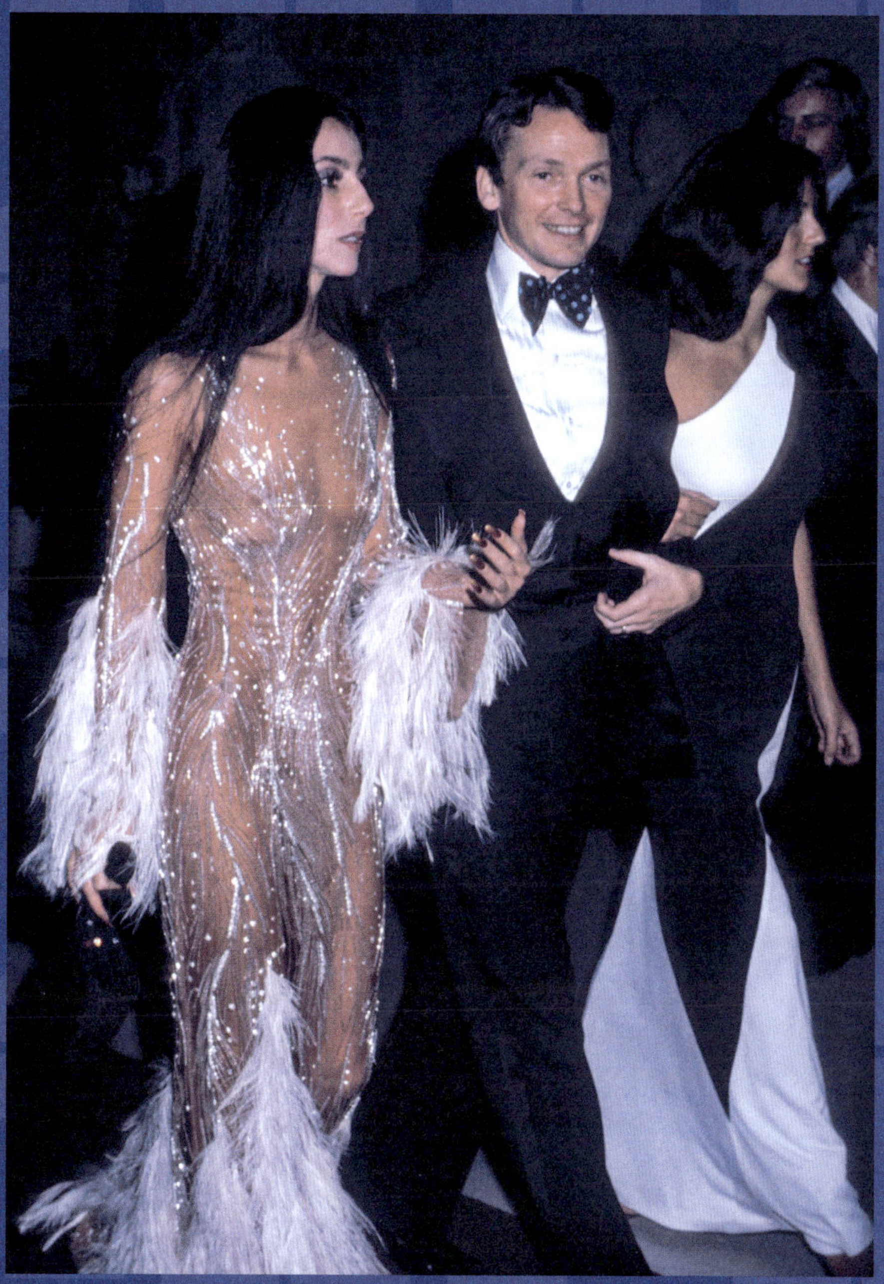

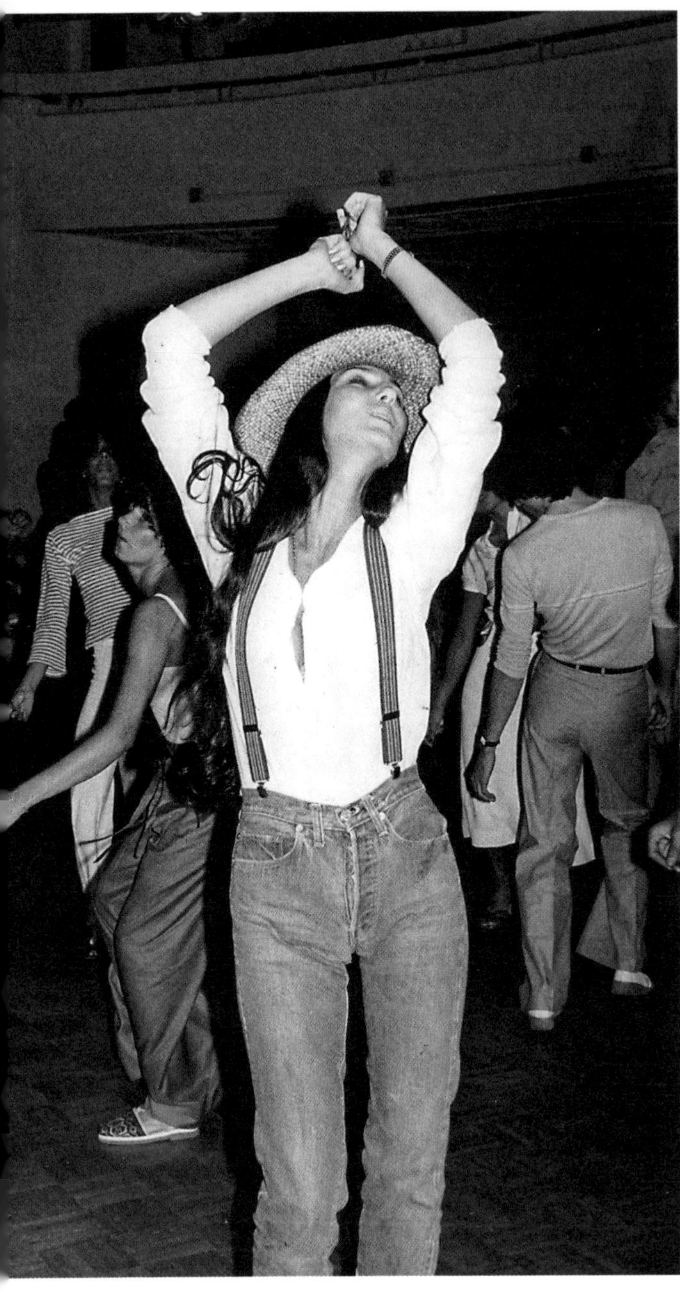

Left: Cher has also always been a fan of jeans, as seen here at Studio 54.

Opposite: Bob Mackie has been a go-to for Cher for decades. He is known for his sheer, body-skimming looks decked out in beadwork and sequins, as worn by Cher at the 1985 Met Gala.

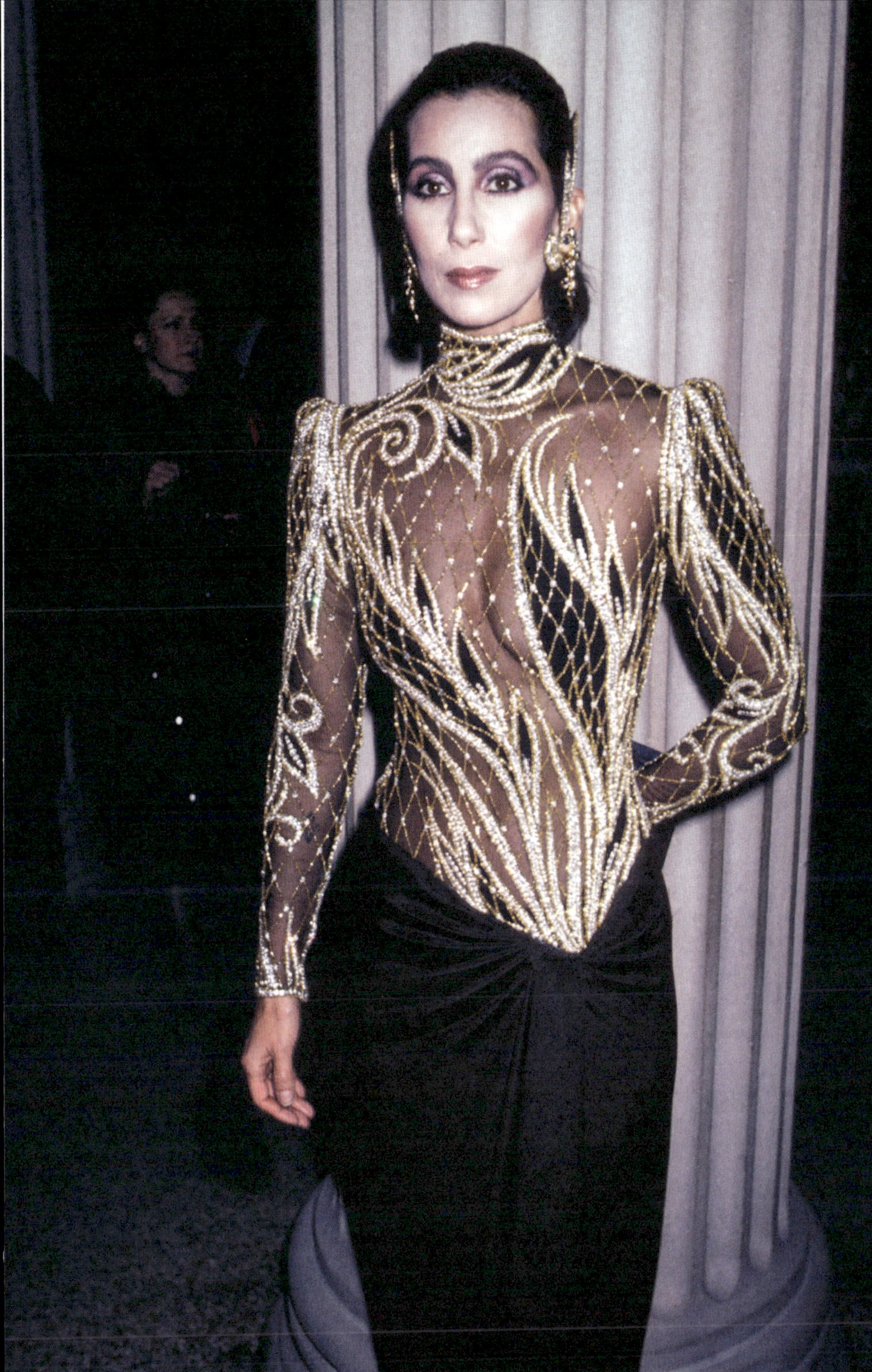

LADY GAGA

Native New Yorker and experimental tastemaker Lady Gaga has often openly credited Cher, as well as Grace Jones, as an inspiration for her own work and style.

Lady Gaga started her career performing in bars and clubs on the Lower East Side, wearing big, dark sunglasses and hooded leotards, much like the Alaïa get-ups for which Jones was so well known. However, as anyone knows, Gaga has challenged the norms as a fashion icon from day one. She's worn a dress made out of meat, a bra that spits fire, and so many other pieces verging on art. But there's something else very distinctly New York that sets her apart: her ability to transform and rebuild her persona, look and aesthetic through each album and era. With *Artpop*, she became living, walking art and with *Joanne*, she turned to a softer, more mainstream palette. Besides that, she changed Met Gala history with her look in 2020 when she made multiple outfit changes on the red carpet.

Even before the concept of going viral existed, Lady Gaga did it multiple times – whether it was crashing Alexander McQueen's first-ever, live-streamed catwalk show because her song was released during the show, or her hot-pants look, which would also influence how some of the biggest performers dress on-stage to this very day.

A supporter of young designers, in 2025 Lady Gaga entered her mayhem era and chose labels such as Ilona. "I'm embracing all of my gothic dreams, and trying to express all of those dark fantasies that I have – but in ways that are both dark, yet also carry the light with them, too," she told *Vogue*. "Theatricality and artistry is a huge part of what I love about fashion, so it definitely has a lot more to do with self-expression than anything else."

Opposite: In 2014, Lady Gaga stepped out of a classic New York City yellow cab wearing an awe-inspiring, fluffy, white look.

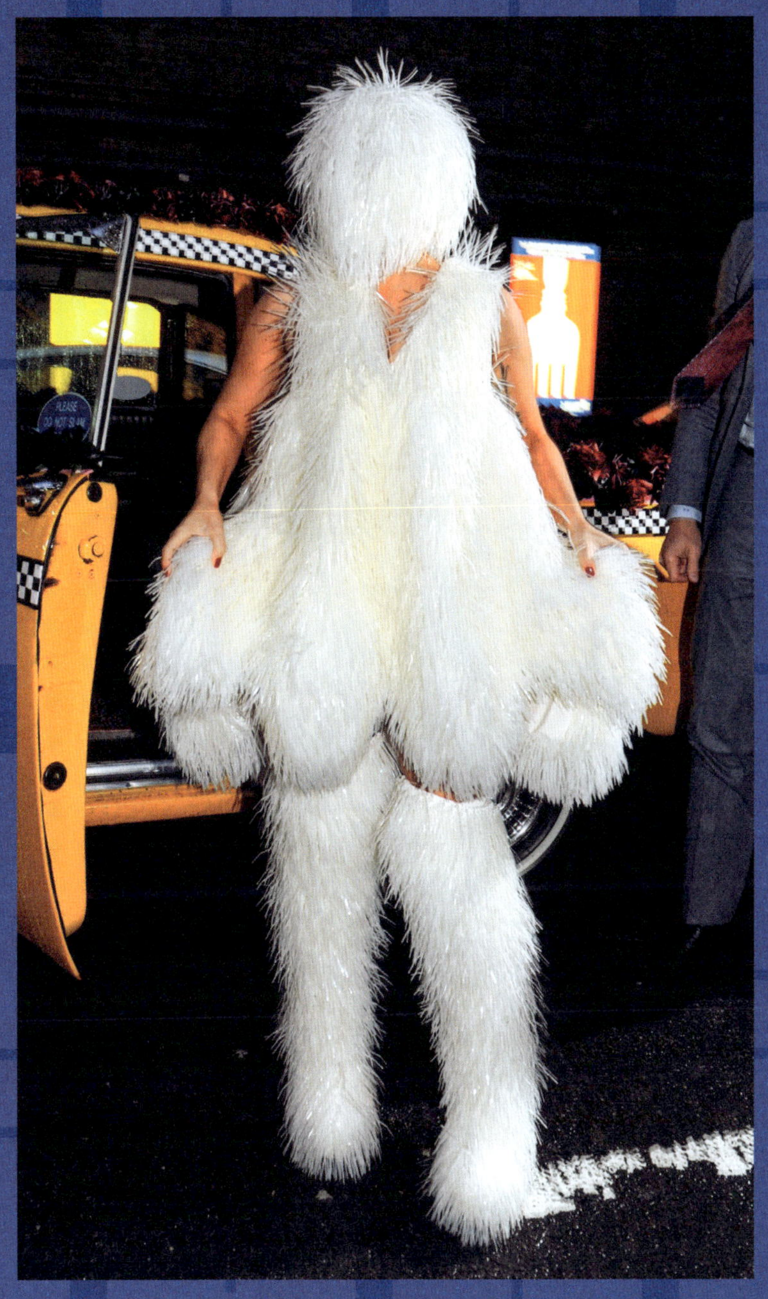
PLEASE
DO NOT SLAM

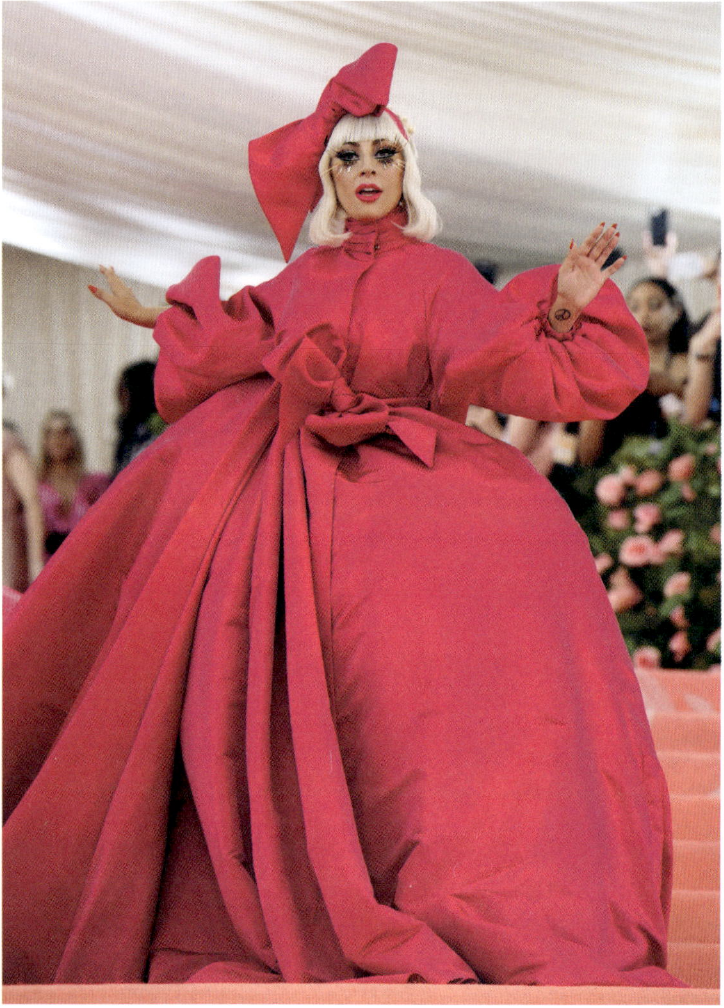

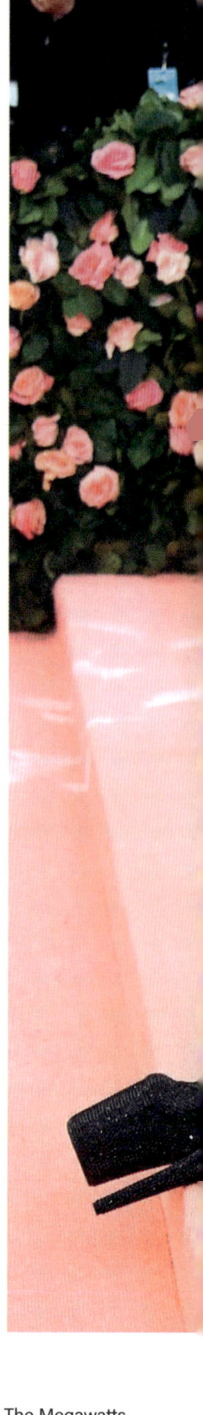

Above: Lady Gaga made fashion history at the 2019 Met Gala when she changed outfits numerous times on the red carpet.

Right: Lady Gaga collaborated with stylist and fashion designer Brandon Maxwell on her 2019 Met Gala looks, which all played to the theme of camp.

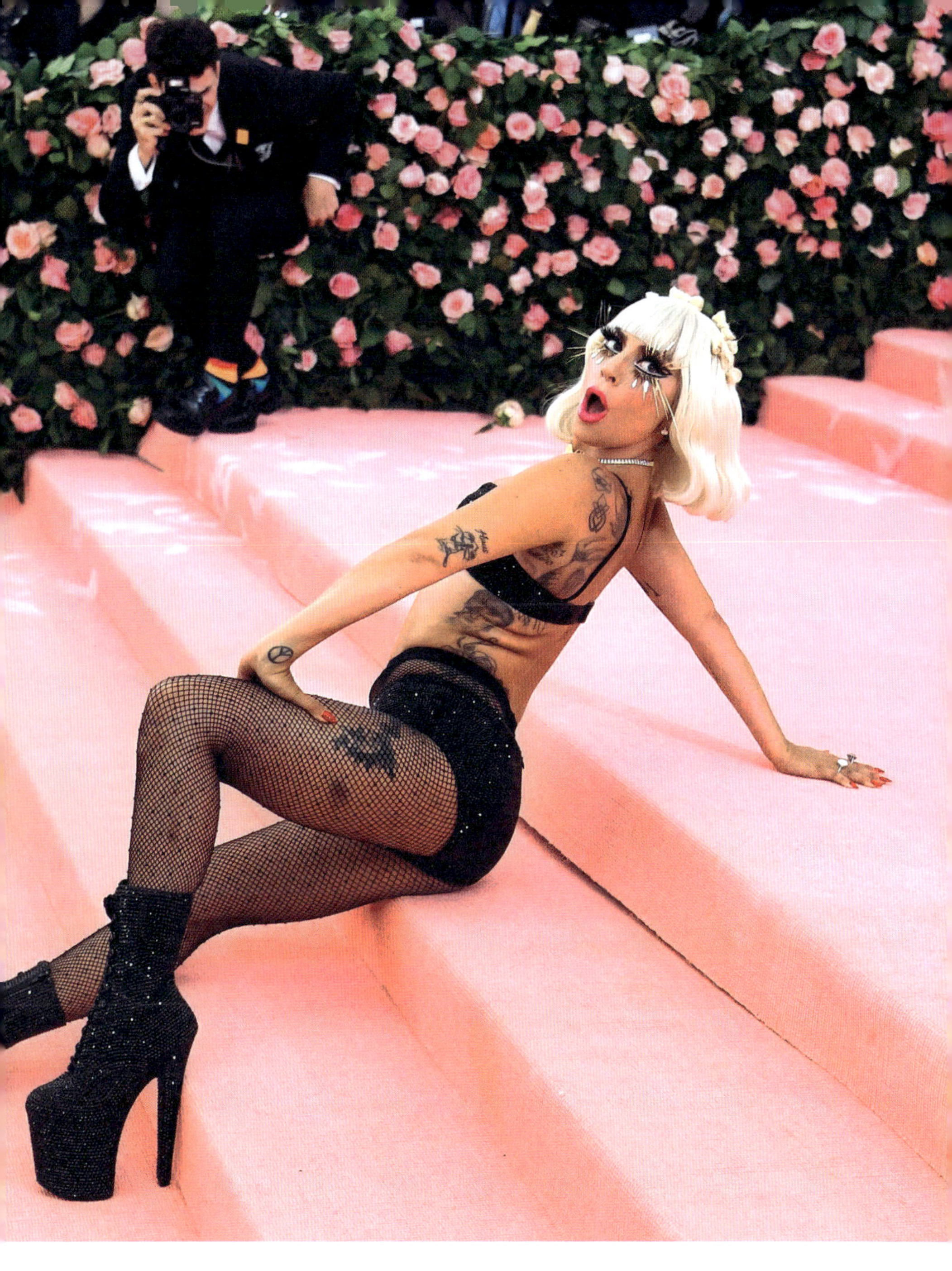

THE HIP-HOP ICONS

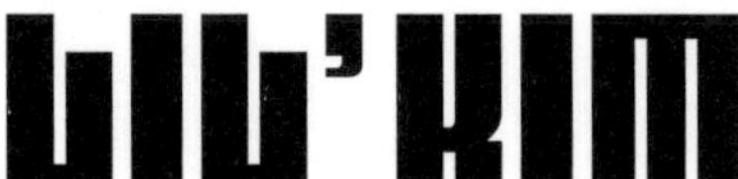

New York's fashion scene would be nothing without the women of hip-hop. Lil' Kim is currently one of the greatest blueprints for celebrity dressing and modern trends, from logomania to pastel furs and brightly coloured hair, all aided by her stylist Misa Hylton. The Brooklyn native rose to fame due to her 1996 album *Hard Core*. For the promotional poster, she wore a leopard-print bikini and feathered cover-up, designed by Patricia Field, the iconic New York stylist behind *Sex and the City*. Before that, she collaborated with The Notorious B.I.G., and was the only woman in his hip-hop group, Junior M.A.F.I.A.

Honorary New York style icon Rihanna was praised for her jaw-dropping, sheer gown covered in 230,000 crystals at the 2014 CFDA Fashion Awards, but Lil' Kim took it even further in a catsuit with 965,000 crystals at the 2019 BET Awards. She was one of the first female rap artists to fully embrace her sexuality when it came to fashion, opting for skin-baring, over-the-top, tight outfits in bright colours and lush, luxurious textures by some of the world's top luxury brands at the time, such as Chanel and Gucci. At the 1999 MTV Video Music Awards, she matched her lilac wig to her sparkly jumpsuit, one breast bared with a seashell-shaped pastie. Versace dressed her in a pink fur to match her hair for the 1999 Met Gala. The same year, she appeared with her body covered in Louis Vuitton logos for *Interview* magazine. She maintains a friendship with designer Marc Jacobs, who was creative director of Louis Vuitton from 1997 to 2013. Lil' Kim's groundbreaking influence is now seen in the wardrobes of almost every single woman rapper.

Opposite: Lil' Kim had one of the most iconic Met Gala looks of all time, wearing Versace to match her hair for the 1999 event.

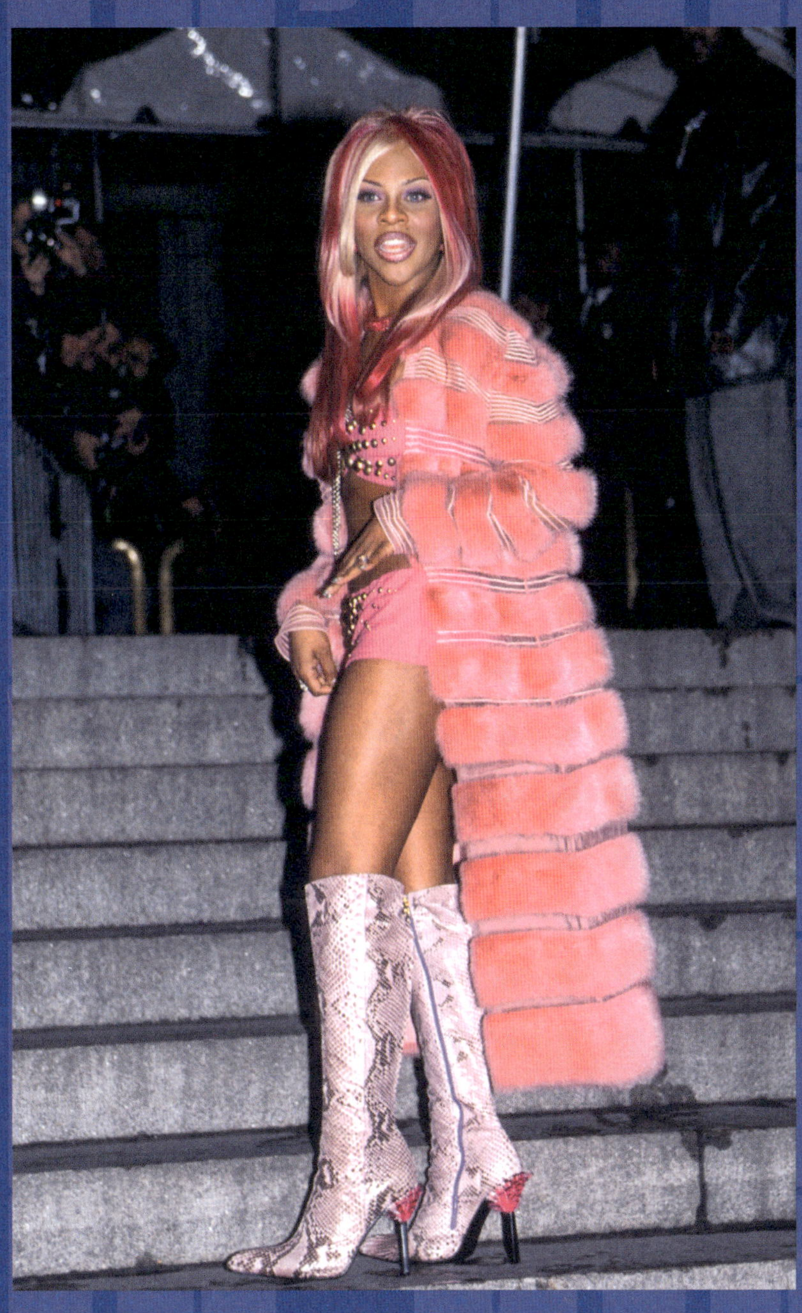

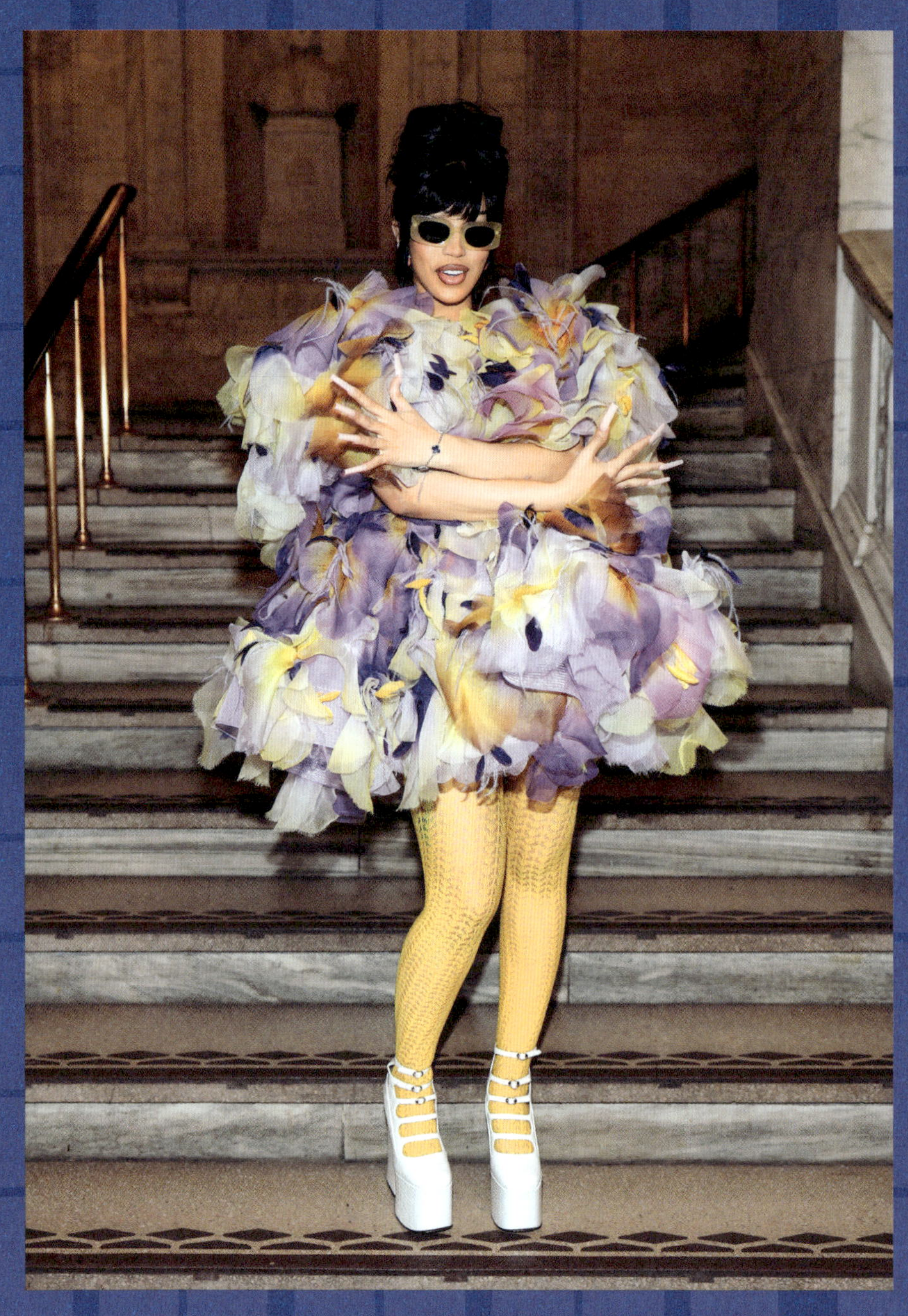

CARDI B

Along with her stylist Kollin Carter, Washington Heights native Cardi B has also become a style icon in her own right. She gained recognition on social media platforms and through VH1's *Love & Hip Hop: New York*, before dropping her debut album in 2018. Style-wise, she goes big and is unafraid to experiment with wild, over-the-top fashion from emerging designers and vintage archives alike.

Cardi B arrived at the Met Gala red carpet in 2018 wearing a maximalist fantasy ornate gown designed by Jeremy Scott for Moschino, full of ecclesiastical references for the "Heavenly Bodies: Fashion and the Catholic Imagination" theme. For 2019, she wore a huge burgundy Thom Browne gown with feathers and a hood that wowed. At the 2024 Met Gala, she opted for an enormous black tulle confection that swanned over the red carpet, a custom gown by emerging Chinese brand Windowsen. She favours long, structured trench coats, bodycon dresses, mini-skirts and lingerie-inspired dressing. Cardi B challenges conventions with her style – especially on the red carpet and at fashion week. She reportedly made history in January 2020 for being the first female rapper to star on the cover of *Vogue*. Perhaps most interestingly, as a woman who isn't afraid to flaunt her curves, she also stuns by boldly taking up ample space with her garments.

Opposite: Cardi B is a native New Yorker and one of music's biggest fashion expressionists. She'll try anything once, like this flowery look she wore to the autumn 2024 Marc Jacobs show.

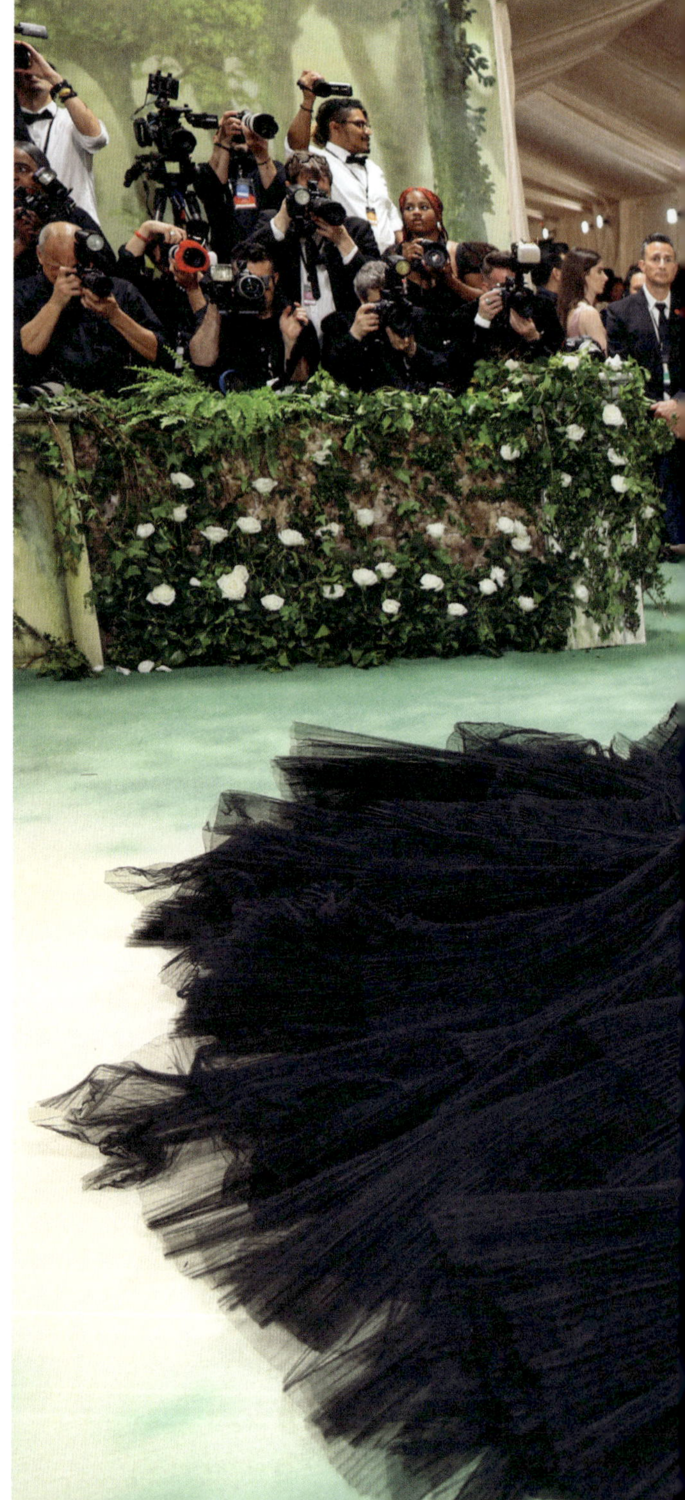

Right: At the 2024 Met Gala, Cardi B wore a massive black dress from emerging label Windowsen.

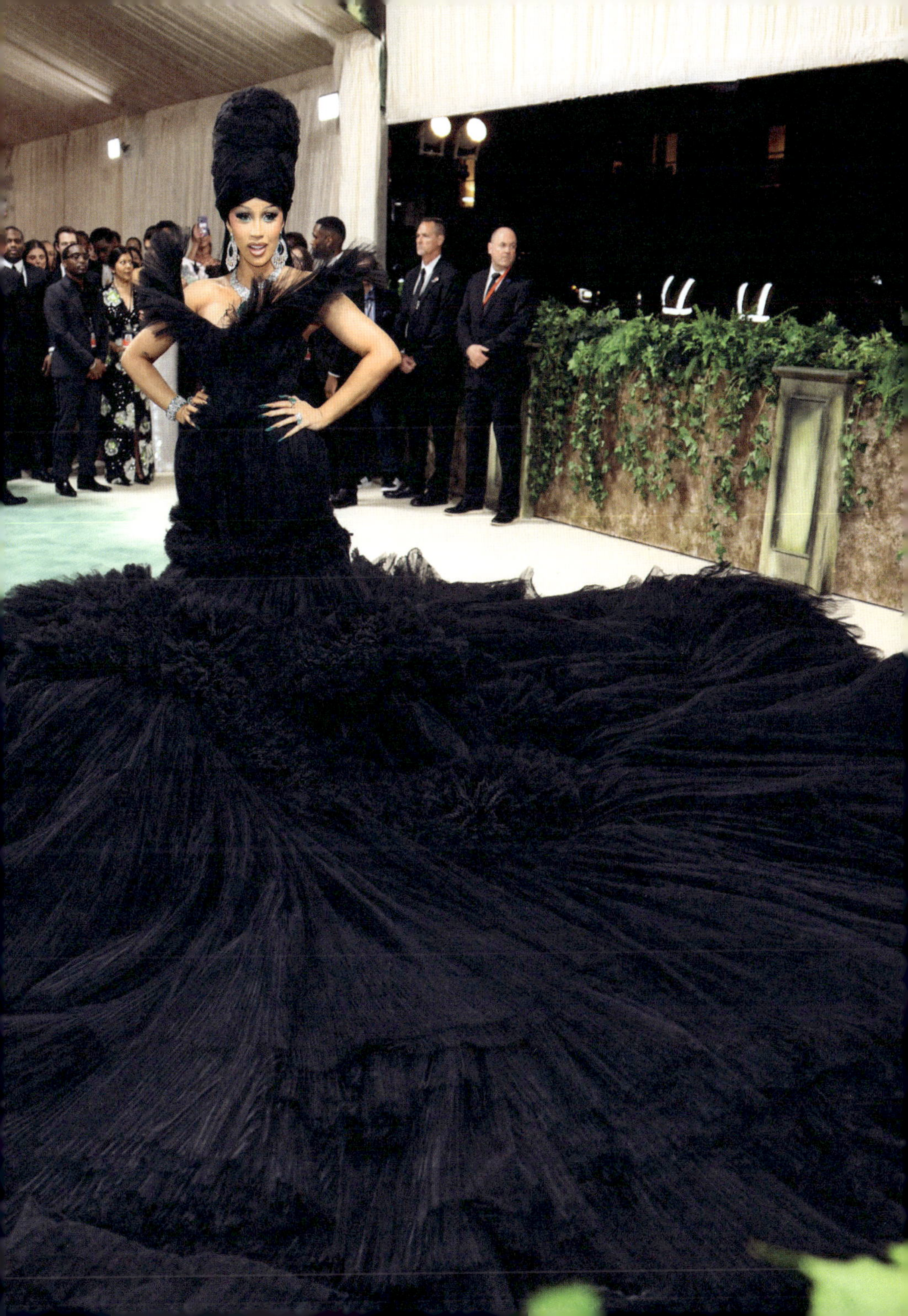

NICKI MINAJ

Rapper Nicki Minaj has been at the forefront of fashion and does things her own way. Born in Trinidad, she moved to Queens when she was five-years-old. In the early 2000s, she rapped in the New York hip-hop group Hoodstars and started uploading songs on her Myspace profile. In 2007, she released her first mixtape.

Not only has Minaj sat front row at major fashion shows and appeared on the cover of *Vogue* and *Vogue Italia*, she has also built relationships with designers like Jeremy Scott, Riccardo Tisci and Marc Jacobs. Her style is extremely experimental and inspired by fantasy characters, such as her alter egos, the loud and bold "Roman" or the soft pink "Barbie", for instance. Minaj has done it all: leopard print hair, chic little Alaïa dresses, crystal corsets and a flower bomb of a dress by Marni for the 2024 Met Gala. She's proof of New York's love of reinvention, imagination and sense of humour. "I like the idea of doing something that everyone else is not," she told *New York* magazine. "I get high off that. Just the idea that other people don't have the balls to do something – that's my thing."

Opposite: Nicki Minaj is extremely experimental and uses fashion as a storytelling method. Here, she is seen wearing runway Marni to the 2024 Met Gala.

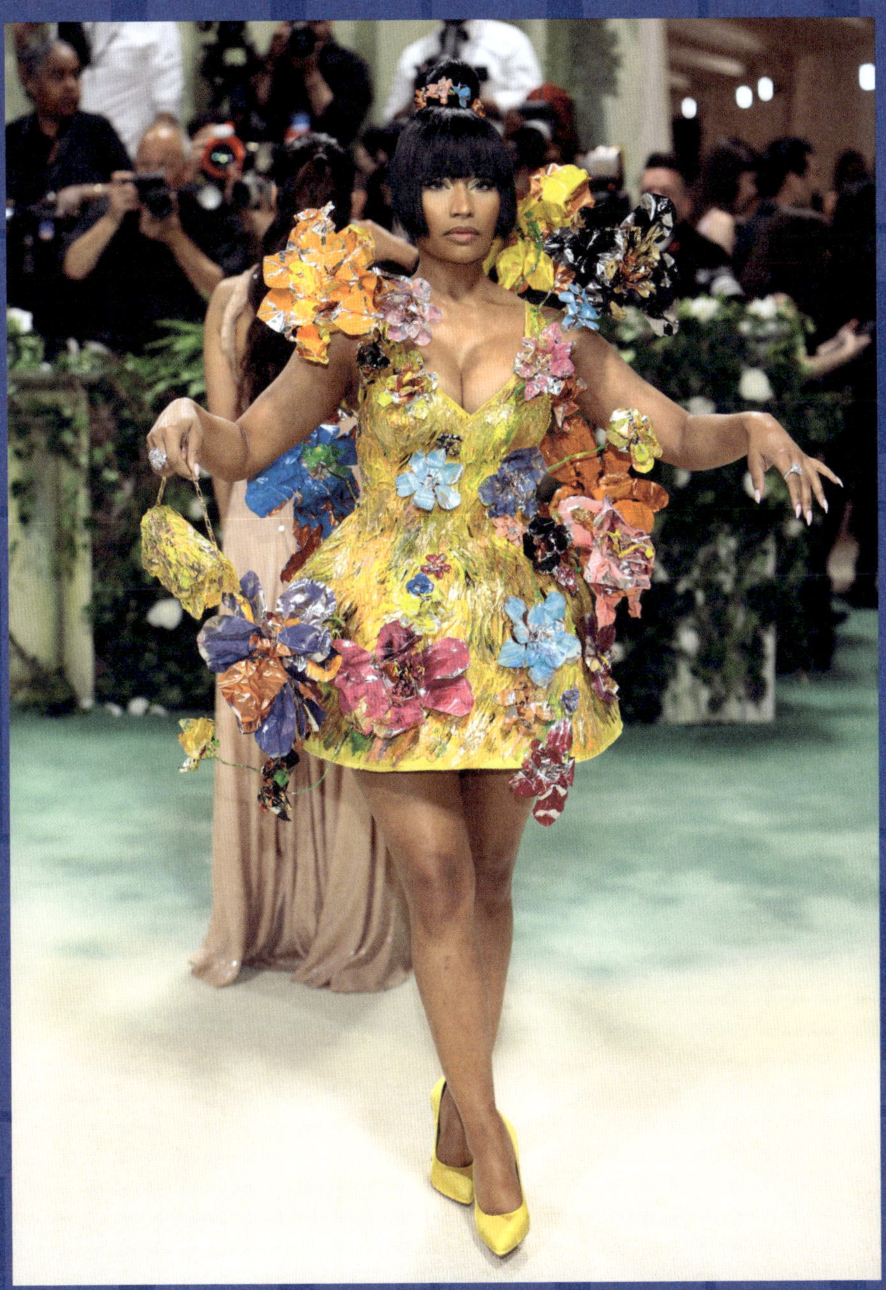

FOXY BROWN

Foxy Brown, a Brooklyn native, served as muse to John Galliano and Calvin Klein in the 1990s. Like Lil' Kim, she loved Versace and Gucci. In her famous 1999 "Hot Spot" music video she wore a metal bikini. In LL Cool J's "I Shot Ya", she mentions Versace, Armani and Gucci, much like many contemporary rappers of today would. In 1999, Dior creative director Galliano invited her to perform at the opening of Dior's new New York store, dressing her in head-to-toe logomania. "Foxy has her own sense of style and all the other ingredients to make it really big," Calvin Klein explained to *Paper Magazine* in 1999. "She's bright, talented, sexy and, most important, she's not afraid to take risks creatively."

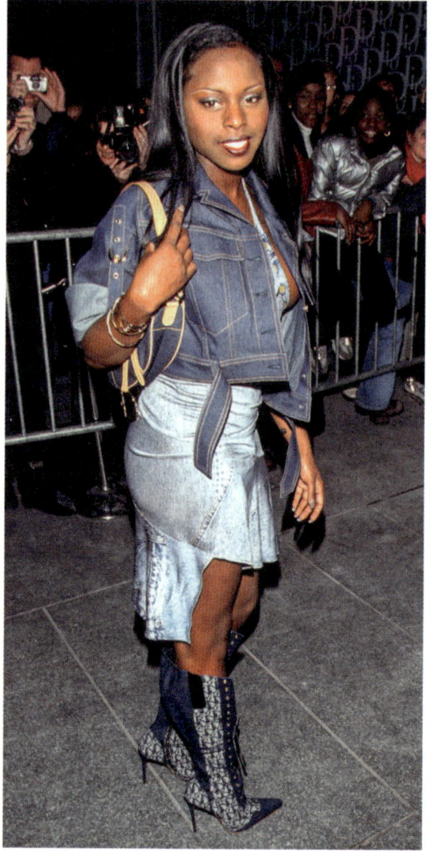

Right: Nineties icon Foxy Brown loved Dior and was an early supporter of logomania.

AALIYAH

When the late Brooklyn-born Aaliyah stepped onto the scene in 1991, she also defined a cool new way of dressing: in bold, baggy leather jackets, sports jerseys, sunglasses, ample amounts of gold jewellery and logo-ified sporty sets from Tommy Hilfiger. She would often wear a thick, white bandana around her hair, a style signature that made her stand out even more. The yellow, zebra-print Roberto Cavalli dress that she wore at the 2000 MTV Music Awards was also iconic. But her look in her "Try Again" music video may have proved most influential. Kim Kardashian was criticized for recreating the outfit for Halloween in 2017, with her white bandana and top to match.

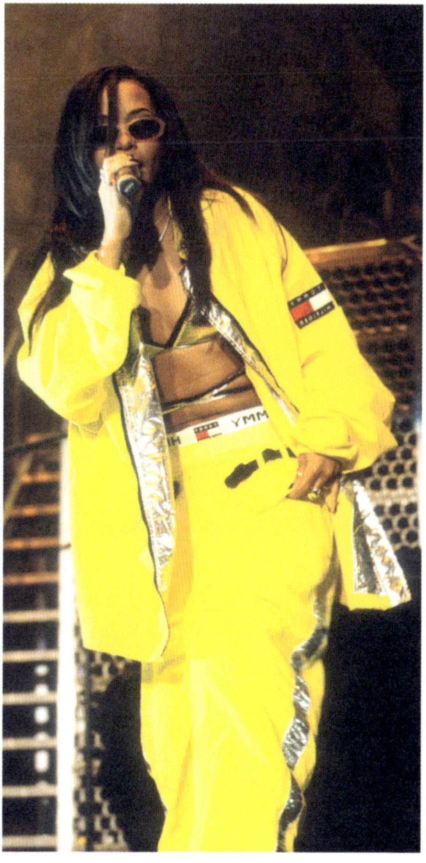

Right: Aaliyah's style was sporty and oversized, as seen here. She favoured designers like Tommy Hilfiger.

THE HIP-HOP ICONS

QUEEN LATIFAH & LAURYN HILL

Around the same time, rappers Queen Latifah and Lauryn Hill, both born in New Jersey, were shaping their own incredibly unique perspectives and styles, which heavily influenced the New York style scene. Even today, transcending decades and geography, both of their aesthetic influences can be seen in the likes of performers like Doechii, who wore a Schiaparelli denim look with a headwrap, which looked like something either of the two iconic aforementioned rappers would wear, to perform at the Louvre in 2025. Hill had one of the most talked about outfits on the 2025 Met Gala red carpet – her first time attending the event. Her larger-than-life, butter-yellow suit was styled with an Hermès Kelly bag in cerulean blue.

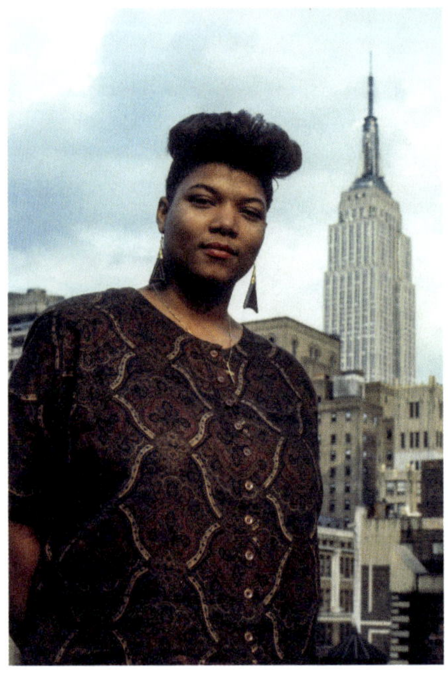

Above: Queen Latifah's early wardrobe was full of multicultural references, as seen here in New York.

Opposite: Lauryn Hill attended her first Met Gala in 2025, donning a yellow suit and carrying an Hermès Kelly bag.

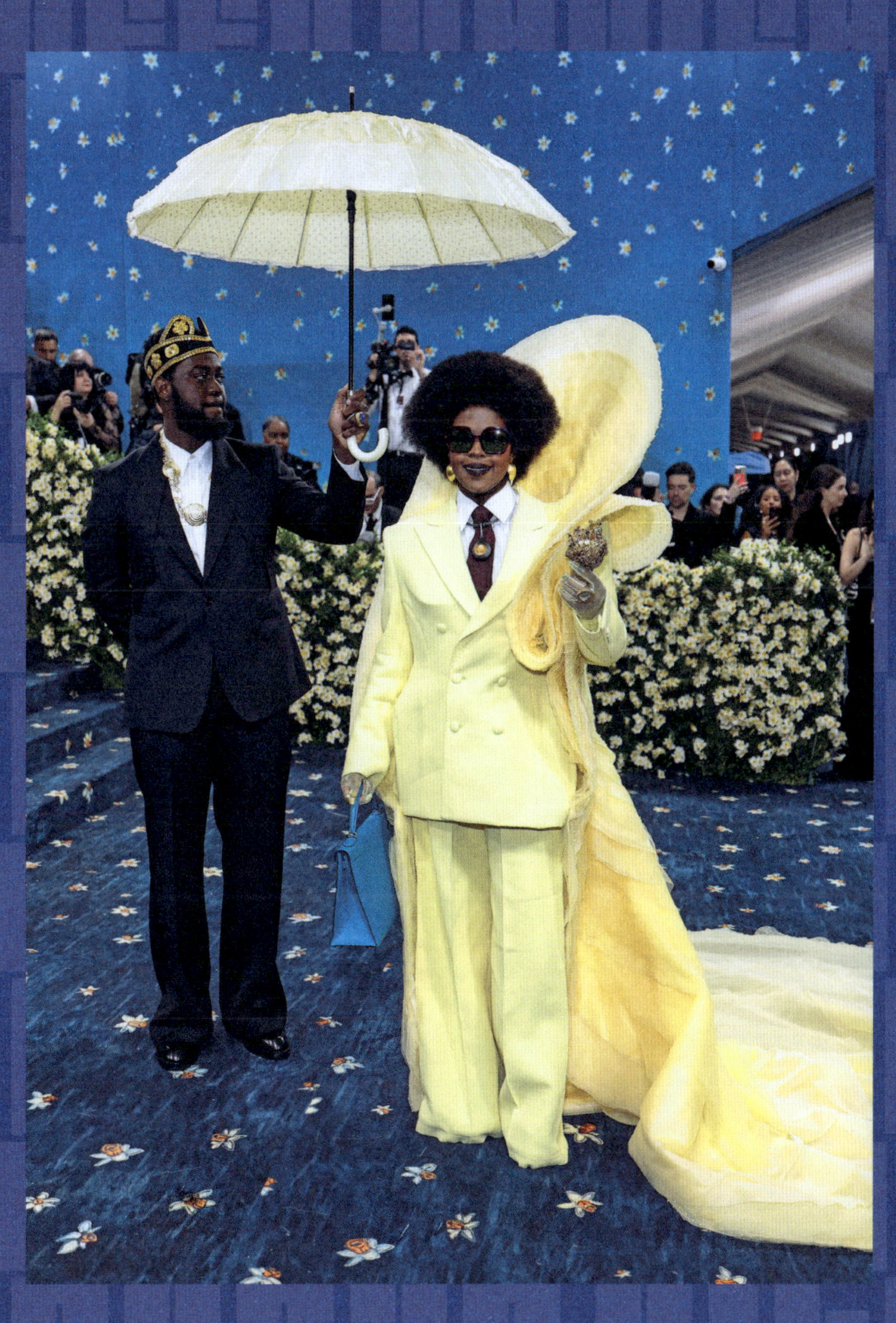

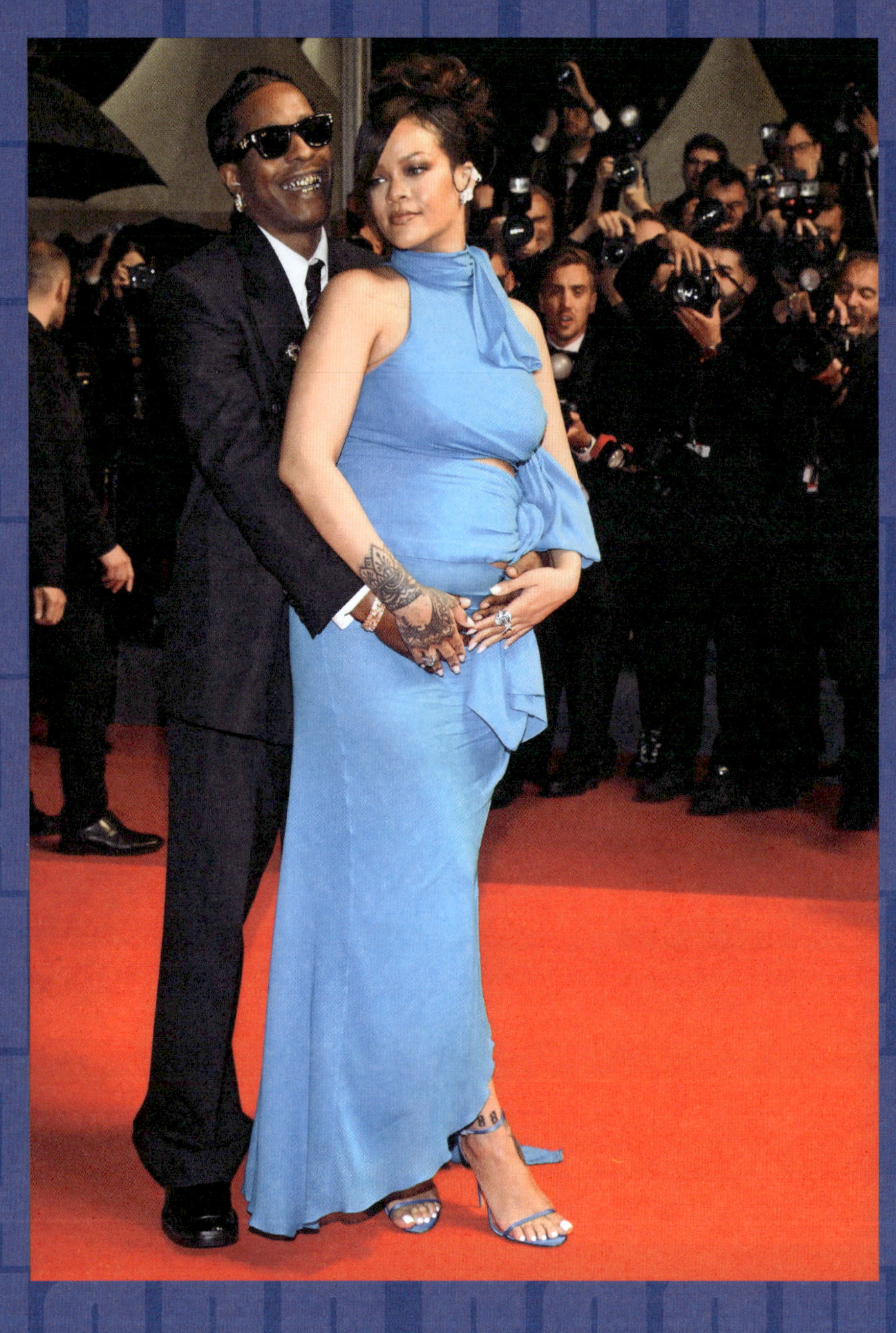

THE HIP-HOP ICONS

RIHANNA & A$AP ROCKY

A$AP Rocky is, without a doubt, one of the most prolific native New York style icons for men in recent years. Following in the footsteps of his iconic wife Rihanna (one of her most memorable outfits of all time was a Victorian-inspired New York Yankees coat designed by Alessandro Michele for Gucci, paired with camo pants), A$AP takes fashion risks and wears everything, from pastel suits to skirts over pants and everything in between, including a massive coat with a trailing train, all made out of vintage quilts, designed by ERL, for the 2021 Met Gala red carpet. His subversive approach to red-carpet dressing has greatly influenced the recent experimental shift we've seen in menswear event dressing.

Always dramatic, Rihanna sets the bar high, whenever and wherever. Take, for instance, her aforementioned jaw-dropping, sheer gown covered in 230,000 crystals at the 2014 CFDA Fashion Awards.

Rihanna practically changed the landscape of pregnancy style in how she dressed – taking her downtown cool sensibility to new heights by wearing a wardrobe of unconventional, non-traditional clothes; showing off her belly in a way that was seen, felt and copied by countless other stylish New York women. "My fashion has always been driven by my mood, and my mood was on mom mode for a minute," she told *Harper's Bazaar*.

Opposite: Rihanna and A$AP Rocky are a style power couple, as seen here together.

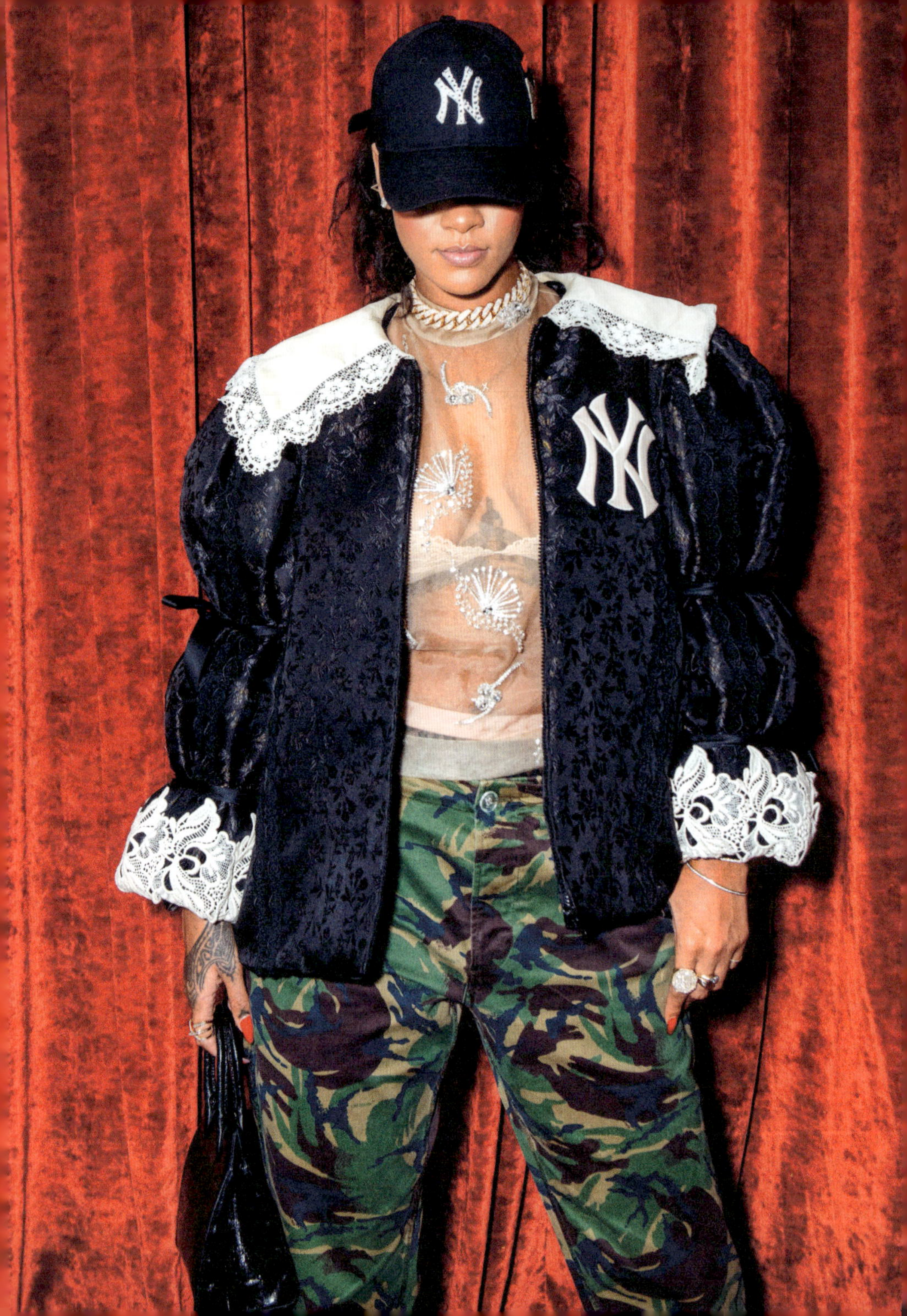

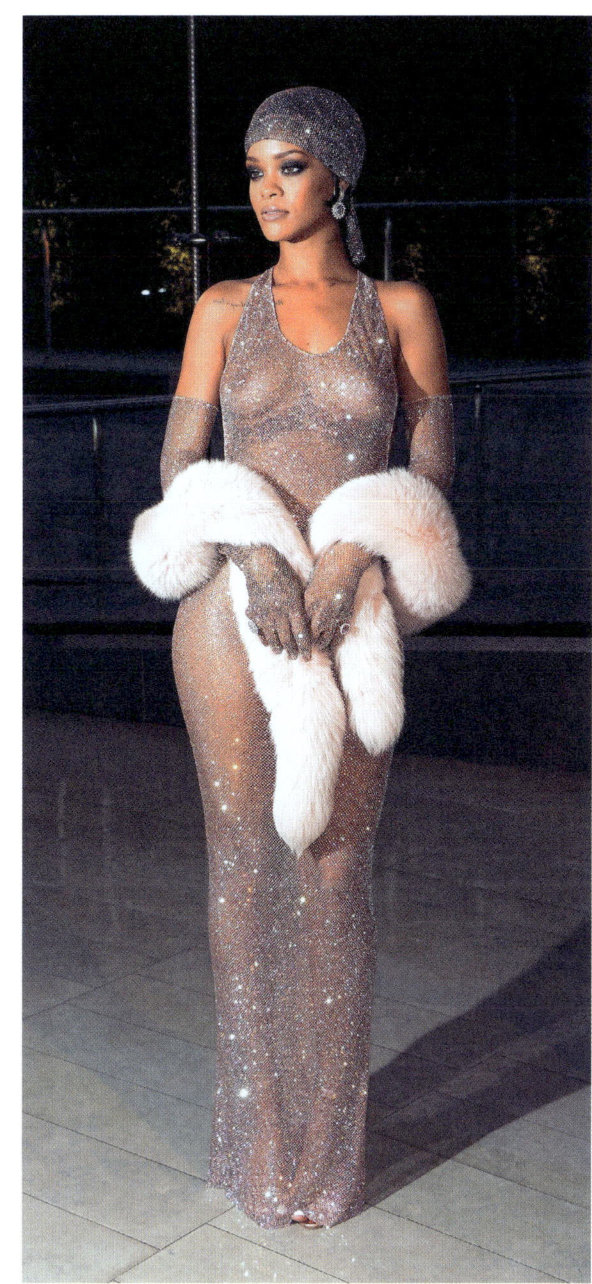

Opposite: Rihanna's style is experimental and fun. Here she wears the Alessandro Michele-designed Gucci x New York Yankees Victorian-inspired jacket with a pair of camouflage pants.

Right: In 2014, Rihanna took a cue from Cher's naked dress and donned a scintillating, shimmery, crystal-encrusted dress to the CFDA awards.

CAROLYN BESSETTE-KENNEDY

What would New York be without its socialite lore and original, rich It-girls? The style codes of High Society New York are worthy of their own tome alone.

Minimalist icon and poster girl for understated 1990s chic sophistication is none other than Carolyn Bessette-Kennedy. The fashion industry It-girl (who started her career in New York at Calvin Klein doing PR) emerged into the spotlight when she began dating John F. Kennedy Jr. in 1994. Just two years later, the duo made the relationship official by getting married on the remote island of Cumberland in Georgia. Her wedding wardrobe of choice? A stunning silk gown by Narciso Rodriguez paired with beautifully beaded Manolo Blahnik sandals. Her bridal uniform and personal style choices made headlines and over the years she became a classic icon of style worshipped by fashion's elite, even decades after her untimely death in 1999 (due to an aviation accident that also took her husband and her sister Lauren Bessette's lives).

Bessette-Kennedy's style was iconic because it defined an aesthetic that is still highly influential today, while also allowing the tabloids a peek into the world of a true fashion-industry executive – a rarity for the time. Her early, off-duty, pre-wedding look is still replicated today by many of the editors, PRs and other industry people in the New York fashion scene. She was often seen on the city streets in well-fitting jeans, plain tank tops, heeled sandals and her style signatures: her tortoiseshell headband or a little bandana over her hair, and her dark, black, little, oval-shaped sunglasses. She loved neutrals: beige, black, grey, navy

Opposite: Carolyn Bessette-Kennedy often wore minimalist looks by designer Yohji Yamamoto, as seen here.

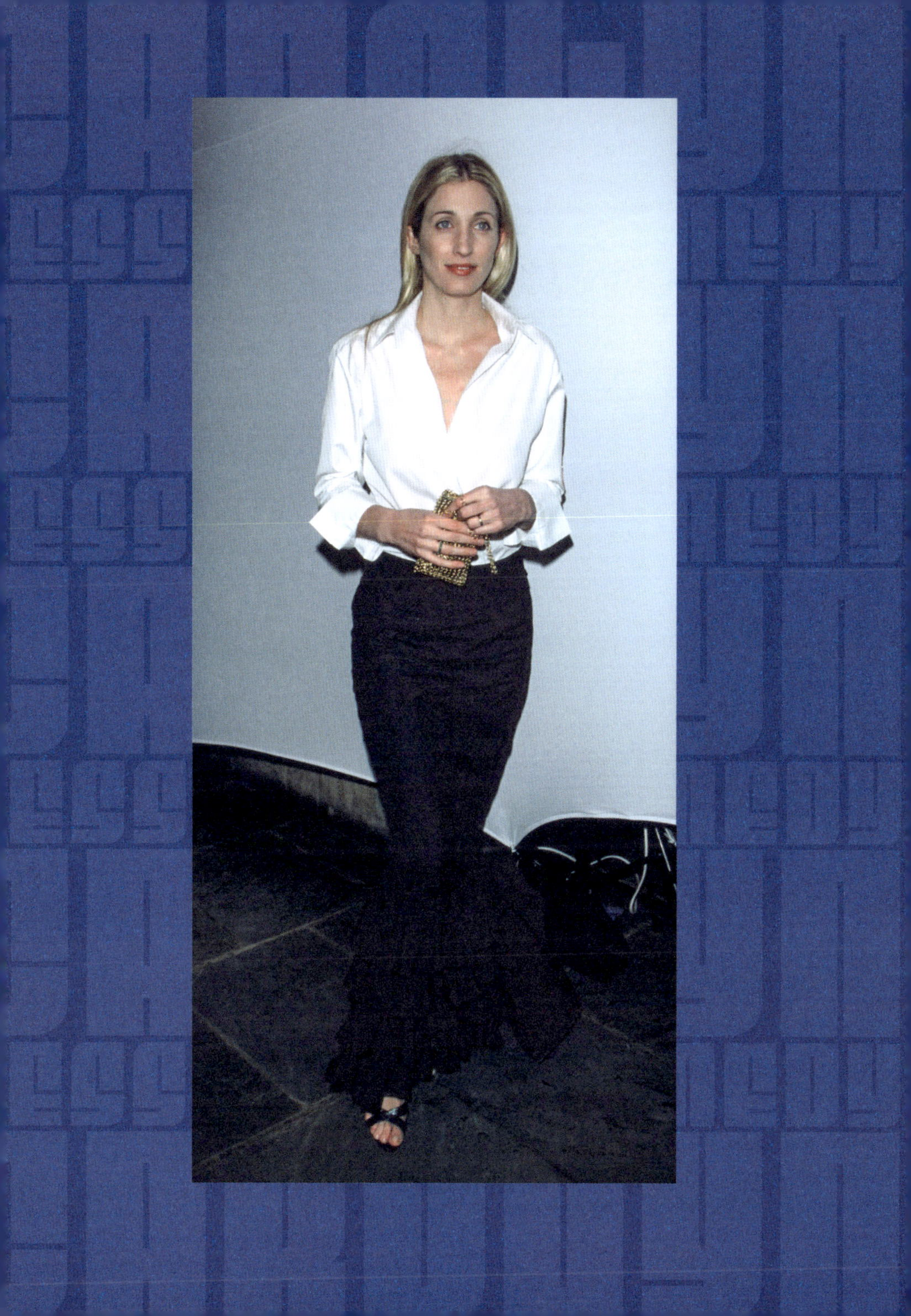

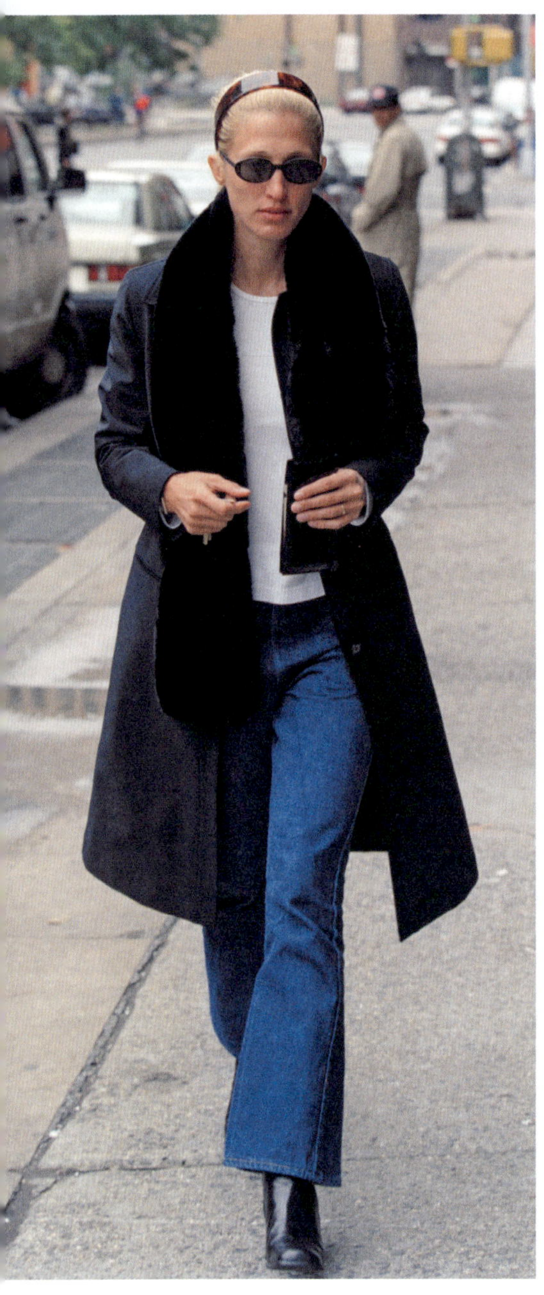

and beyond. When she did wear colour, she'd opt for a flowy, floral mini-dress with kitten heels.

Once she was more in the spotlight, Bessette-Kennedy reclaimed her look in a new way. Instead of wearing an over-the-top gown to a gala, she opted for a white, button-down shirt and a long, black maxi-skirt (both by avant-garde designer Yohji Yamamoto) and black strappy sandal heels for the Whitney Museum of American Art Gala. Most interesting was the unassuming way she wore high designer pieces. She was a huge fan of Yohji Yamamoto, and frequently shopped at the legendary New York department store Barneys for his pieces. She opted for his off-kilter, ruffled blazers and structured suiting, while most high-society tabloid favourites were wearing designers like Oscar de la Renta, or Dior, as did Princess Diana. Her commitment to wearing Yohji Yamamoto over what everyone else wore cemented her as someone who had a strong point of view about her image, one that would make a lasting impression.

Left: Carolyn Bessette-Kennedy's style staples were a tortoiseshell headband and skinny, dark, oval sunglasses.

Opposite: At events, Carolyn Bessette-Kennedy opted for toned-down, chic, black, tailored looks as opposed to the bright colours and overtly feminine outfits society counterparts were wearing at the time.

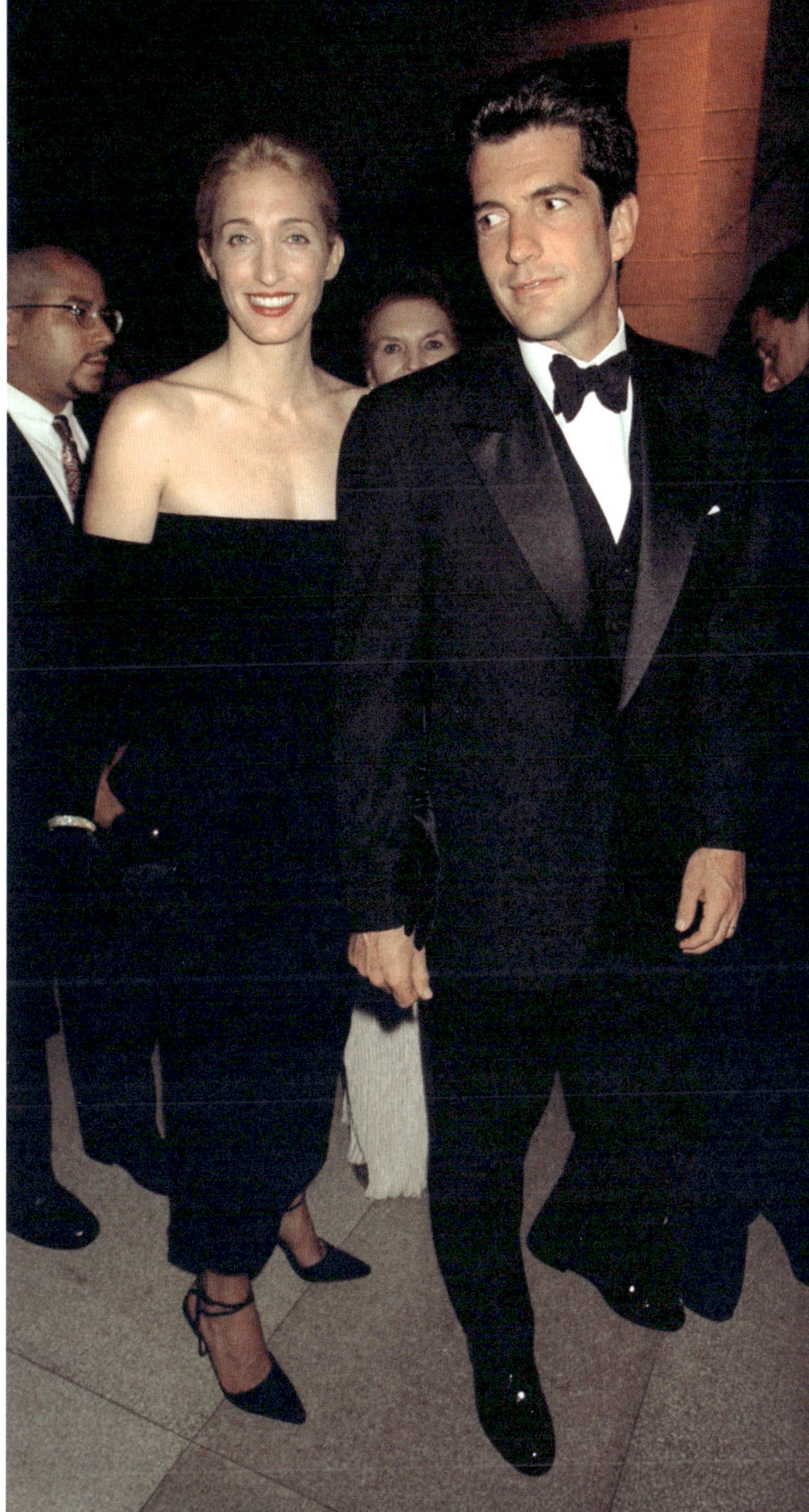

THE SOCIAL SET

TINSLEY MORTIMER

In the early to mid-2000s, a new class of cool, young socialites dominated the New York style icon scene. One of the most famous of all was Tinsley Mortimer, originally from Virginia and a descendant of multiple First families.

She went to college in New York at Columbia and appeared in the 2008 season premiere episode of *Gossip Girl*, as herself, later starring in her own CW reality show, *High Society*, in 2010. In 2017, Mortimer joined the cast of Bravo's reality television series *The Real Housewives of New York City*. *Town & Country* labelled her "once the most photographed woman in New York City". At the height of her fame, she cemented her style with signature, middle-parted, beachy, blonde waves that looked as if they came fresh off the pages of a magazine editorial, along with floral mini-dresses, strappy heels, long, silk or lace maxi-gowns, and ample printed frocks.

Even all these years later, her personal style doesn't waver. She was reportedly a huge inspiration for the aesthetic of the main characters in *Gossip Girl*. "If you put Blair and Serena together, you get Tinsley Mortimer. Tinsley's hair is always set and she always looks perfect, but she takes risks," costume designer Eric Daman told *Vanity Fair*.

Opposite: Tinsley Mortimer appeared in the original *Gossip Girl* series wearing her signature strapless dress style. Costume designers Eric Daman and Meredith Markworth-Pollack cited Mortimer's style as influencing the looks of characters Blair and Serena.

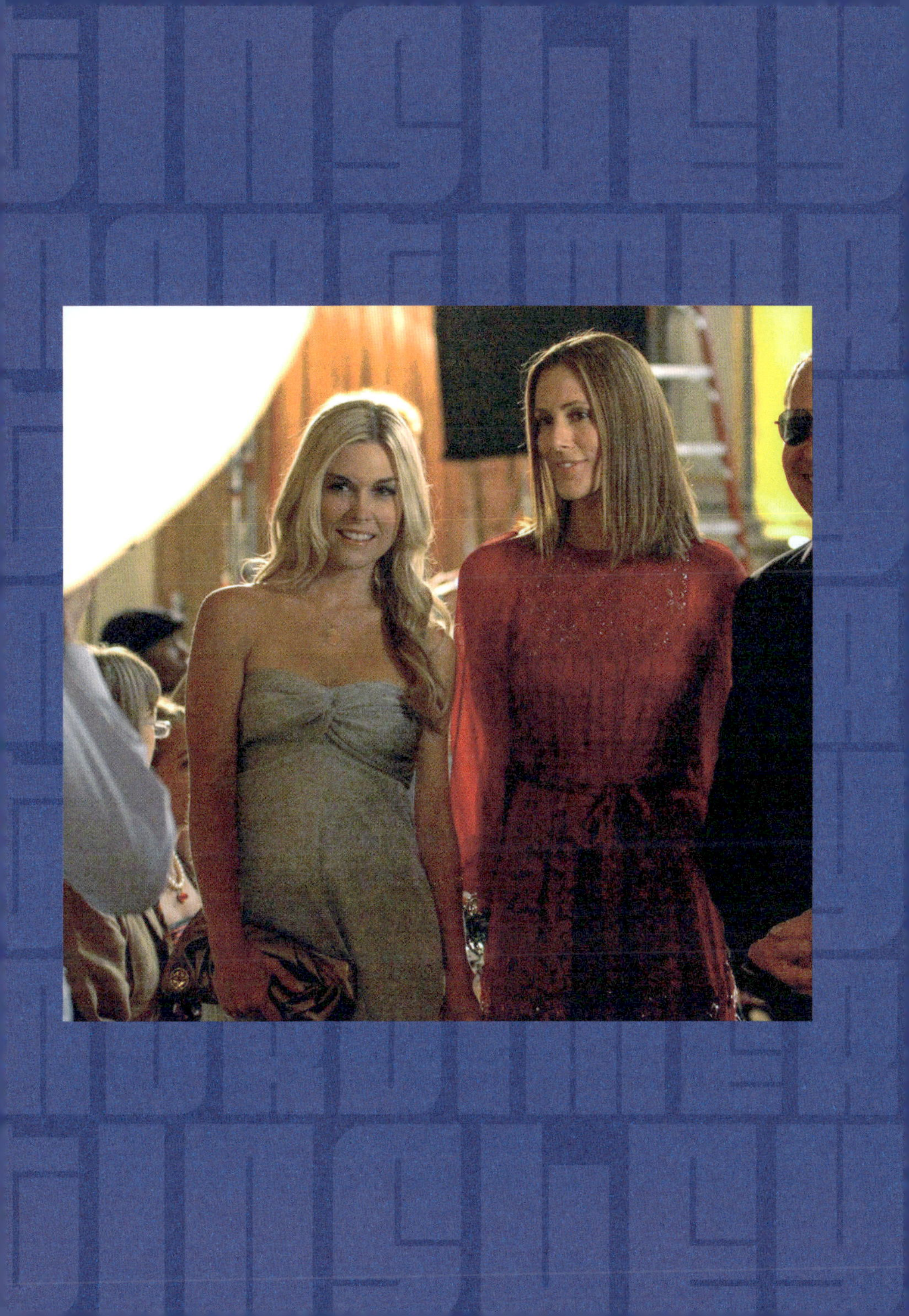

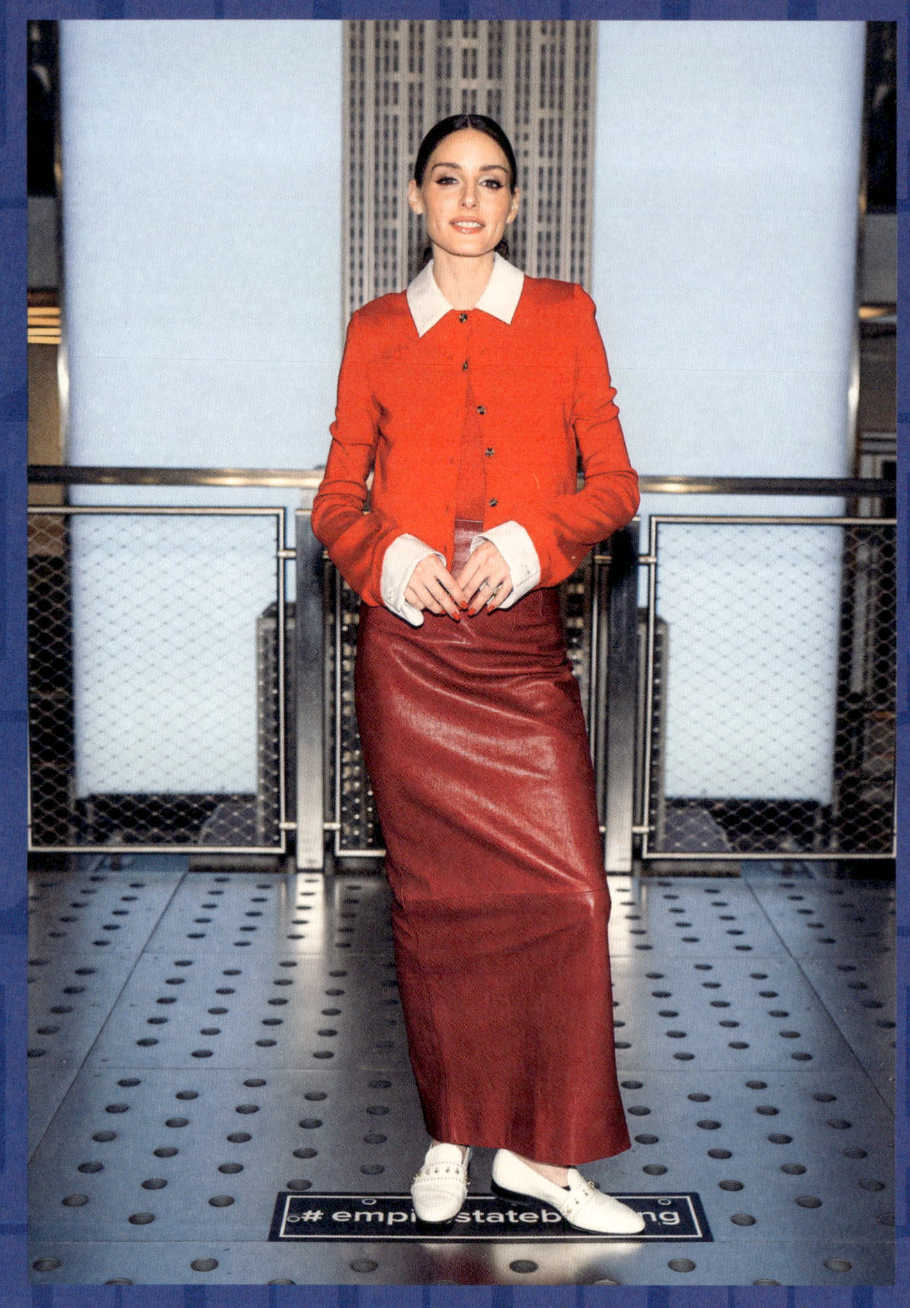

OLIVIA PALERMO

Also in the mid-2010s, Olivia Palermo became one of the most watched people in New York when it came to the world of fashion. Born to a real-estate developer father and interior designer mother, she was raised on the Upper East Side, of course with time spent in Greenwich, Connecticut. She was spotted by photographer Patrick McMullan (known for his agency that photographs top events and society gatherings) at an auction. In 2008, she gained major attention when she starred in *The City*, the fashion, New York City version of the infamous US series *The Hills*. There, the reality show followed her as she worked at Diane von Furstenberg and *Elle* magazine. Her style is polished and yet approachable, with a curated hand that makes everything look expensive. She dresses modestly and with reserve, shying away from anything flashy or controversial. With over eight million followers across her social media platforms, today she continues to collaborate with brands and keep up ongoing partnerships with her extremely curated, polished image.

Opposite: Olivia Palermo's minimal, modest style had a major influence on the New York landscape, most particularly in the mid-2000s.

THE SOCIAL SET

GLORIA VANDERBILT

Long before the reign of early 2000s society queens such as Mortimer and Palermo, Gloria Vanderbilt took her socialite style and turned it into a business. Born in 1924 in Manhattan to railroad heir Reginald Claypoole Vanderbilt, she began modelling for fashion magazines, including *Harper's Bazaar* when she was 15. Later, she committed to acting, and eventually her passion, which was painting.

In the 1970s, Vanderbilt ventured into the fashion industry with licensing agreements that would change history. Often credited as starting the first designer denim brand, Vanderbilt partnered with businessman Mohan Murjan to release her line of jeans. She acted as the spokeswoman, and in doing so, she made her extremely expensive taste accessible with high-waisted, slim-fit jeans marked with her signature swan-shaped logo. With striking dark hair, mesmerizing eyes and a love of glamour, Vanderbilt dressed in beautiful formal dresses by exclusive label Mainbocher, antique garments she collected, structured feminine suits, and always – accessories, whether it be a little silk neck scarf or hoards of jewels. She epitomized taste and glamour.

Opposite: Early Gloria Vanderbilt style was ultra-feminine and poised, before the socialite created her own designer denim brand.

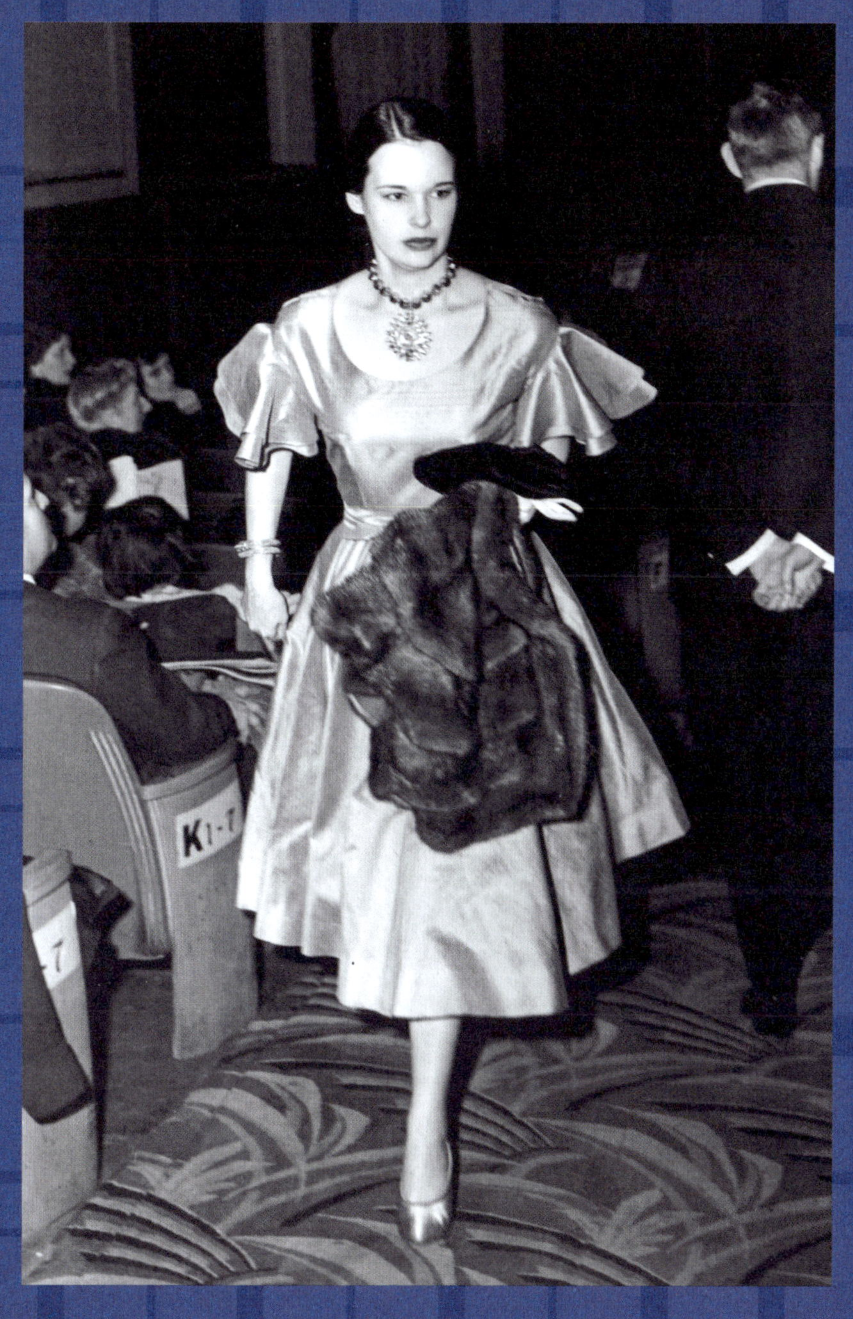

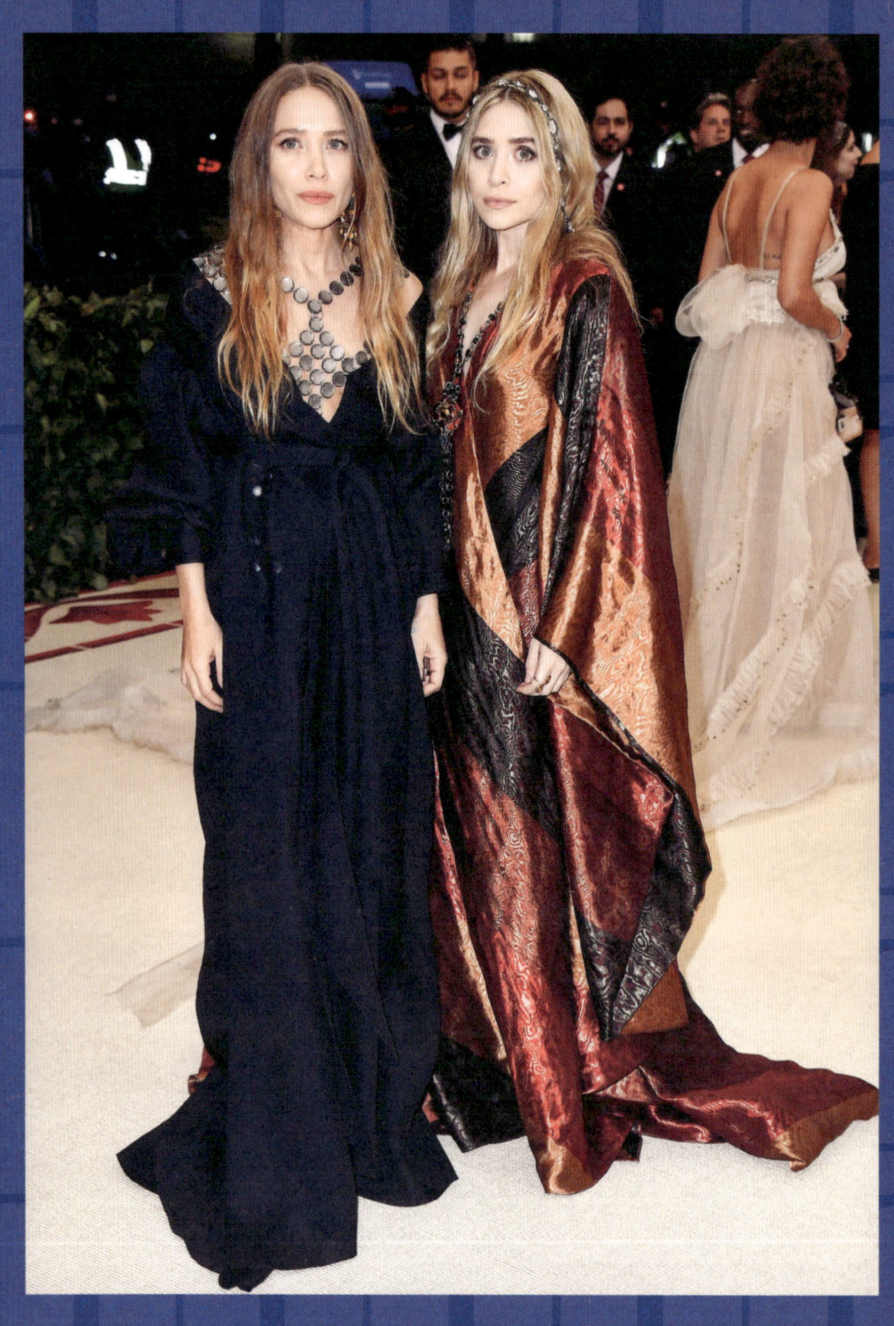

THE OLSEN TWINS

When the Olsen twins moved to New York City in 2004, no one knew they would change fashion history. The duo became famous for starring in sitcom *Full House* (1987–95) and later became pre-teen icons from their series of TV shows, movies, video games and media created under their own production company, Dualstar.

Mary-Kate and Ashley originally moved to New York City in 2004 to attend New York University's Gallatin School of Individualized Study. They'd eventually drop out, and in 2006, they founded their award-winning, New York-based fashion line The Row.

Despite becoming two of the wealthiest women in the entertainment industry of all time at a young age, and moving in elite New York social scenes, the Olsen twins did things their own way. They are some of the first major celebrities to publicly wear rare designer vintage in place of current season runway items and they also popularized the "bag lady chic" style of excessive, messy layering in the early 2000s. Think dark sunglasses, hugely oversized sweaters over white T-shirts, and open, button-down shirts, baggy pants and flat shoes. They've worn funky hats and huge shades as power moves to hide themselves. After living their entire childhood on display, who can blame them for doing things their own way? The Row echoes their coolly private sentiment, eschewing advertising and sometimes banning guests from taking photos on their phones at their runway show. But the aesthetic is expensive, understated and eponymous with the quiet luxury trend that dominated media in the mid-2020s.

Mary-Kate made fashion history (and echoed Jane Birkin's ethos of *using* your designer bags) in the way she wore her overly used and abused,

Opposite: The Olsen twins wore vintage Paco Rabanne to the 2018 Met Gala.

stained, mint-green Balenciaga Moto bag and perfectly visible, worn-in, box-calfskin Hermès Kelly. The Olsen twins' predilection for vintage is best seen on the Met Gala red carpet. When they first attended the event in 2005, as freshmen at NYU, Mary-Kate wore a vintage slip, while Ashley chose a strapless Oscar de la Renta gown. The theme? Chanel. Ashley's stunning, sheer, vintage, tangerine-hued gown worn to the 2013 Met Gala is a fan favourite, while the archival lambskin leather Chanel get-ups of their 2019 Met Gala appearance will live forever in the minds of vintage fashion lovers.

Below left: Mary-Kate's wine-stained Balenciaga City bag is one of the most famous It-bags of all time, let alone in New York fashion history.

Below right: The Olsen Twins were some of the first celebs to wear vintage clothing on the red carpet before it became mainstream, as seen here when Ashley wore vintage Dior to the 2013 Met Gala.

Opposite: The duo wore vintage Chanel ensembles for the 2019 Met Gala.

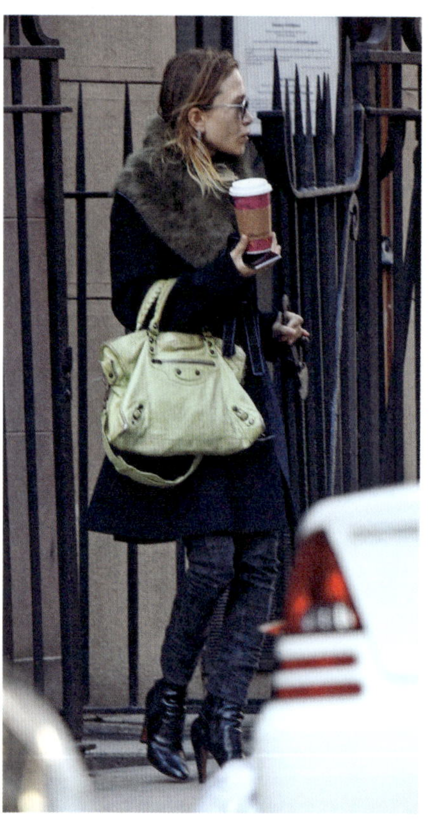

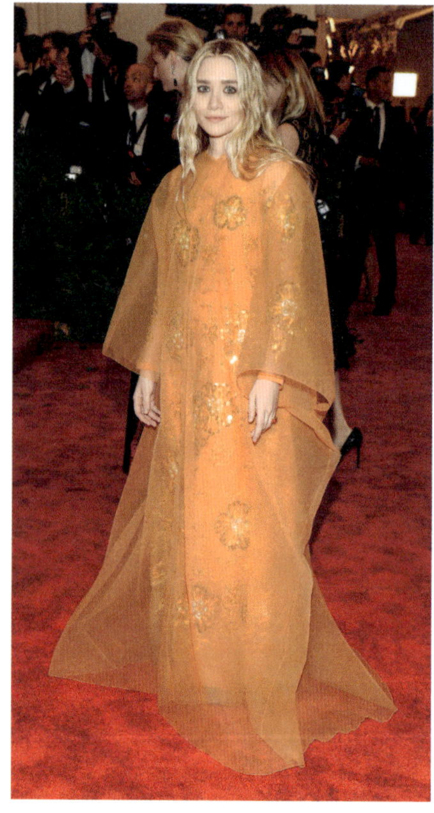

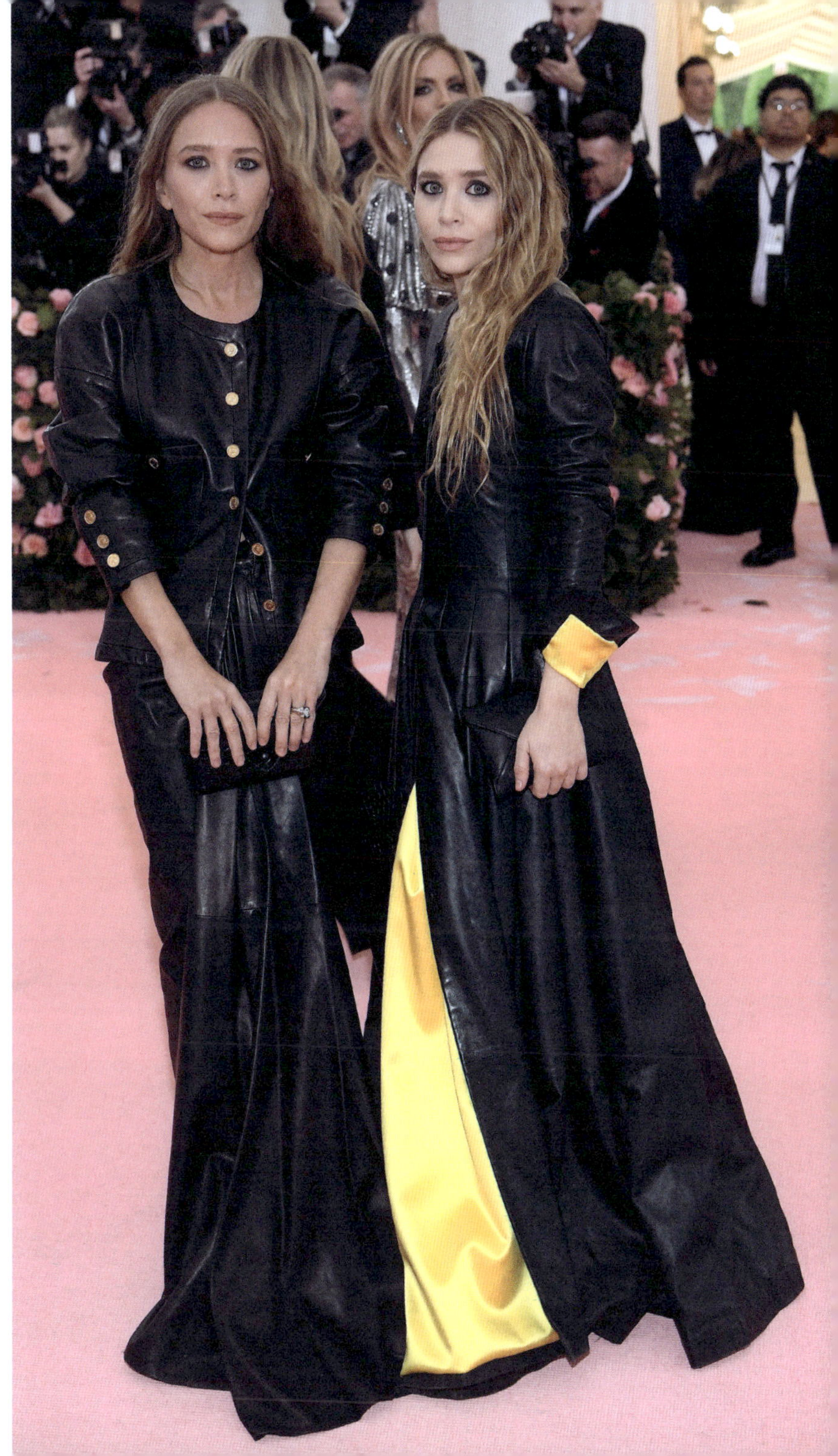

MOST WATCHED ECCENTRICS

LITTLE EDIE & BIG EDIE

Style feels most authentic when it's personal. That's part of the reason why Little Edie has become one of the most iconic and least conventional social circle icons of all time. Immortalized in the 1975 *Grey Gardens* documentary, mother and daughter Edith Ewing Bouvier Beale (1895–1977), "Big Edie", and Edith Bouvier Beale, "Little Edie" (aunt and first cousin of Jacqueline Kennedy Onassis and Lee Radziwill), lived in a decrepit mansion in the Hamptons with their cats. While their story is overwhelmingly sad and the famously loved documentary may also raise questions about exploitation, Little Edie's sense of whimsy and personal style has inspired oddly eccentric maximalists for decades. In her younger days, she dressed conservatively in pretty dresses for New York society events. But her *Grey Gardens* era is the most defining. Her influence has been seen on the runway, especially during creative director Alessandro Michele's reign at Gucci. In the film, she wears scarves tied around her head, with large brooches, skirts as capes, layered sweaters, tights, big fur coats and bathing suits.

Opposite: Little Edie, inspiration to all maximalists and eccentrics, outside her *Grey Gardens* home in her signature fur coat and headscarf.

Overleaf: Little Edie and her mother, Big Edie, wore a collage of different found items in their later years and were most extensively explored in the documentary *Grey Gardens*.

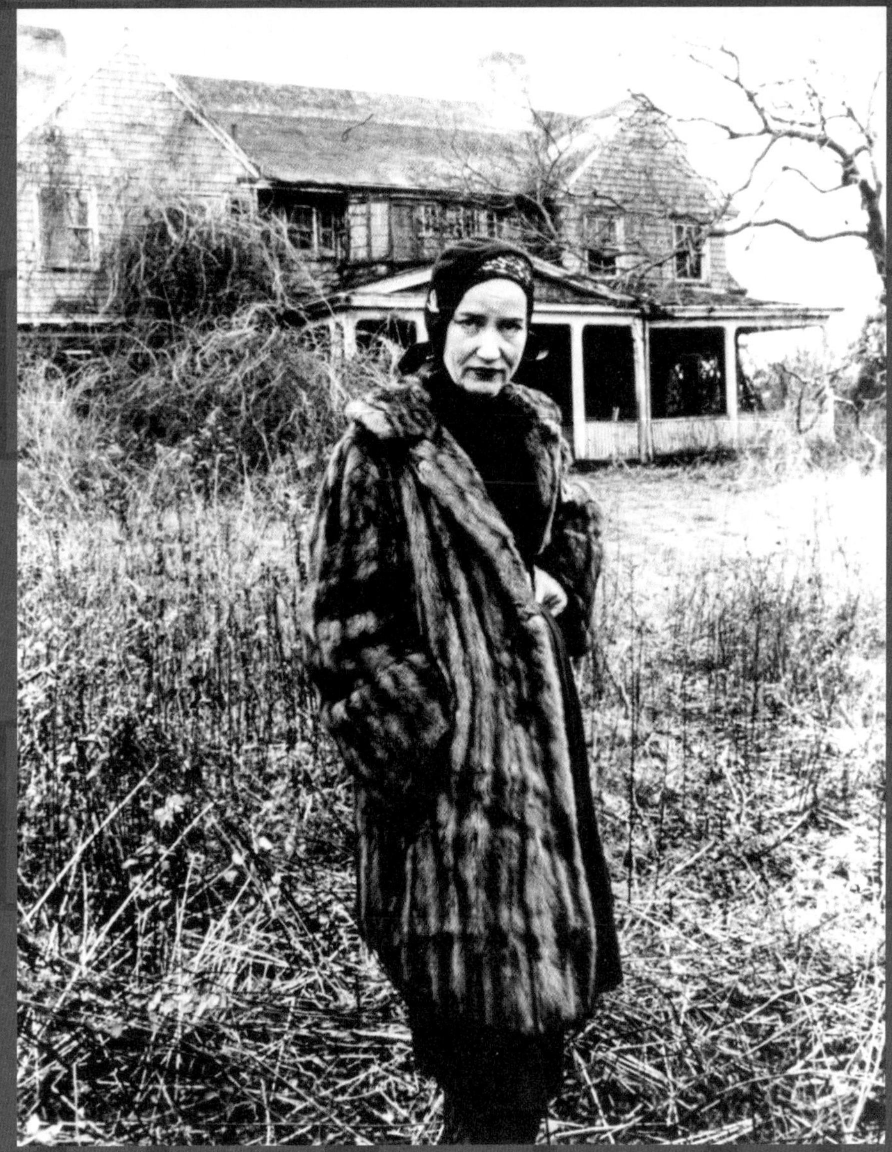

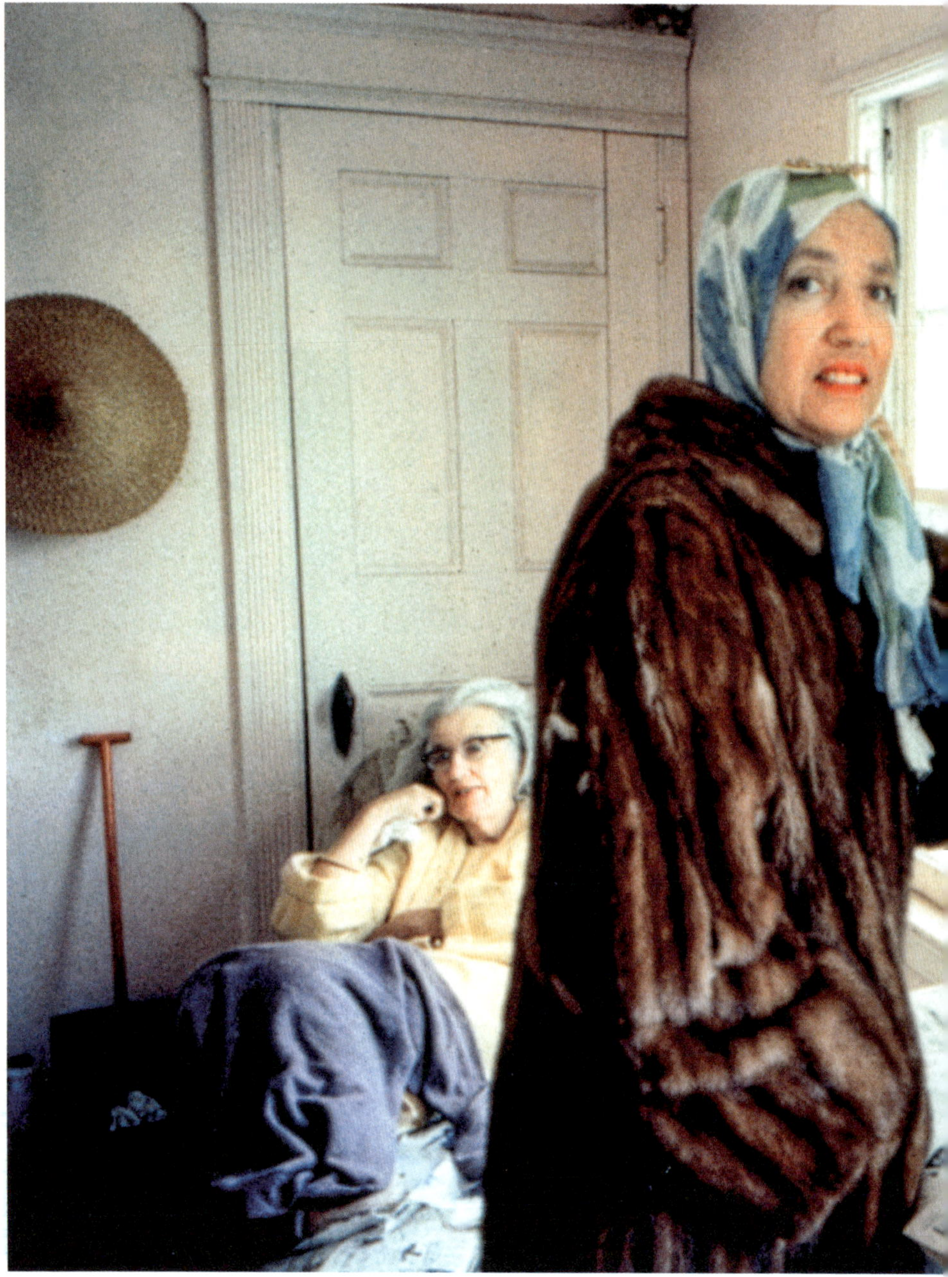

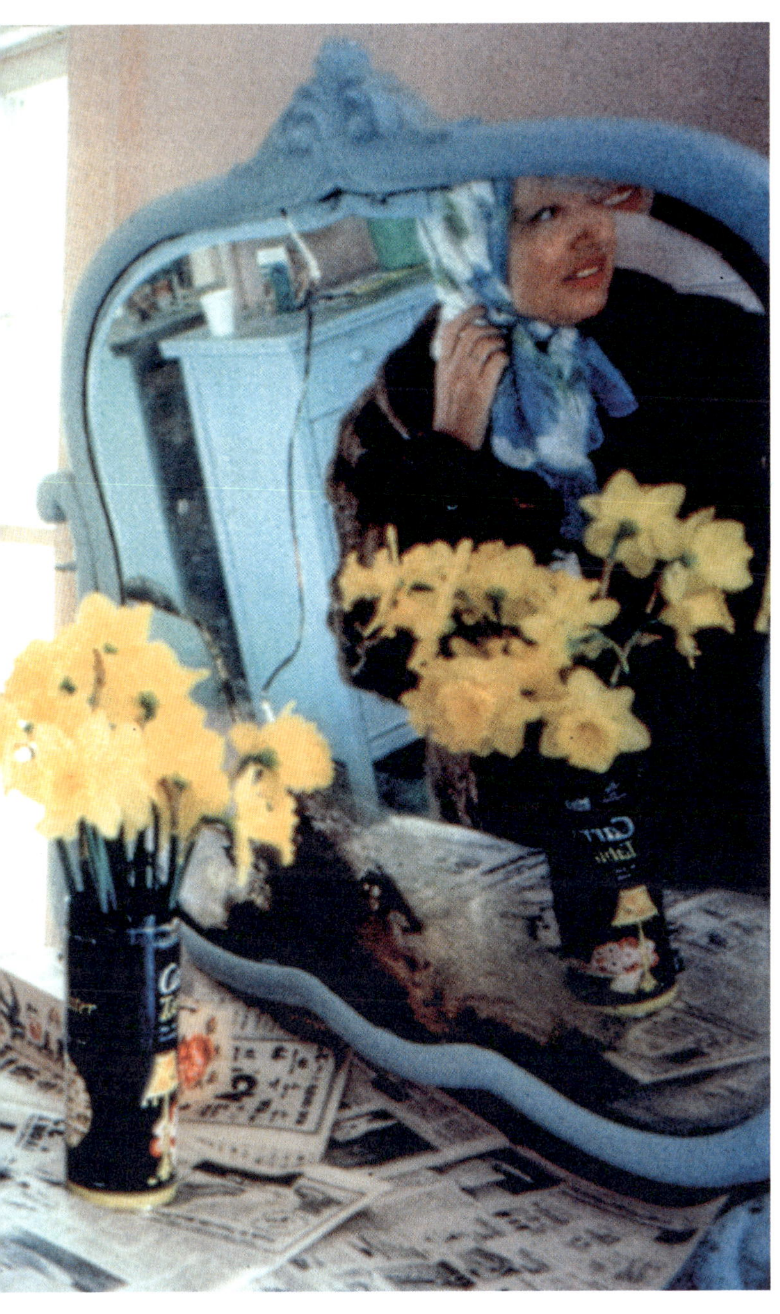

FIRST LADIES & SWANS

Eccentric is the opposite of how you'd describe Jackie Kennedy, who is considered the ultimate timeless, classic icon. Born in Southampton, New York, to a stockbroker father and socialite mother, she made her debut on the social scene before going on to marry John F. Kennedy and, later, Aristotle Socrates Onassis.

She defined a legacy of New York style, with her signature Chanel suits, pearl necklaces, pillbox hats and dark, oversized sunglasses. She adored careful accessorizing – brooches, ladylike handbags, wide ornate belts and white gloves – but she also didn't shy away from a full leopard-print suit and matching hat. In the 1970s, she lived in printed maxi-dresses and menswear-inspired suiting.

Above all else, the New York social scene doyennes of the 1960s laid the groundwork for other society style makers to come. Take socialite Nan Kempner, for instance. This muse to Yves Saint Laurent made history when she was refused at the famed La Côte Basque restaurant in 1972 because she was wearing the designer's Le Smoking tuxedo instead of a skirt or dress. She reportedly took off her trousers and walked in wearing just the jacket. She lived for extravagance and had one of the biggest collections of haute couture fashion in the country at the height of her fame.

Opposite: Jackie Kennedy's style shifted throughout the years. She is well remembered for her oversized sunglasses, minimal tailored looks and statement jewellery in her later years, as seen here.

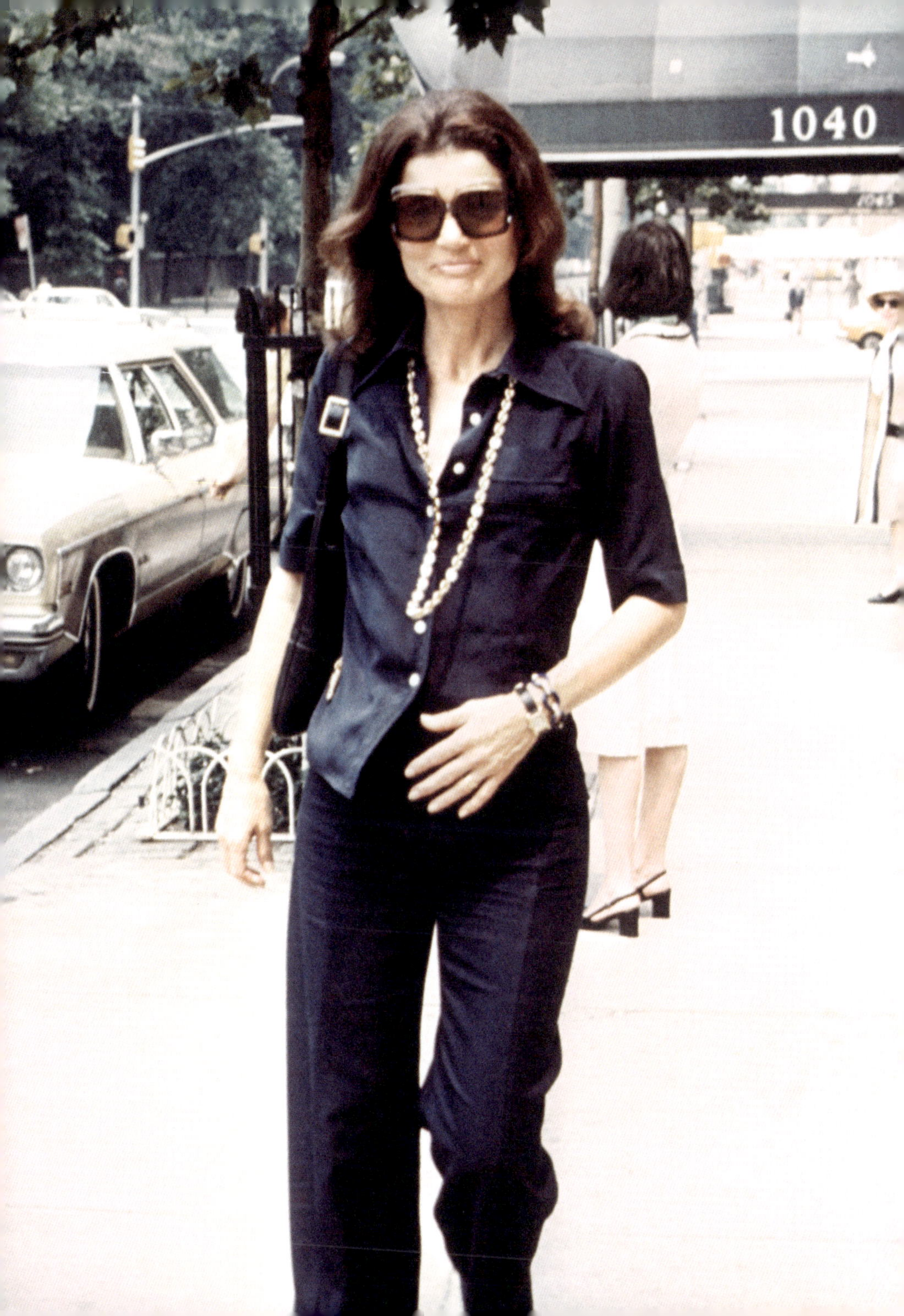
1040

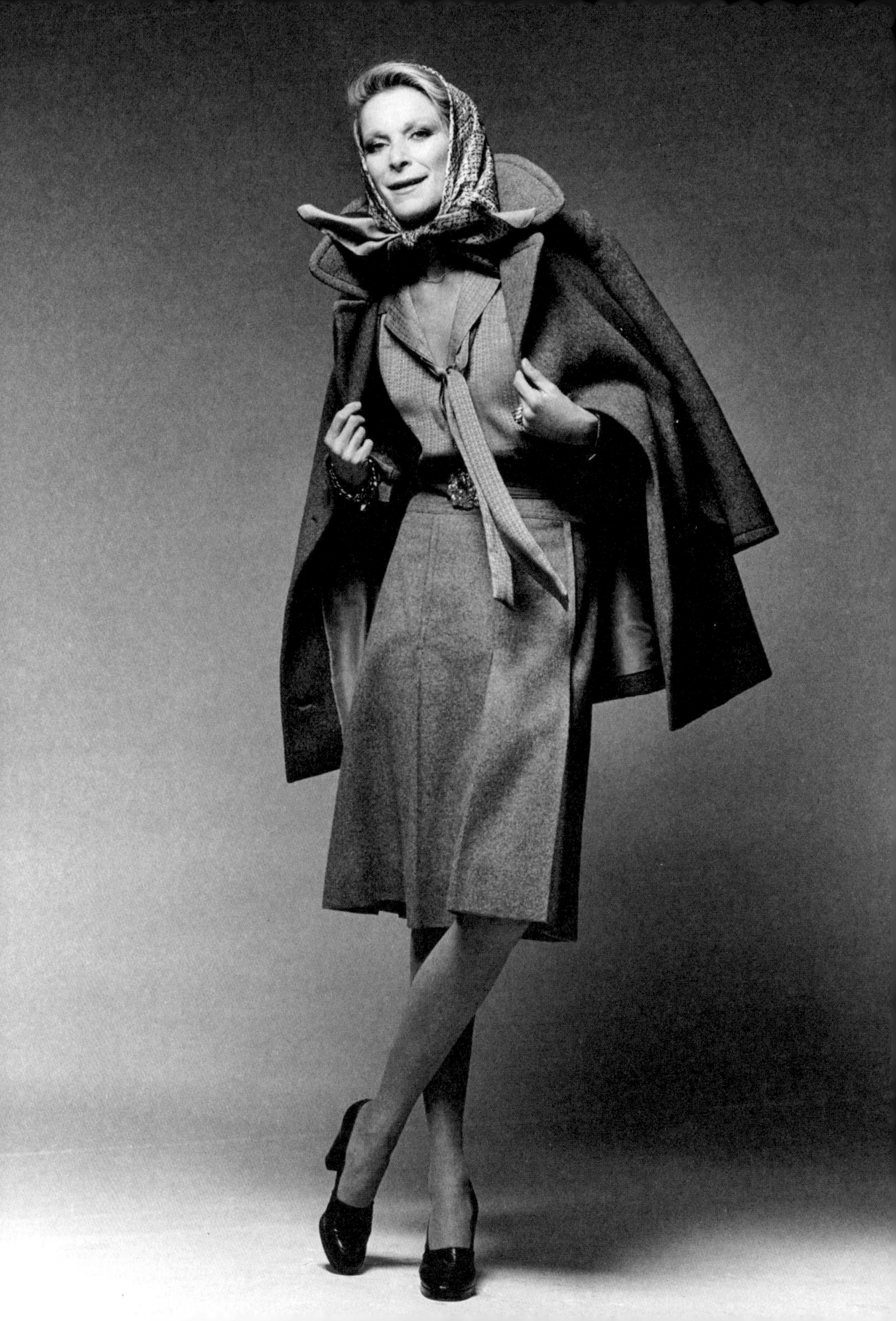

The so-called Swans of famed writer Truman Capote's friend group let him accompany them to glamorous vacations, upscale lunches, galas and more in exchange for friendship, before he betrayed them by airing their personal affairs in a tell-all. The group was composed of Lee Radziwill, C.Z. Guest, Slim Keith, Babe Paley, Ann Woodward, Gloria Guinness, Marella Agnelli and Pamela Harriman – some of them more editorial in their style choices than others.

Paley, in particular, was known for her style. A former *Vogue* editor, she loved colourful and playful details, big bags, closed-toe shoes, antique jewels and tradition. She was known for tying Hermès scarves to her bags before it was a major trend. In 1944, in an essay for *Vogue*, she wrote, "Color, in fact, is my weakness. I fall in love with a pale blue coat (even though it spends its life at the cleaner's). I like the pansy blue of the paper-silk shantung suit photographed on this page. I like the quick red of the Flower Show rose that blooms on my black-and-white, checked cotton beret. I like the giddy dinner hat, with its bright sprawl of pink cabbage roses and green velvet leaves, sprinkled with pearl and paillette dewdrops."

Likewise, Slim Keith was known for her classic, cool, untouchable aesthetic. She is rumoured to have inspired the main character in the 1944 film *To Have and Have Not*. She brought the tall, blonde, athletic California girl look to New York, with flannel pants, easy maxi-skirts and dresses without embellishment. In 2023, *Vogue* called C.Z. Guest "the most elegant and enigmatic of Truman Capote's Swans". She favoured lots of white, plus practical American sportswear inspired by her life as a horticulturist and equine enthusiast, on top of being a socialite, with a twist of elegance from Ralph Lauren, Michael Kors and Oscar de la Renta.

Lee Radziwill, on the other hand, who was a PR executive at Armani after working as an actress and interior decorator, was the picture of timeless American glamour with a careful injection of personality: in silky sets, sequinned gowns, sophisticated beige neutrals, embellished suits and gold leather jackets.

Opposite: Nan Kempner was a New York society and couture-collecting legend, known for her bold personality and exquisite taste.

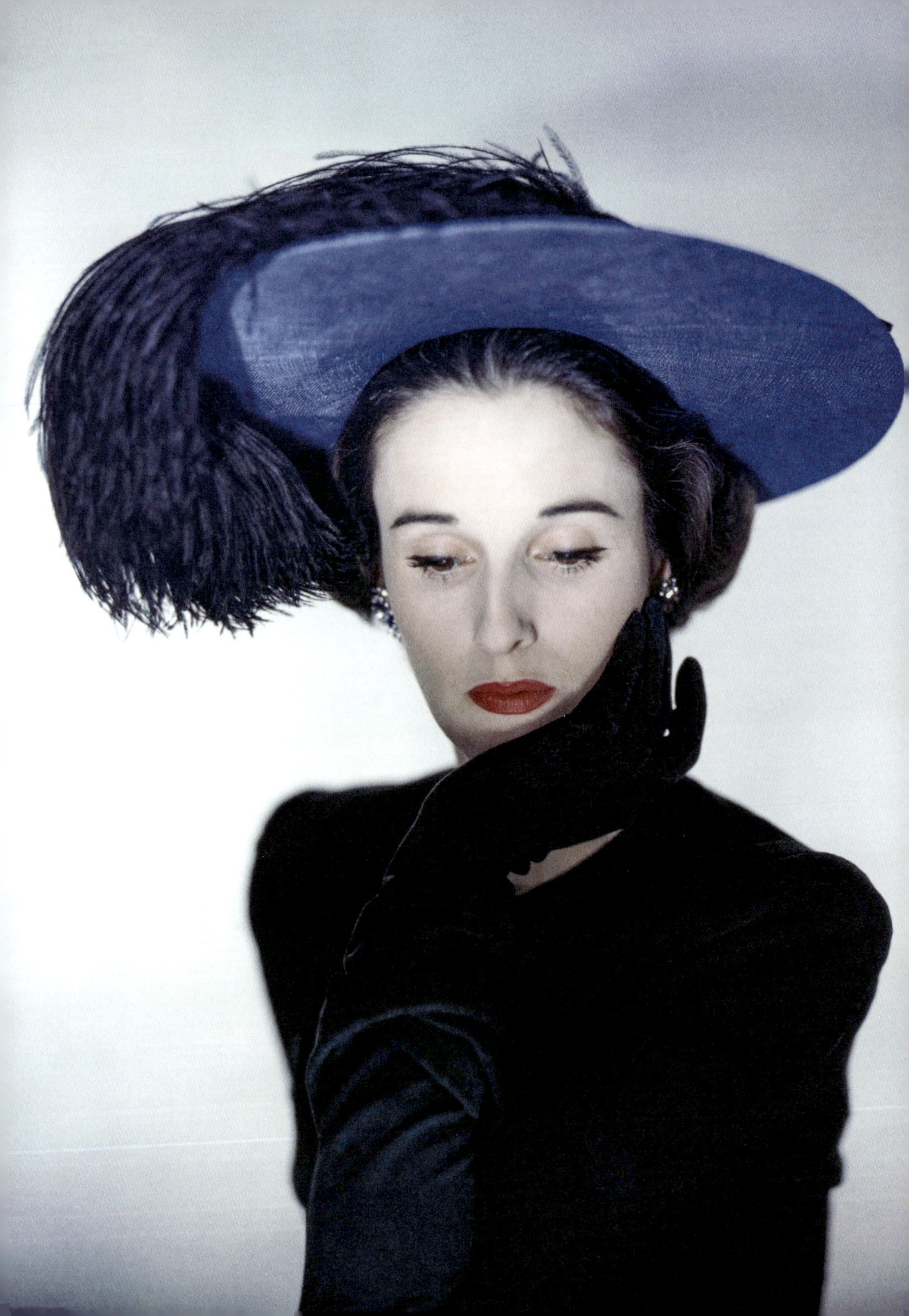

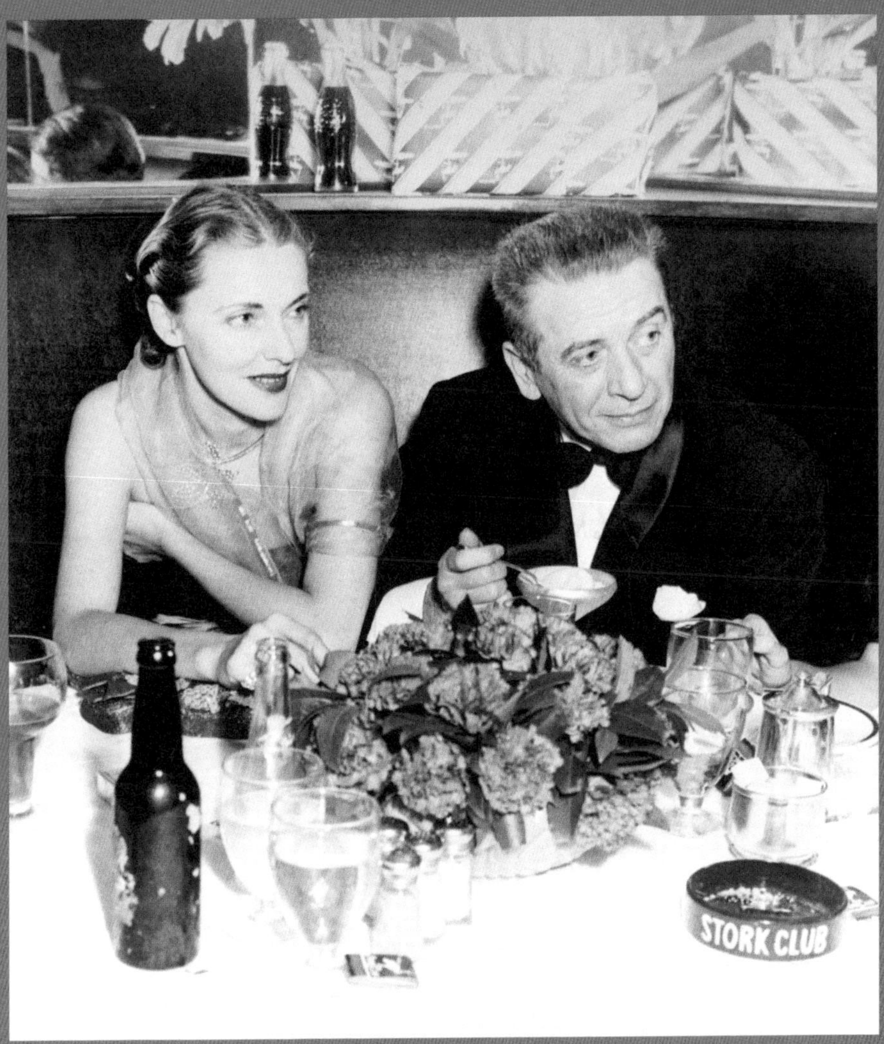

Opposite: Magazine editor and socialite Babe Paley wears a striking and dramatic feathered hat.

Above: Slim Keith, seen here with theatrical producer Leland Hayward.

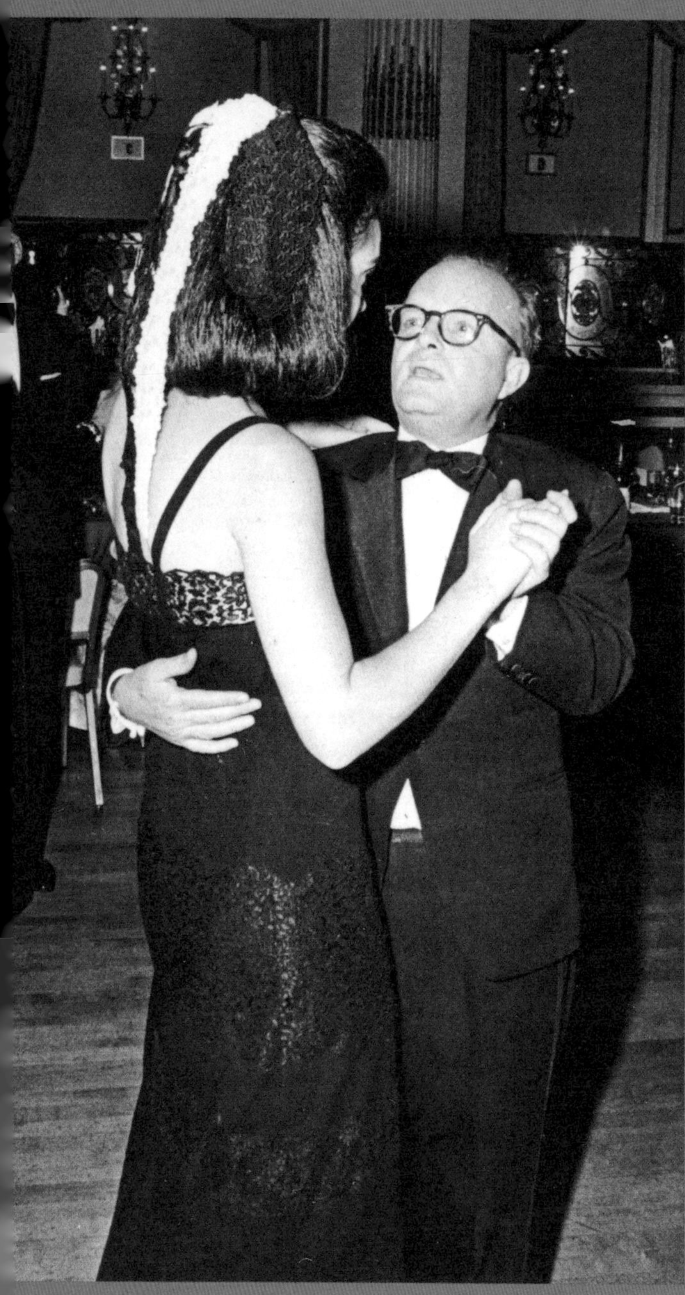

Left: The writer once at the centre of New York style society: Truman Capote dancing with Wendy Vanderbilt (later Lehman) at his Black and White Ball in 1966.

Opposite: Lee Radziwill, a Truman Capote Swan who also became a muse to Dior creative director Jonathan Anderson in 2025.

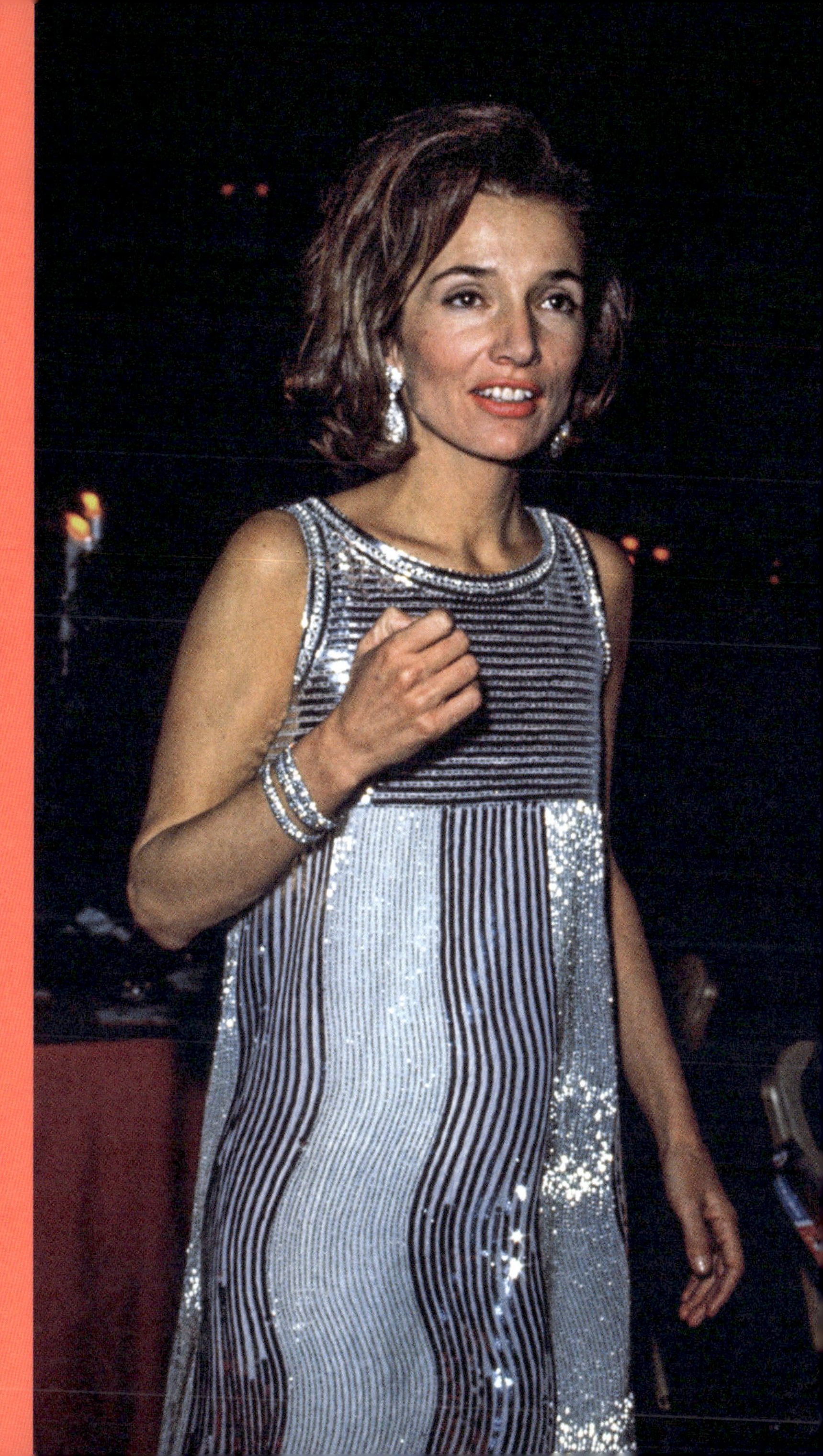

CHAPTER 5:

FASHION INSIDERS

In one of the world's most expressive cities, it's no wonder the beating heart of the fashion industry contains some of the most divinely expressive dressers. From designers to stylists and editors, the fashion insiders who keep it all alive serve as a driving force for tastemaking, trends and, of course, a devotion to the celebration of self and style.

ANNA SUI

There's a wild cliché in the world of fashion that designers are often minimalists, only wear their own work, or live in a bubble of neutrals so as to not interfere with their curated aesthetic. But not here in New York. Some of the most iconic designers who have made a name for themselves also have an incredibly memorable way of dressing – cementing their legacy beyond designing and into the stratosphere as iconic style icons.

The designer Anna Sui has her own aesthetic that dives deep into the world of rock 'n' roll music culture when she's designing her epic runway shows. However, Sui herself is also a lifelong vintage shopper and devotee, and can often be seen wearing rare pieces from her personal collection, such as antique Bakelite jewellery, vintage Yves Saint Laurent dresses and pieces from Prada's spring 2008 fairy-themed collection. She came to New York to attend Parsons in the 1970s, and wore Kenzo, mixed with 1940s vintage dresses and jackets with shoulder pads and platform shoes, and scarves tied in her hair. In the 1980s, she wore lace petticoats with tuxedo jackets and band T-shirts or a corseted top. "When I arrived in New York, there was a whole glam rock thing going on, which switched into punk really quickly," she says.

With her blunt fringe, her look is so iconic that Barbie created a doll version of her in 2025. Sui founded her ready-to-wear label in 1981, and came of age in New York City famous haunts like CBGB and Max's Kansas City, which had a huge influence on the development of her look. "Nobody had any money back then, but everybody looked like movie stars," she says. "Everybody dressed in vintage clothes, and there were lots of

Opposite: Fashion designer Anna Sui has always been inspired by music, culture and vintage fashion.

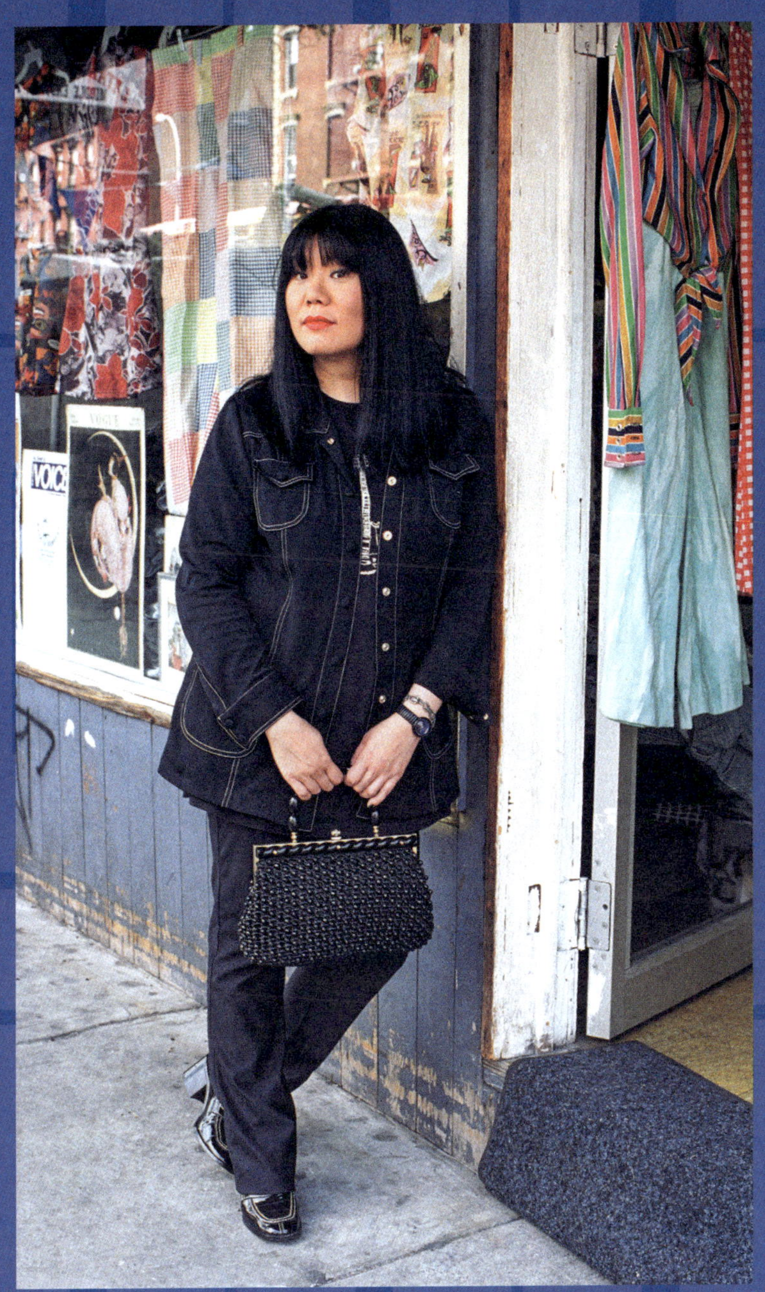
VOGUE

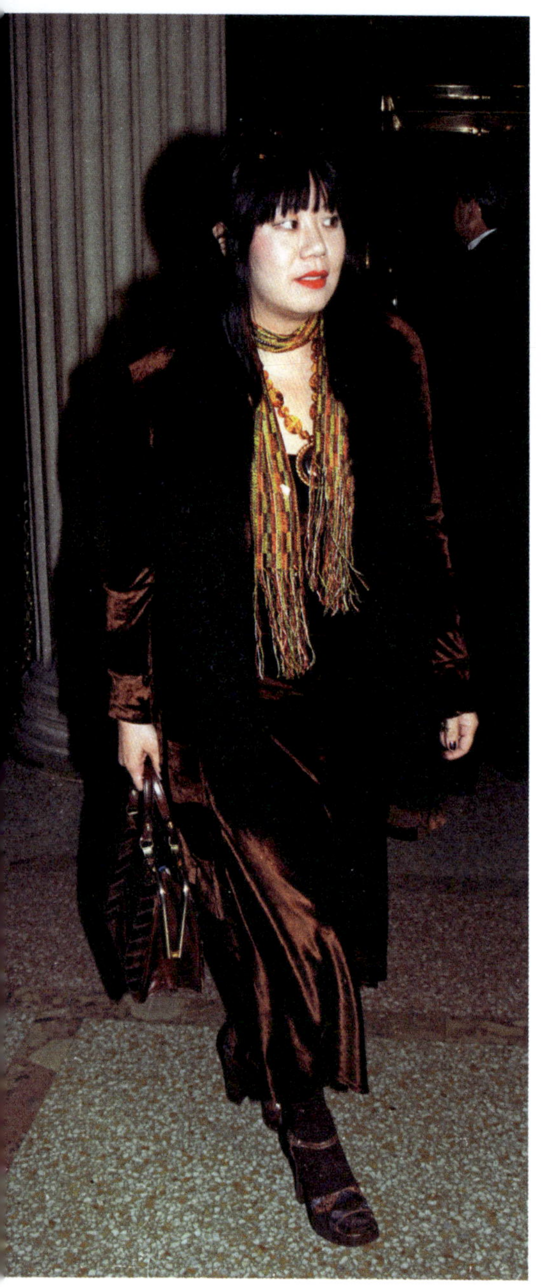

girls wearing 1960s cocktail dresses and they had these little 1960s handbags that they would get in their arms and they always wore these 1960s stiletto shoes. But with fishnets or black stockings, lots of heavy make-up." As a teen, she covered herself in chunky vintage jewellery and piled on ruffled baby-doll dresses. Her personal style would later form the basis of, and become essential to, her namesake brand. Alongside her vintage-leaning aesthetic, as Sui developed her brand, she pulled from lots of the underground subcultures that served as the backbone of New York style: punk, goth, clubs kids and beyond.

"When I went to Parsons, I had made a lot of clothes for myself, and I think what I loved was that whole, folkloric, rich hippie look," Sui says of her early style. "I found some Liberty of London fabric and made some peasant skirts. I had a velvet peplum jacket. I had some suede boots that were embroidered. I made a denim jacket that was like a peplum jacket. I was trying to emulate that."

Left: In her early days as a fashion designer Anna Sui wore plenty of prints, long scarves and lush, vintage-inspired fabrics.

Opposite: Anna Sui's autumn 2025 collection had many vintage influences, including Art Deco-inspired jewellery, leopard prints, turbans and Peggy Guggenheim-inspired butterfly sunglasses.

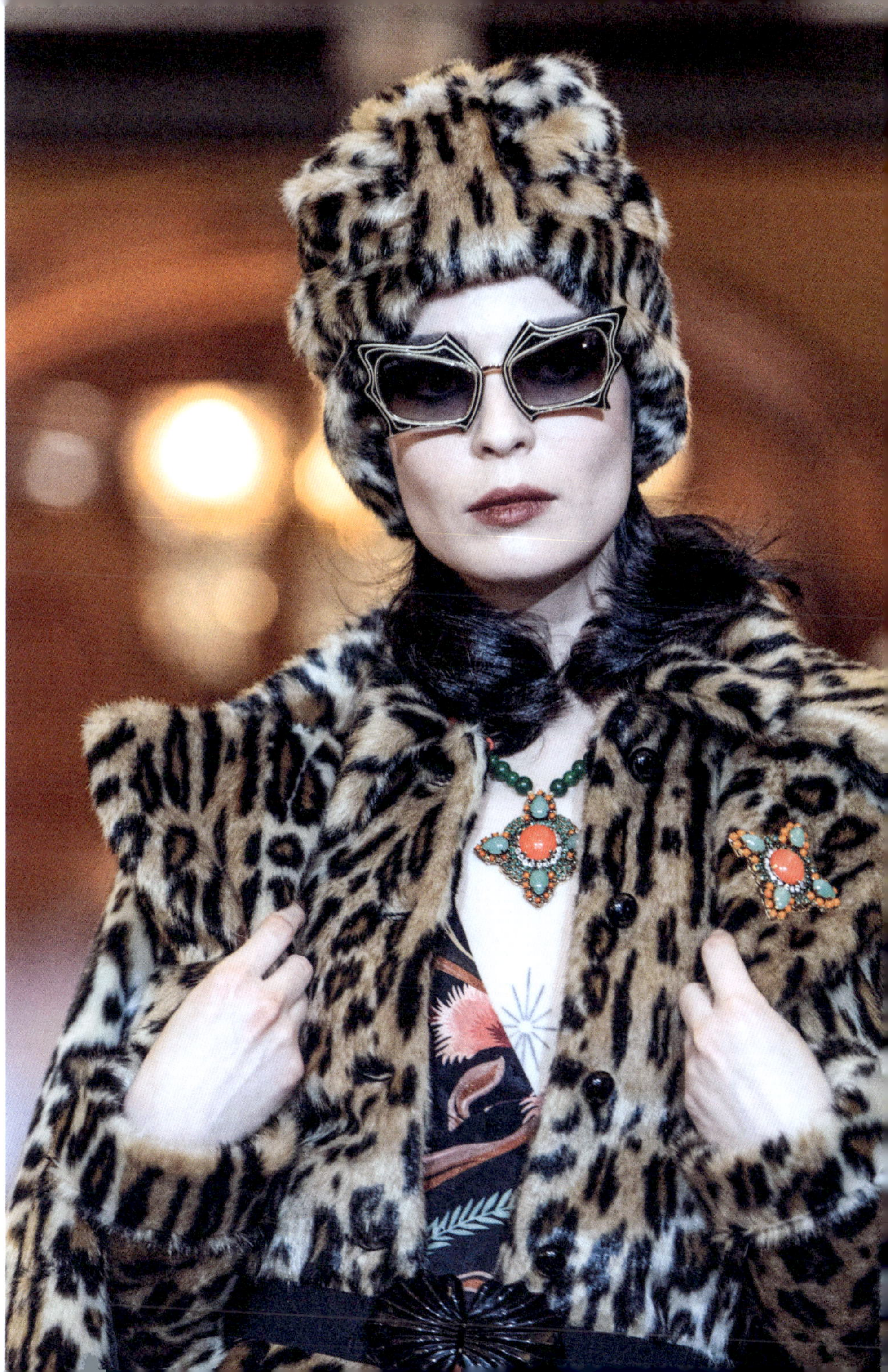

NORMA KAMALI

Many of the legendary contemporary female designers of New York were deeply inspired by vintage and had their own vibrant sense of personal style prior to kicking off their labels. Norma Kamali was one such designer. The native New Yorker opened her first boutique in the city in 1969. An avid collector of vintage jewellery, Kamali herself lived her brand: chic, pleated pieces that referenced the 1940s and tailored sweatsuit materials and silhouettes with massive sculptural volume, like her heavily influential sleeping-bag coat. "If I were to pick, 1939 was my favourite year in fashion," she told *Vogue* of her personal style. "I would put a shoulder pad in anything!" She would wear denim on denim with gold necklaces piled one on top of the other, or floor-length coats.

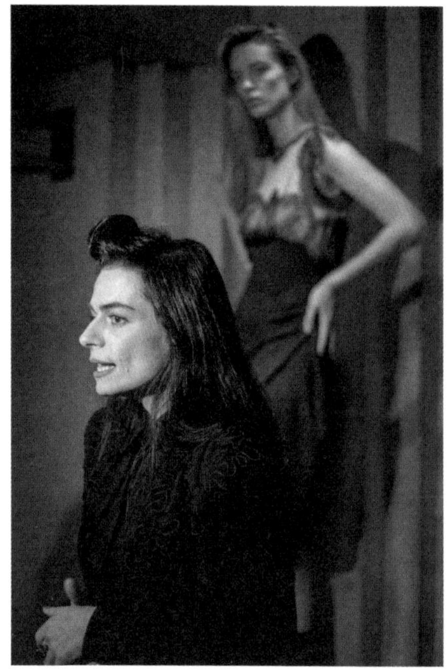

Above: Designer Norma Kamali lives her own brand ethos and is a collector of vintage jewellery.

Opposite: Norma Kamali in 1981 in one of her own designs, which combines comfort with avant-garde sensibility.

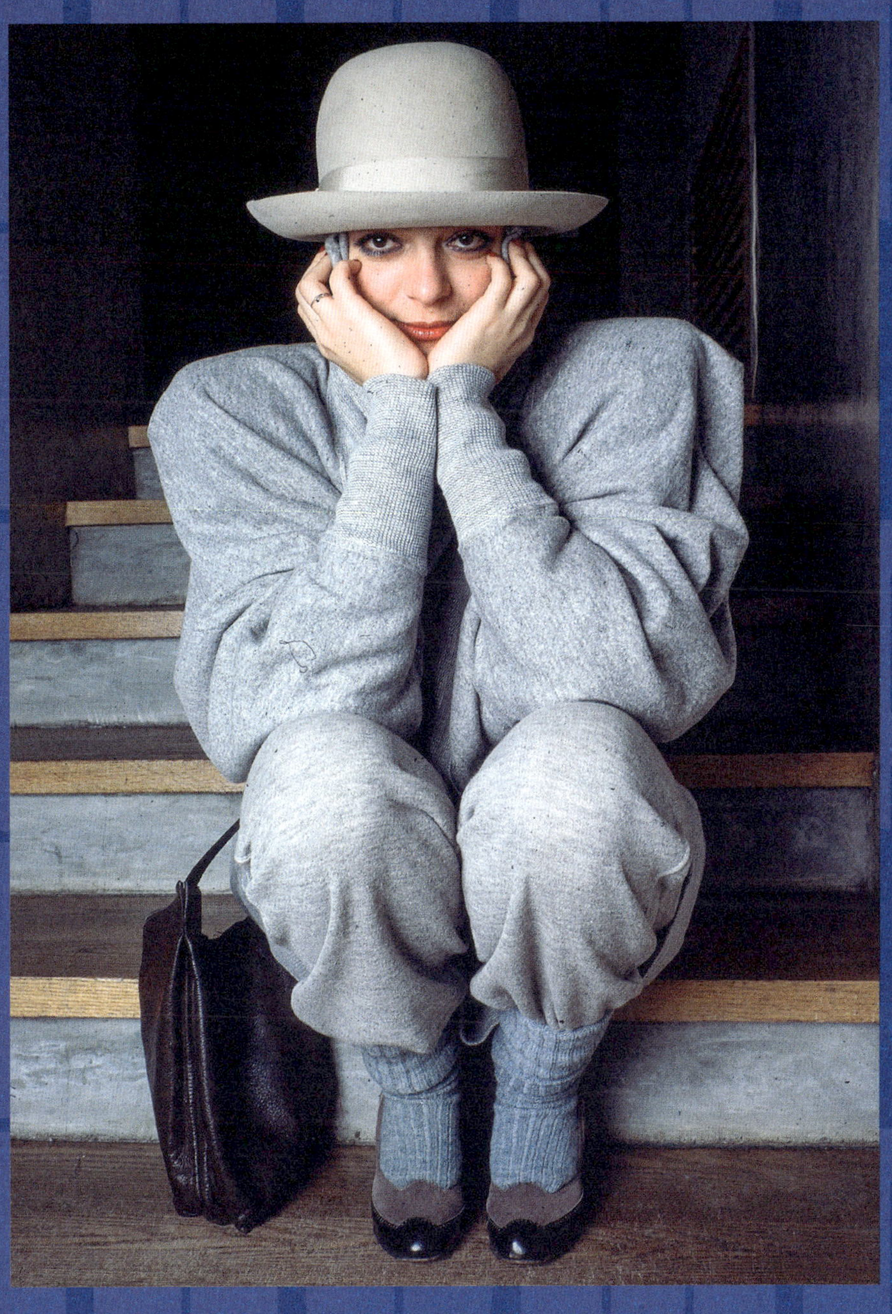

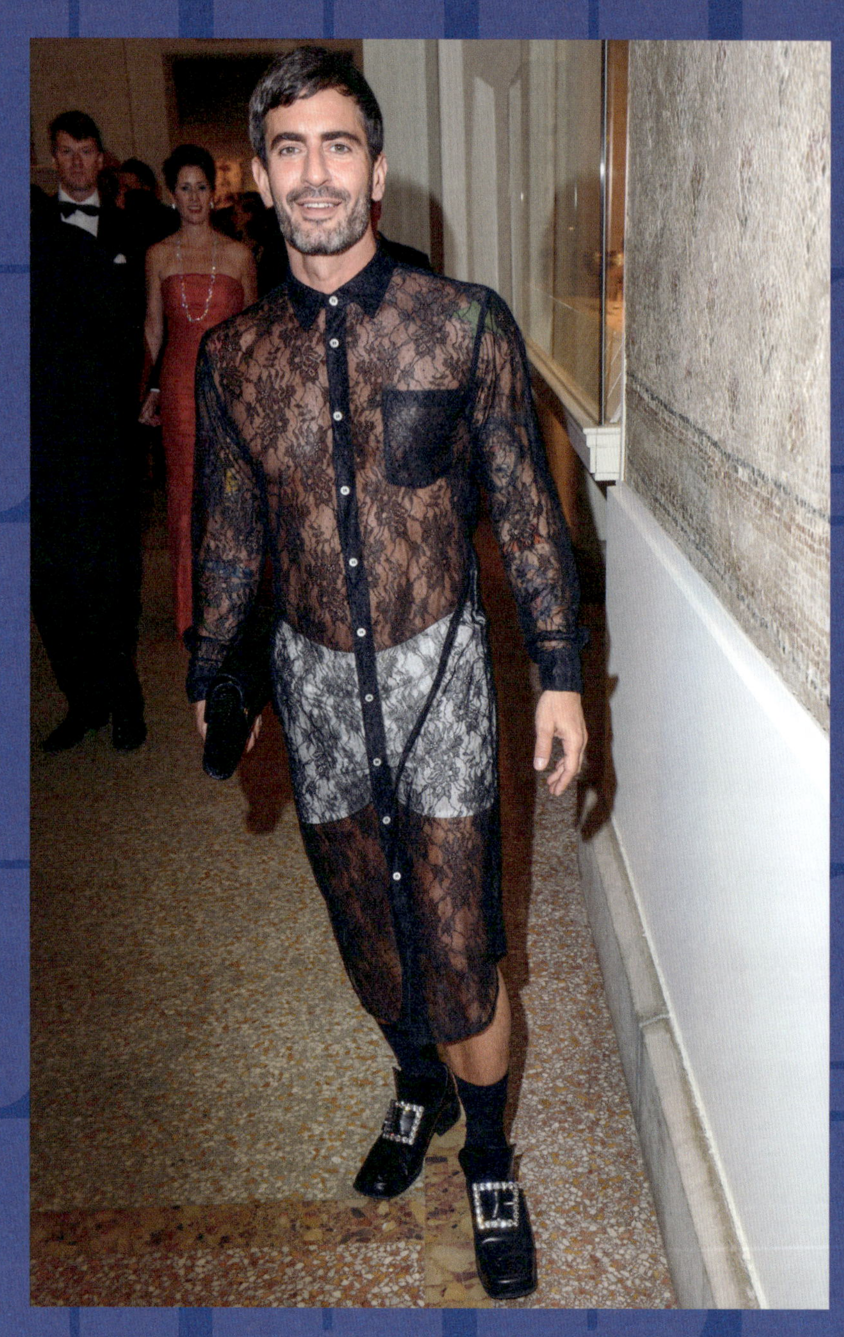

MARC JACOBS

Born in 1963, Marc Jacobs came of age in New York and grew up idolizing the subcultures and nightlife in the city, as well as some of the most iconic retail stores of all time. Jacobs reportedly went to the exciting beacon of retail Fiorucci, constantly, for inspiration. When he was a young designer, he dressed casually in sweatshirts, oversized trench coats and denim, which coincided with the popular grunge aesthetic trending at the time – and which he also brought to the Perry Ellis brand for whom he was creative director. He was later fired from the brand as a result of creating that same collection. But later in his career, Jacobs would further develop his personal style into something instantly recognizable and slightly camp. For example, he wore a sheer Comme des Garçons black lace dress on the 2012 Met Gala red carpet. Jacobs likes to push at conventional boundaries with his own wardrobe and personal beauty choices. He has gone through phases in which he often appreciates and wears dramatic nail art, including unique hand-painted shapes or extra-long tips covered in crystals.

Opposite: Marc Jacobs wearing sheer lace Comme des Garçons to the 2012 Met Gala.

RALPH LAUREN

Some New York designers perfectly embody the brands they build and have therefore become personal style heroes by association. Even people who aren't interested in fashion would probably recognize Ralph Lauren, the man. Dressed in worn-in denim, rustic leather belts, button-down shirts and other American prep workwear Western staples that define his brand, he lives it. Born in The Bronx, Lauren had a unique influence on the Lo Life subculture of New York in the late 1980s and 1990s. The Brooklyn-based movement was led by rapper Rack-Lo. They sought to recontextualize conventional prep fashion and wore Polo Ralph Lauren from head to toe.

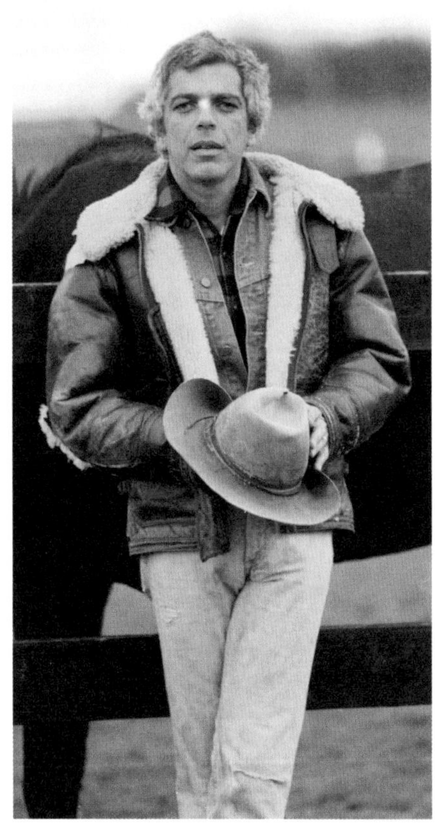

Right: Designer Ralph Lauren epitomizes his own aesthetic, wearing denim, leather and Western-inspired get-ups.

Opposite: Ralph Lauren, Bronx native, dresses as an American-style archetype.

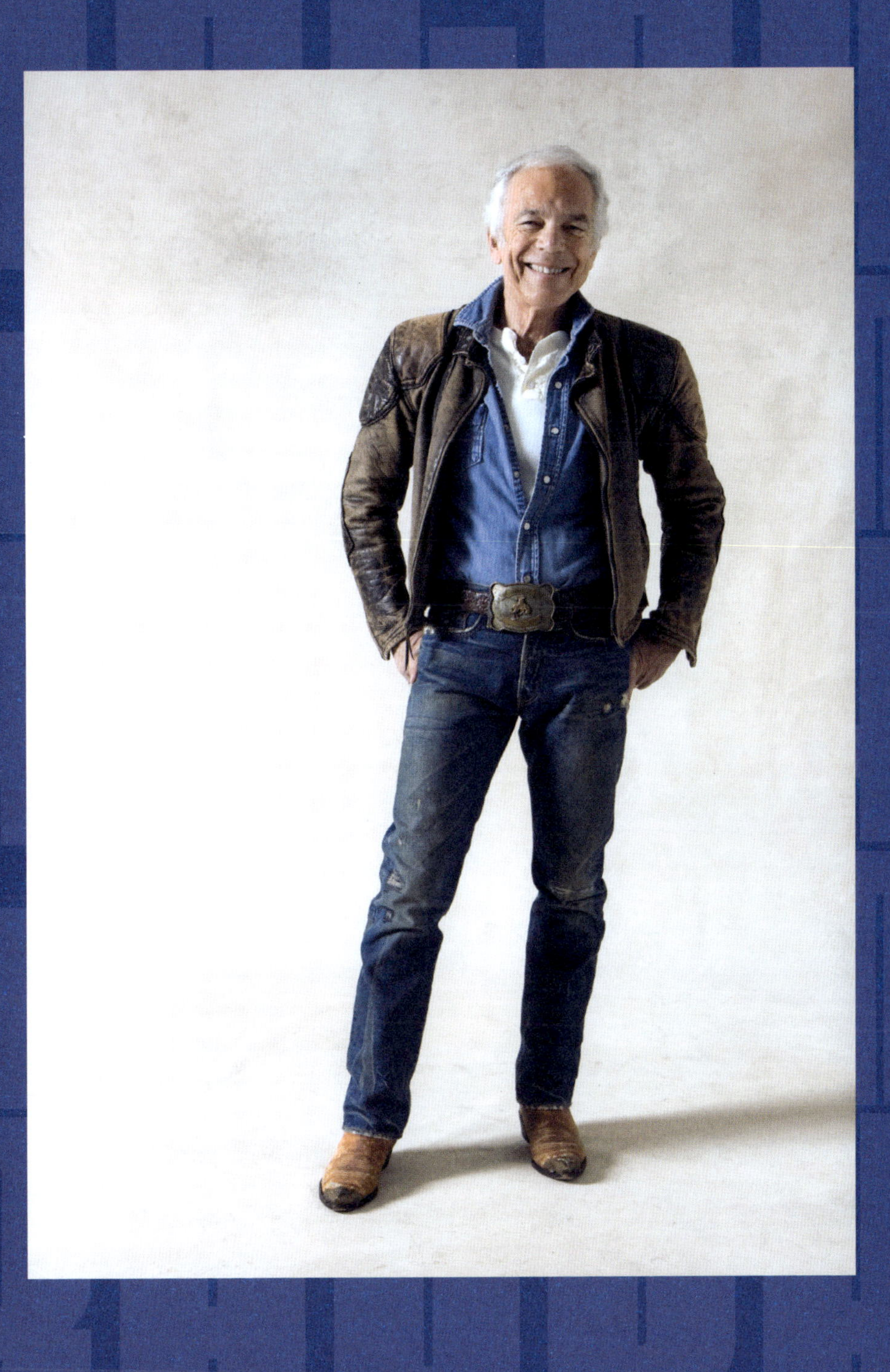

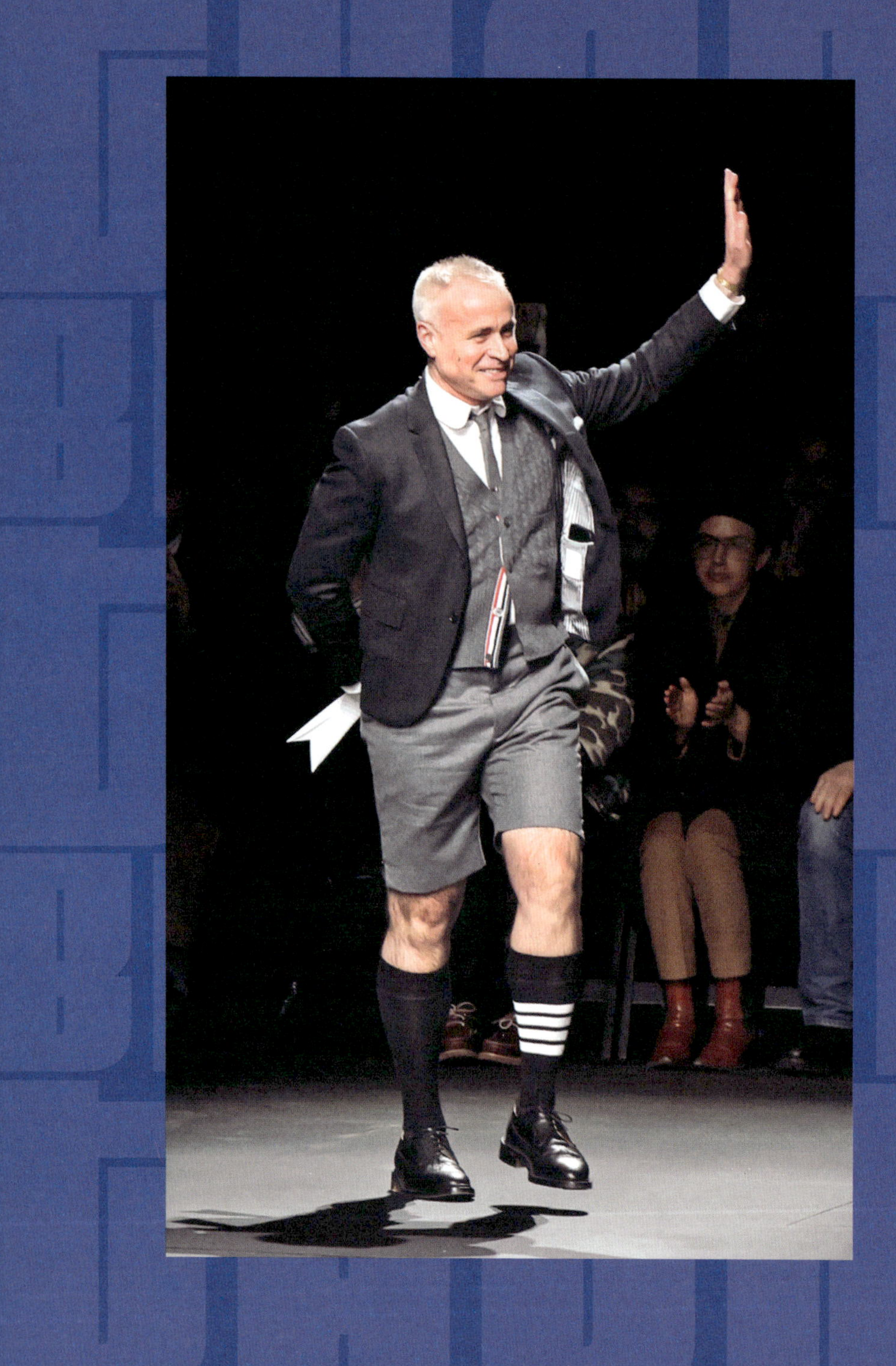

THOM BROWNE

Thom Browne, the incredibly recognizable American designer based in New York, has his own sort of uniform. Originally from Allentown, Pennsylvania, he tried his hand at acting in Los Angeles before finding his passion for making custom suits. He moved to New York in 1997. The designer can be found around town, always in his signature short, tight, grey suits with their red-white-and-blue-striped, grosgrain ribbon details. Browne is one of the few designers who almost always wears the same thing and he completely embodies the brand aesthetic. Interestingly, his own signature work is also a frequent heavy hitter on the red carpets across the globe. Janelle Monáe has become well known for wearing very extreme, surreal takes on the classic Thom Browne grey suit at the Met Gala. Other celebrities – everyone from Adrien Brody to Khloé Kardashian – have worn simpler takes on the classic Thom Browne wardrobe. Browne plays with infinite extremes and everyday formalities in both his work and his own style of dressing.

Opposite: Thom Browne is always seen in his own uniform: a short suit creation of his own, of course.

VERA WANG

Designer Vera Wang, who is famous for her wedding dresses and tailored gowns, often makes an appearance in luxurious pieces that embody the label – minimalist, quietly chic gowns at red-carpet events. It's no surprise she herself is so stylish. After all, she debuted her bridal brand in 1990 because she couldn't find a dress she liked for her own wedding. Wang favours dark colours like charcoal and inky blacks, with a flash of surprising embellishment, whether it be a big necklace, jewelled headband or large watch. She reportedly tries on every wedding dress she designs, to this day. "I don't know a woman designer that does not inhabit her work... It really is a very different relationship to work, to your process, and to what you create," she told *People*.

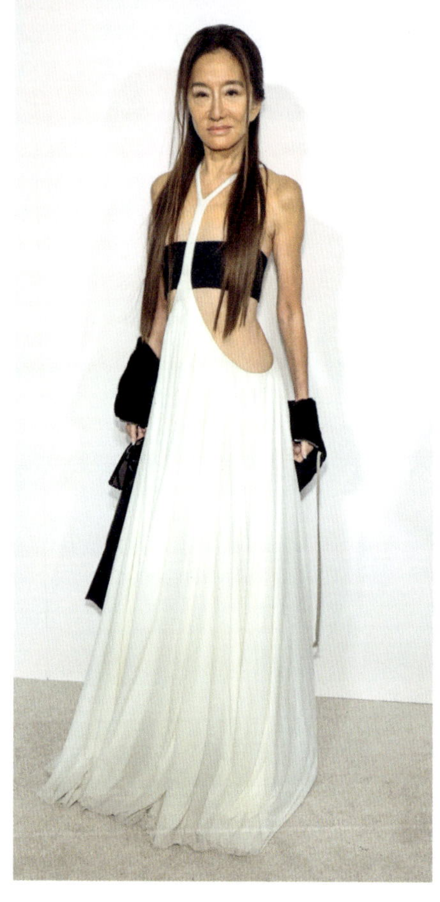

Right: Designer Vera Wang often makes an appearance on the red carpet in flowing, black-and-white gowns.

Opposite: Vera Wang often wears her own romantic work, as seen here at the 2024 Met Gala.

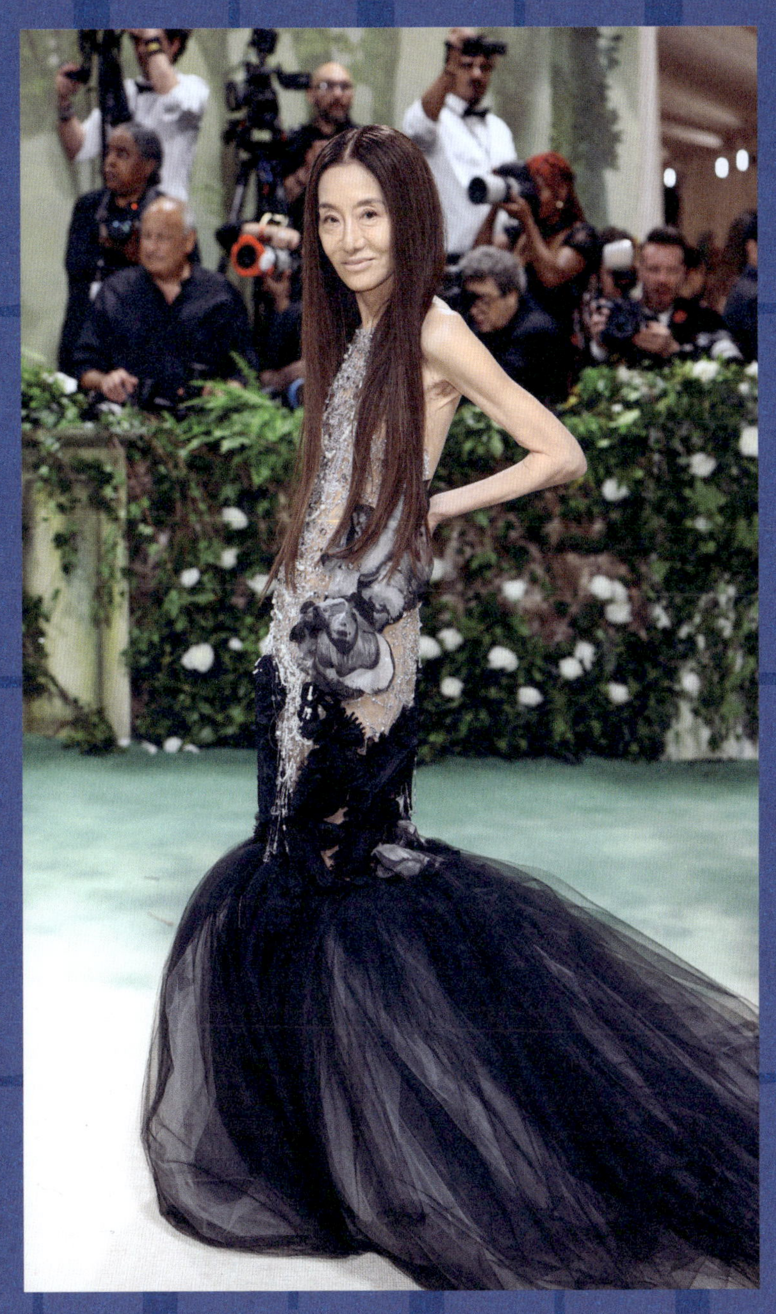

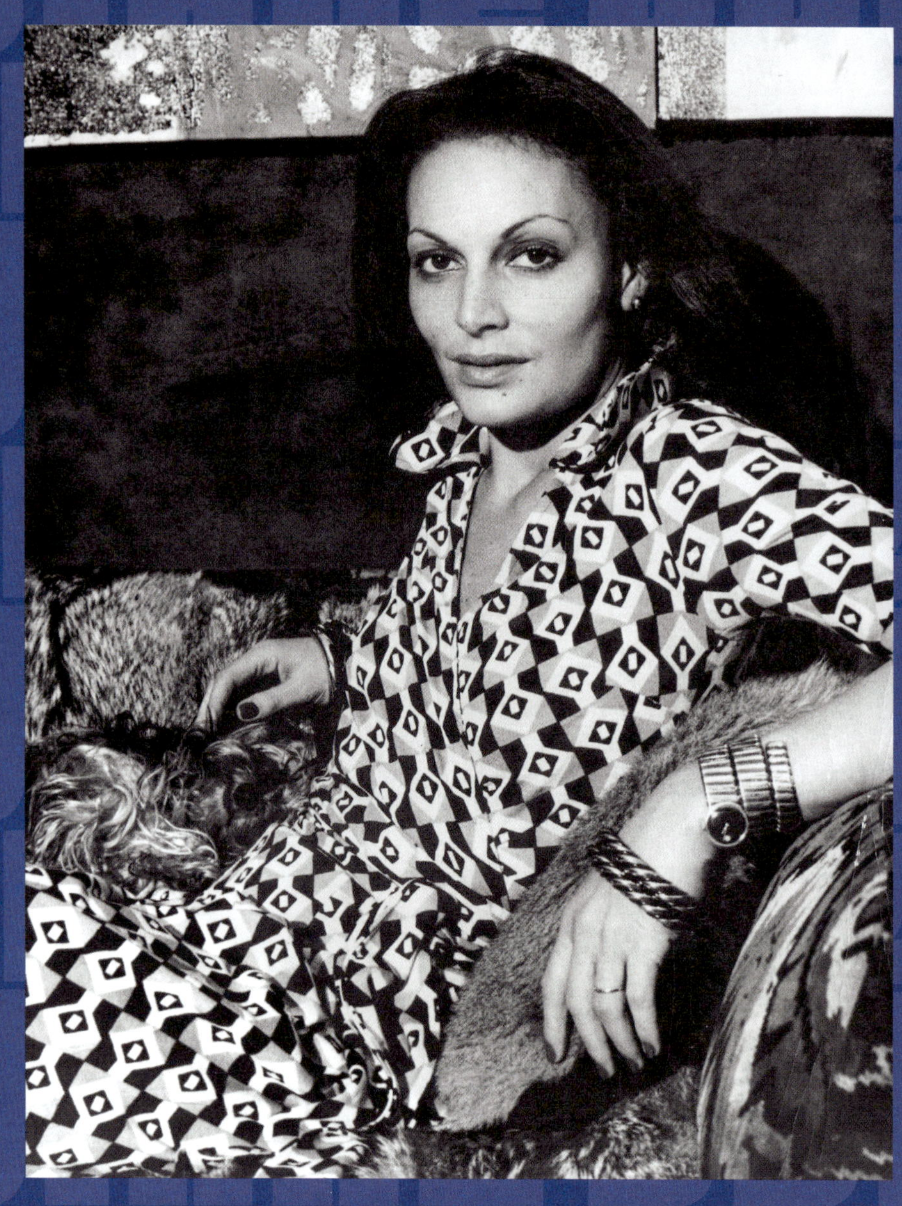

DIANE VON FURSTENBERG

Another of the most prominent New York designers with a sense of style to match is Diane von Furstenberg. She has always stood behind powerful, strong silhouettes that empower women and go along with their lifestyles. Her personal style and work aligns with her manifesto for confidence. "The best tip to truly owning it, is to really have a good relationship with yourself and not be delusional and practice the truth," she once told me in an interview for *New York* magazine. One could say she ultimately dresses and designs for women through the female gaze. In the 1970s, when she was freshly starting her career, she wore tailored pinstripe suits. Early on, she transformed her look with a product that would soon become such a style signature: the printed wrap dress. She wore it, along with plunging jersey dresses, leopard print, lace and ample prints at premieres, on red carpets, at galas and beyond. She's as instantly recognizable today as she was decades earlier.

Opposite: Designer Diane von Furstenberg, seen wearing one of her own infamous wrap dresses.

LYNN YAEGER

Between all the stylists, retail leaders, editors and writers in New York there are always standouts whose imagery lives on forever. It's one thing to work in the industry, but yet another to build a strong visual aesthetic personally. New York industry tastemakers are some of the best people to look to when it comes to style DNA. They break rules, lead the way and inspire entire generations to think – or dress – differently. And they carefully consider their look from head to toe, hair included.

One such fan favourite is Lynn Yaeger. The longtime writer can be seen traipsing around the city streets, in her West Village neighbourhood, on the subways and at the best antique fairs across the globe in her signature poufy dresses, flat shoes and antique jewellery.

Yaeger worked for *The Village Voice* for three decades before becoming a contributor to top publications, including the *New York Times* and *Vogue*. She favours girly dresses from London designer Simone Rocha and big skirts from Comme des Garçons.

Yaeger can be spotted a mile away not just because of her unique sense of style, but also due to the iconic beauty look she developed. An avid antique collector, she wears doll-like blush, a 1920s-inspired, short, red bob with baby fringe and a deep, exaggerated cupid's bow-drawn lip. "Early on, I decided to ignore the industry's dictates – so stifling, unattainable, judgmental – and make my own rules," she once wrote for *Oprah* magazine. "I had long admired women with strong signature looks – Anna Piaggi, Diana Vreeland, Isabella Blow – for whom the fashion world seemed to make an exception."

Opposite: Writer Lynn Yaeger is every eccentric's favourite New York dresser. She often combines Simone Rocha, Comme des Garçons and vintage in her own quirky way.

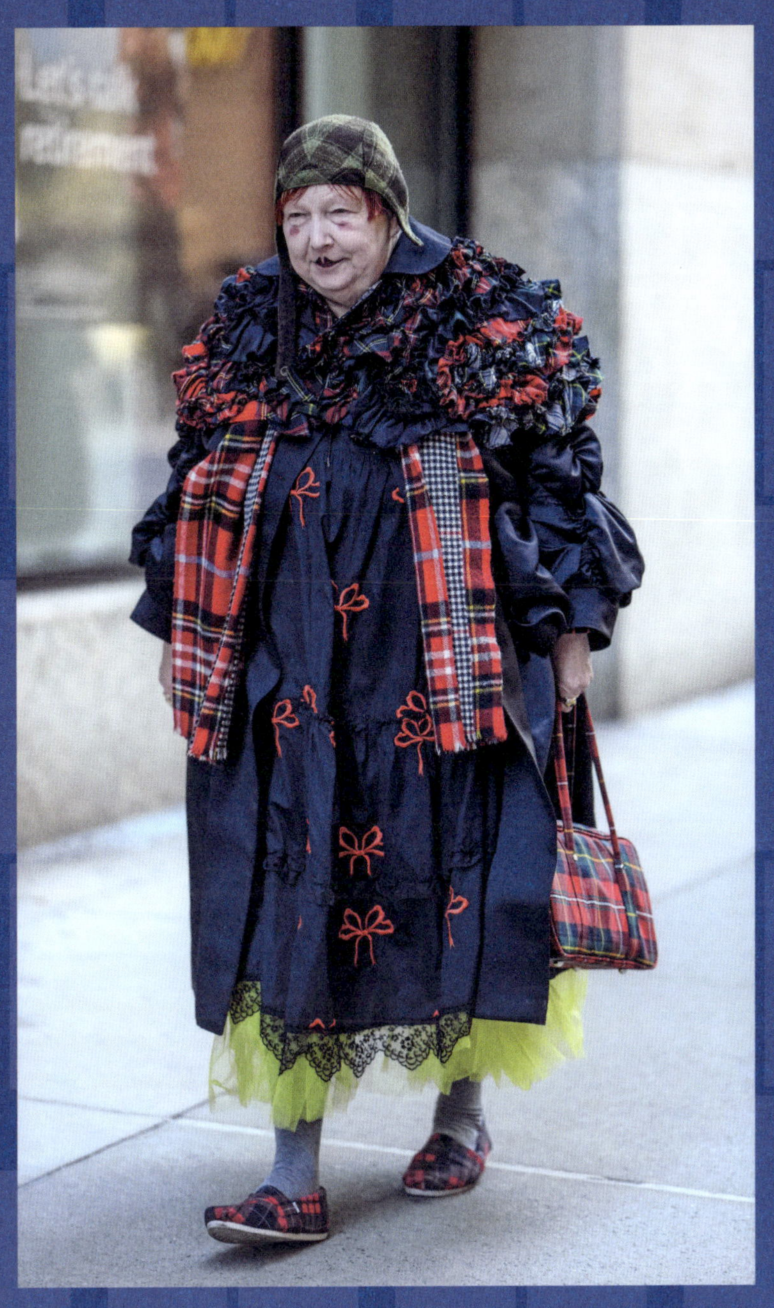

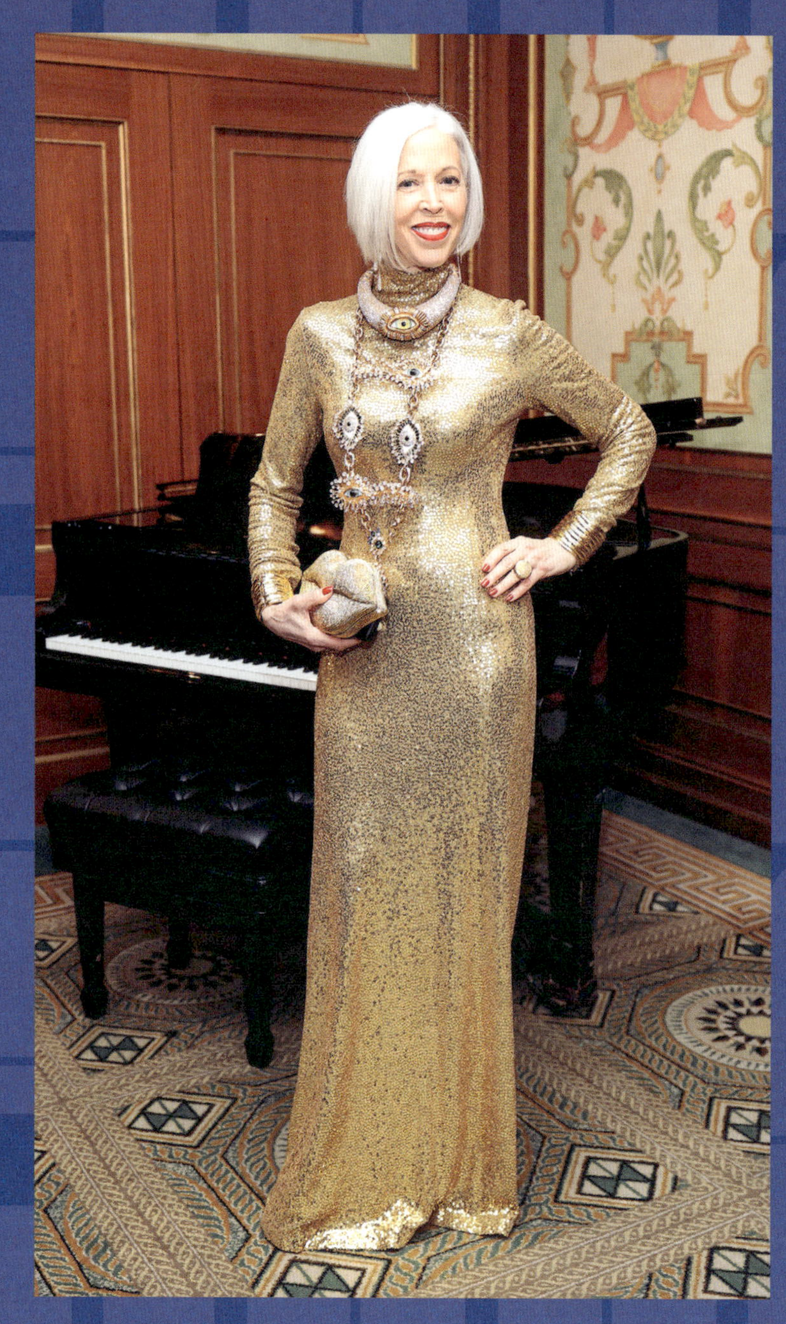

LINDA FARGO

As senior vice president of the fashion office and the director of women's fashion and store presentation for the legendary Bergdorf Goodman department store, Linda Fargo also has an iconic beauty look.

With her ice-blonde, perfected, sleek bob and never without a swipe of red lipstick, she epitomizes style, grace and a signature uptown look with a twist. Leopard print and unexpected staples from Japanese brands like Sacai and Comme des Garçons are her go-to, paired with jeans, bright red suiting or carefully considered prints. She always looks expensive and is one of the very few faces of retail giants who has ever been such a regular favourite of street-style photographers during fashion week.

Originally from the Midwest, Fargo began her fashion journey with a love of vintage, and grew up wearing French twist up-dos. "I think New York City is really the perfect playground for my particular style because it embraces everything, just like the city itself," says Fargo. "It's from glamour to cool, to edgy, to casual, to shocking. It's like anything and everything plays out in New York and it's kind of reflected in the range and the acceptance of all of this range of styles. I mean, I sometimes leave the house for work at nine in the morning and what to some people might look like I am fully in cocktail attire looks like perfectly normal here. I really think New York is really a fashion lover's paradise."

"I would say that vintage was probably my first real love and exploration of fashion and style," she tells us. "Maybe it was because of movies, but I just loved all the style from vintage eras and plus it fit my budget as well. Today, I think I'm pretty graphic and sculptural. A lot of times I rely on black and white, probably because it's so vivid and sharp.

Opposite: Fashion industry icon Linda Fargo epitomizes elegance: always dressed impeccably and with a smile.

ANNA WINTOUR

How could a book about New York City style be complete without mentioning Anna Wintour? The former editor-in-chief of *Vogue*, global editorial director of *Vogue* and chief content officer at Condé Nast is one of the most-watched figures in fashion globally, let alone in New York. She's created an undeniably iconic look for herself, most notably pegged to her meticulous, never-changing bob and dark sunglasses. It's proof that one can create an aesthetic based on hair alone. She has reportedly had her hairstyle since she was 14.

Wintour herself has described her own style as "safe", and often leans towards long, colourful dresses, printed coats and florals. She almost always wears her bright, antique-style, collet-set collar necklaces. Her love for these accessories allegedly started when she bought a purple, Georgian-era necklace at the English jeweller, S.J. Phillips Ltd, which is rumoured to have cost $20,000. Another distinct style code of Wintour? You'll almost never see her carrying a handbag, or any other bag, for that matter. She only carries a bag on very select occasions. This adds to her lore, authority, mystery and status.

Opposite: Anna Wintour stuns in a decadent pink look for one of her Met Gala outfits. The famed editor reportedly never wears all-black.

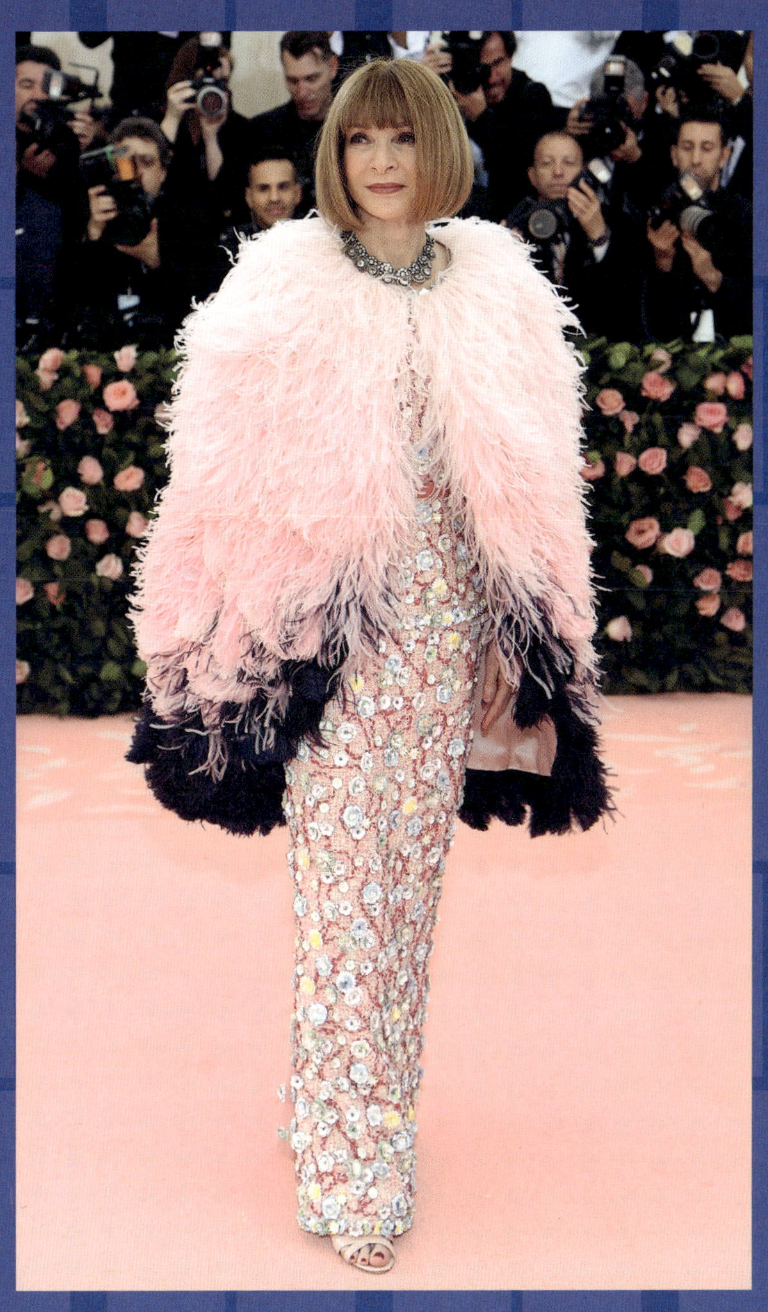

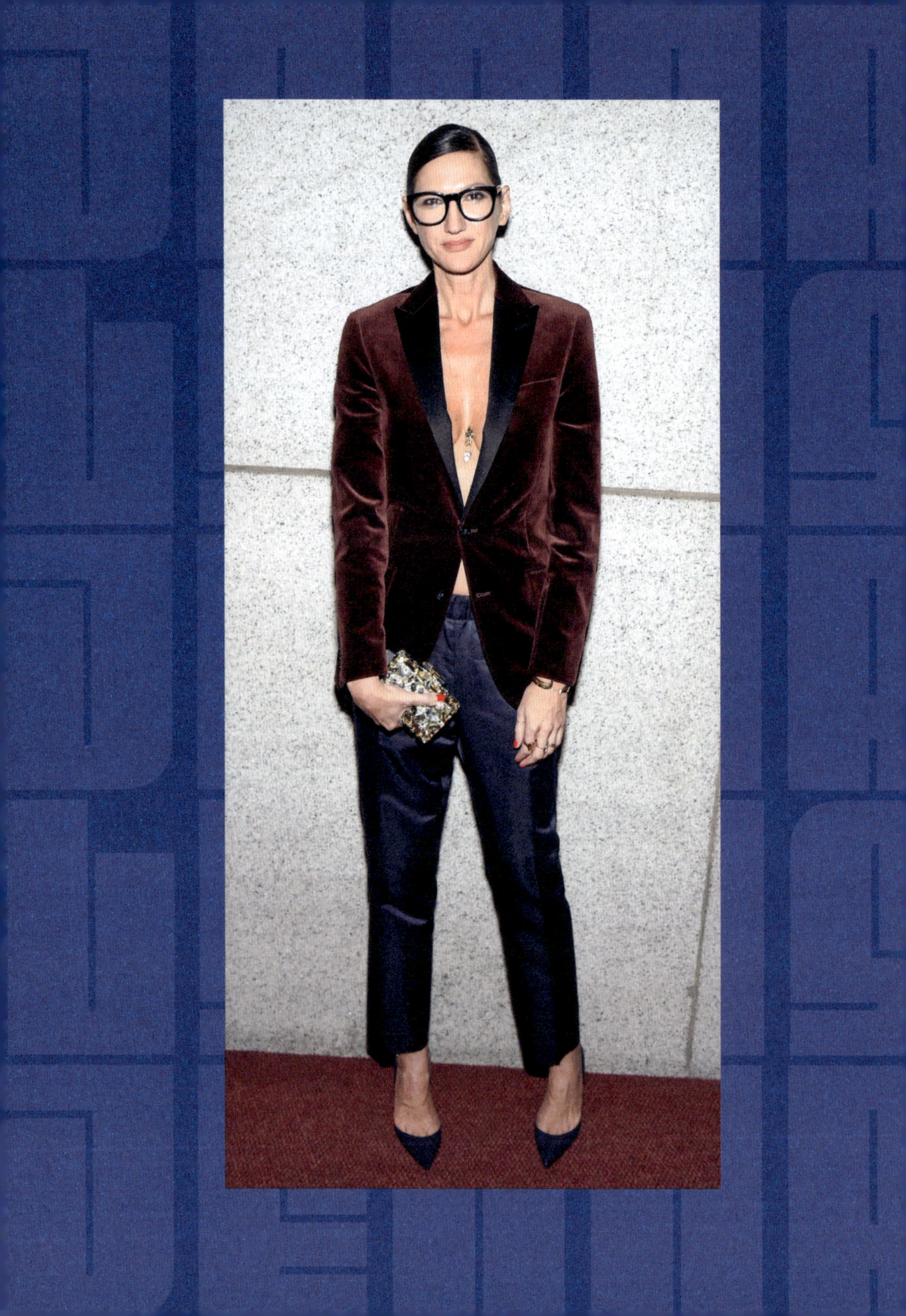

JENNA LYONS

Few people from the retail world have made such an impact as style icons like Linda Fargo, but Jenna Lyons is another figure who emerged from behind the scenes with a strong personal style ethos. In 2013, the *New York Times* ran a story titled "Jenna Lyons, the Woman Who Dresses America". She was the executive creative director and president of retailer J.Crew from 2010 until April 2017, and remains a style influence as well as a past cast member of *The Real Housewives of New York City*. She is instantly recognizable for her thick-rimmed glasses, chic suiting, cool, boxy tailoring and in her J.Crew-era, bright pops of colour, casual pieces like T-shirts or denim shirts with formal accents like ballgown skirts, sequins and statement necklaces.

"I think one of the things that I love, or I'm probably inspired the most by, is the power of transformation and the way that people can reframe their vision of who they are or of somebody else," Lyons told *Vogue* in 2017. "It's nice seeing someone put something on and look at themselves in the mirror and see themselves differently and hopefully better." When she was younger, she was first inspired by Tina Chow, Grace Jones and Jerry Hall, women she saw in the pages of books and magazines. "What was interesting or beautiful about them was their personality and their style and their individuality, not the fact that they looked the same," she says. Today, Lyons represents the same kind of sentiment – standing out in a bold and brave way that totally captures and captivates any room.

Opposite: Former J.Crew exec turned reality television star Jenna Lyons is a style icon known for her take on tailored suits, dark glasses and mixing formal and casual.

JUNE AMBROSE

Stylist June Ambrose grew up in The Bronx and gained notoriety for styling the likes of Missy Elliott and Jay-Z in their Forward Vision music videos in the 1990s. On her social media platforms, she documents her minimalist eccentric outfits with lots of suiting, cool sneakers and exaggerated hats. "I love anything that makes my face look tiny. It's a trick. I like to play with scale," she told *L.A. Times*. "I'm like an animated version of myself. These silhouettes and shapes make me feel like a little girl. I really tap into sense memories of childhood. What did I feel the most effortless in? What did I feel the most useful in? What made me want to dance?"

One of the most iconic looks from Ambrose's body of work is Missy Elliott's video for "The Rain (Supa Dupa Fly)", the first single off her first solo rap album, *Supa Dupa Fly*. She opens the video wearing what looks like an inflated trash bag. "[During] my early career in hip-hop culture, I was forced to design the looks in order to get the couture attention that the culture needed," she told *Bustle*. "It had no stitching, it was all seamed with tire glue. The outer layer – which was the patent leather vinyl – we were able to sew up. Any little leak could throw off the inflation."

Much like her experimental, groundbreaking work in the world of music, Ambrose takes fun fashion risks that pay off. She mixes formal and casual and adores wearing unusual silhouettes from Japanese brands, including Junya Watanabe and Sacai. When she's front row at fashion week, she always stands out. For a brief period of time, Ambrose also served as a designer, when Puma appointed her as a creative director in 2020. "I'm pretty eccentric at times," she once told Refinery29. "I love a hat."

Opposite: Stylist June Ambrose is almost never without a dramatic hat, as seen here.

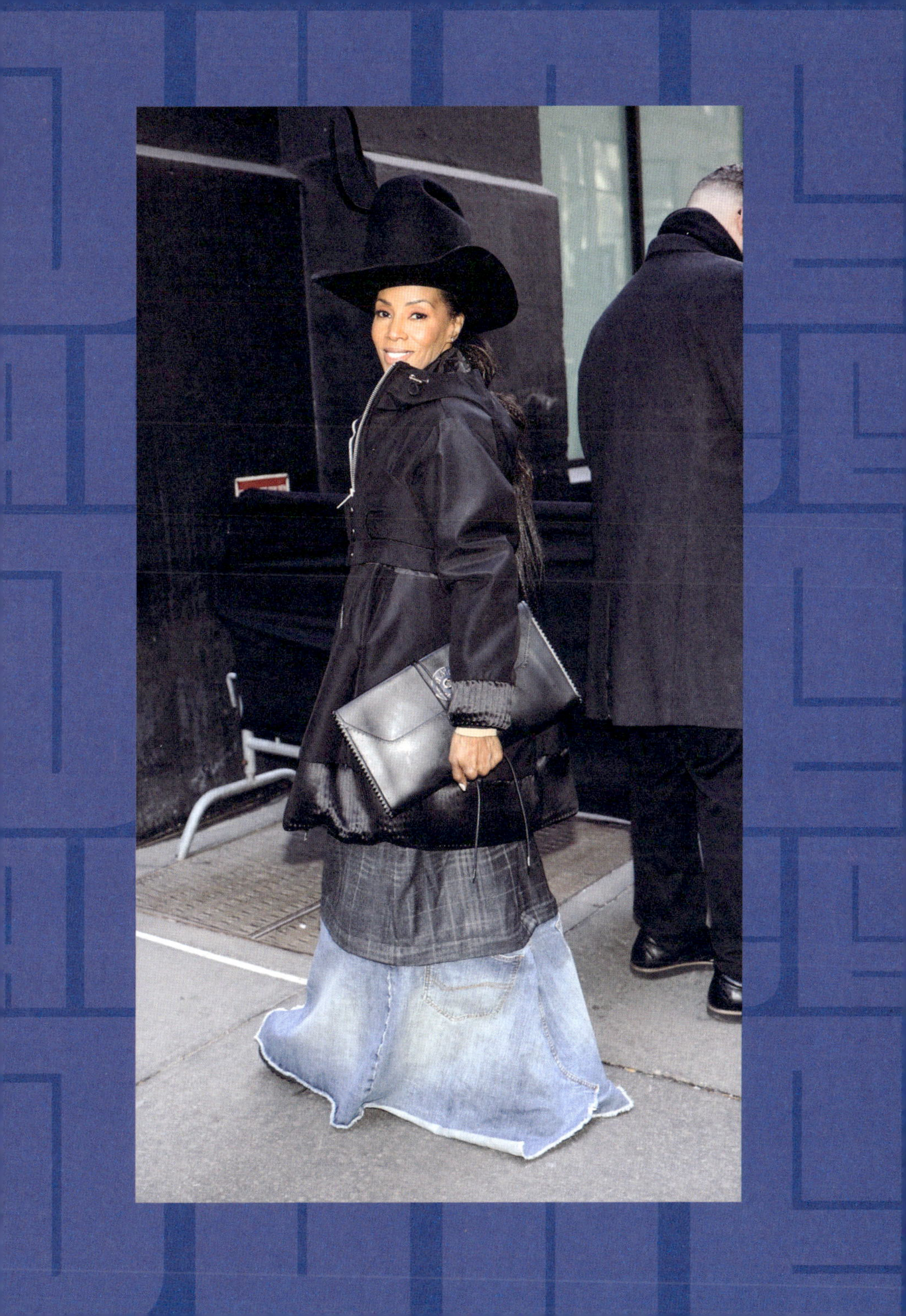

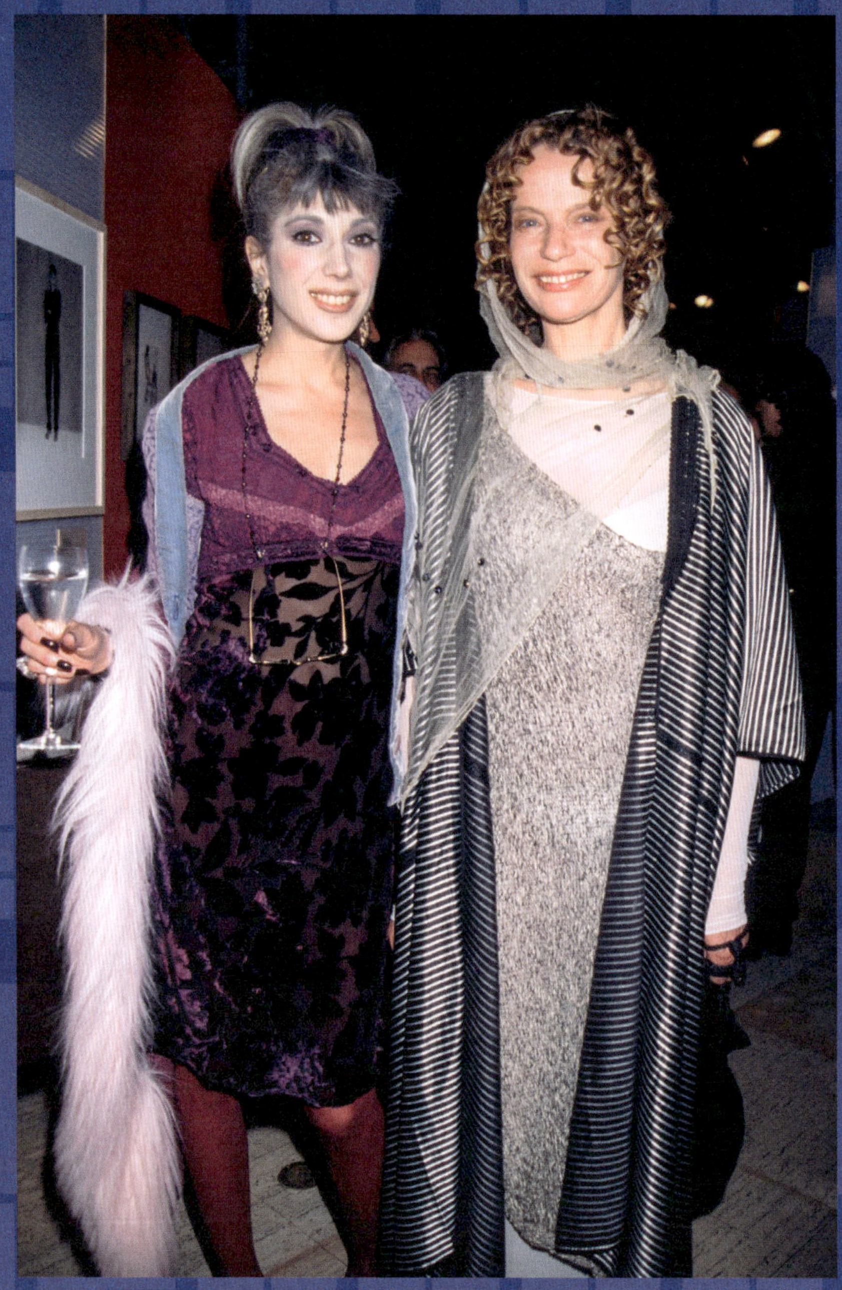

LAUREN EZERSKY

Another highly influential New York tastemaker of the 1990s is undoubtedly Lauren Ezersky. The snarky, sardonic television host and journalist was the queen of *Behind the Velvet Ropes*, a fashion-focused cable television series that aired from the mid-1980s to 2012. Many of the New York fashion industry's elder millennial population grew up watching her. Born in Yonkers, a suburb outside of New York City, her boisterous, drawn-out accent is so iconic and distinct. When she was younger, her long, black hair was streaked with grey and she wore cool printed dresses and fun denim. Today, she can be seen wearing a mix of archival fashion from the likes of Tom Ford mixed in with huge, bold, gold accessories from Schiaparelli by Daniel Roseberry.

In 2022, *Vogue* called Ezersky New York's "Most Unjaded Fashion Journalist". It's no wonder. Could anyone today pull off what she did when she got in bed with Alexander McQueen at his hotel to interview him? Said *Vogue*'s former creative director Sally Singer in the same article: "People might remember her look as being tough or hard because of her voice and her eye make-up, but she wore incredibly beautiful and fragile clothes. Very romantic, sometimes with a utility edge like a biker jacket, but most of her clothes were the clothes of dreams." Today, her distinct chic look is reminiscent of a cool, real-life Cruella de Vil.

Opposite: Lauren Ezersky, seen here with model Veruschka in 1990.

THE FUTURE OF FASHION ICONS

In a city as bold and expressive as New York, there's bound to be a constantly moving cadre of new creatives who shake things up. They define their looks with boldness.

Take, for instance, the brand Collina Strada, run by designer Hillary Taymour. She founded the label in 2008 and lives for sustainably fuelled, bright colours, ethereal fabrics and an incredibly inclusive casting on the runway. Taymour herself is very recognizable for her big sunglasses, oversized, tie-dye, spun fits and is often featured in fashion week street-style shots. Elsewhere, there's absolutely no denying the power of accessories in the evolution of personal style in New York, either. Stylist Gabriella Karefa-Johnson is an inspiring, colourful beacon of light in a neutral-hued world. She mixes and matches different prints and piles on playful, quirky jewellery. She loves stripes, denim and sporty staples and has styled It-girls and models, including Gigi Hadid, Kendall Jenner and Ashley Graham. Icons like the model Alex Consani define style through her ever-growing social media presence. Actress Hunter Schafer wears her out-of-this-world, red-carpet looks, styled by Dara Allen.

Street style photographers like Phil Oh, Tommy Ton and so many other rising names document the real-world style on the streets during fashion week. Elsewhere, model Paloma Elsesser is defining the next generation of model style, with a curated wardrobe of mixed emerging designers, classic hits and vintage. Iconoclasts, like the Green Lady of Brooklyn, have created their own versions of iconic New York style. Ari Seth Cohen, known for his AdvancedStyle content, continues to document the older style set that so iconically defines the city.

In the past decade, new names have continued to pop up, always with their own distinct aesthetics and ideas. The next icon could be you.

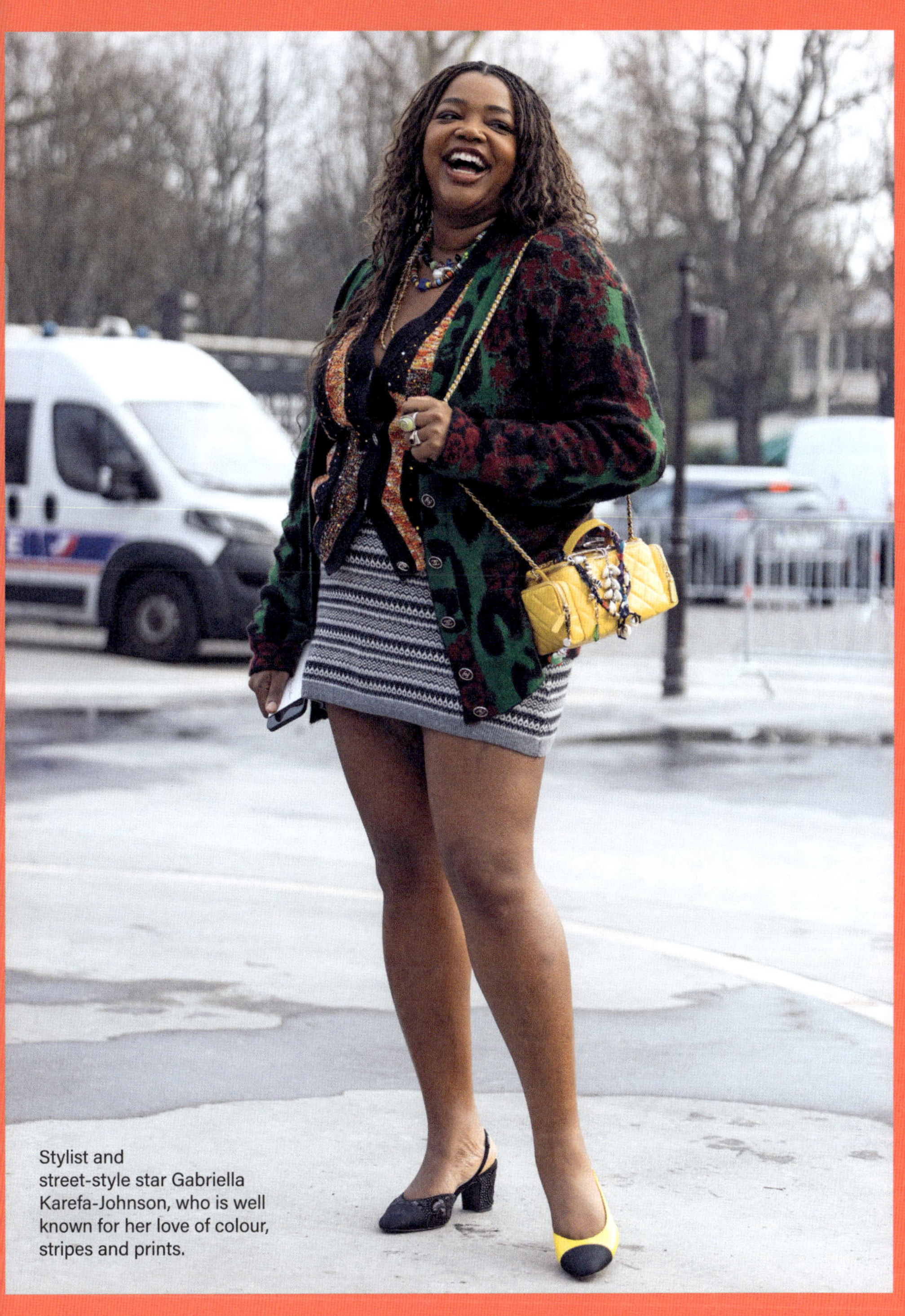

Stylist and
street-style star Gabriella
Karefa-Johnson, who is well
known for her love of colour,
stripes and prints.

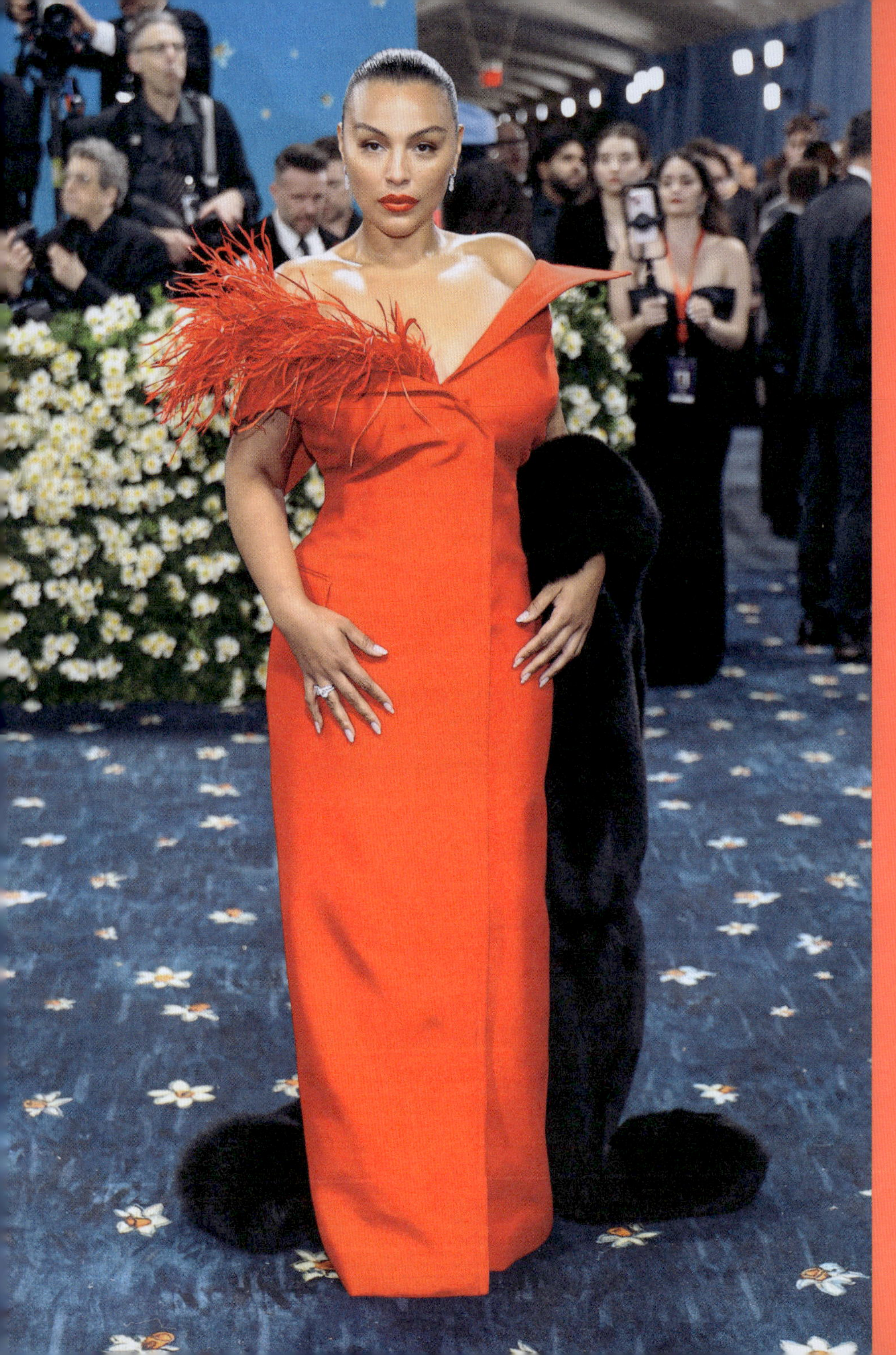

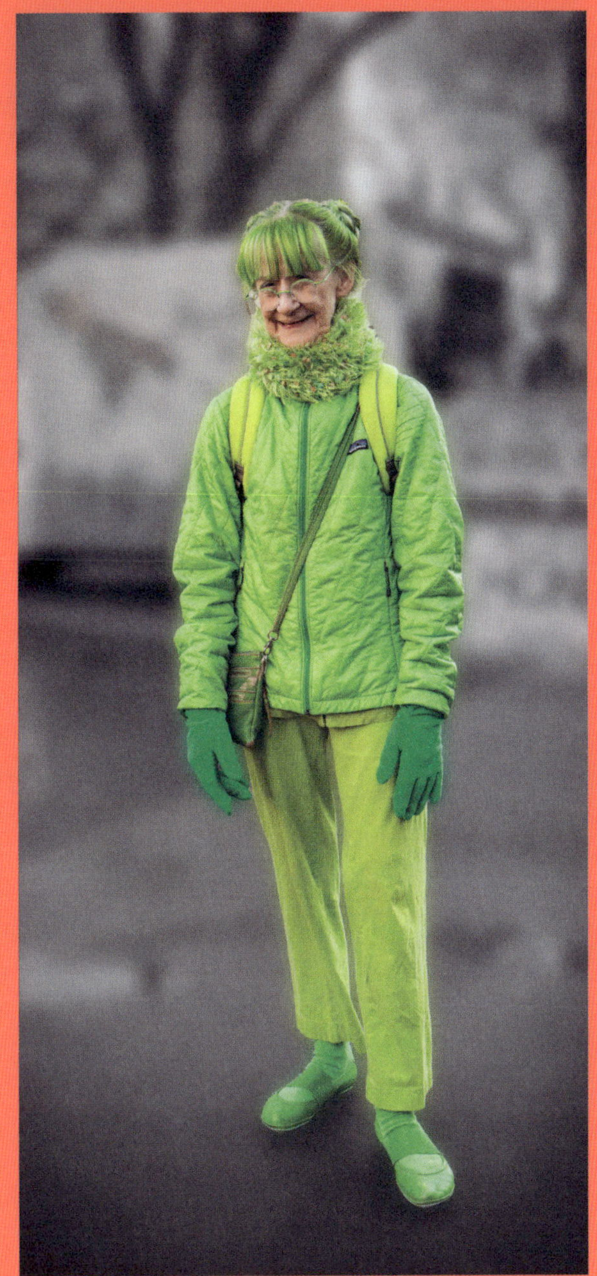

Opposite: Model Paloma Elsesser wearing a Ferragamo gown by Maximilian Davis at the 2025 Met Gala.

Right: Elizabeth Eaton Rosenthal, known as the Green Lady of Brooklyn, who has had a cult following for decades for her imaginative, all-green looks.

INDEX

CREDITS

The publishers would like to thank the following sources for their kind permission to reproduce the pictures in this book.

Alamy Stock Photo: Aj Pics 32; /Album 23; /Allstar Picture Library Limited 39; / Ira Berger 203; /Bettmann 167; /Erwin Blumenfeld/Condé Nast via Getty Images 166; /Everett Collection 149, 160-161; / Landmark Media 21, 28-29; /PA Images 78; /Pictorial Press 15, 24; /PictureLux/The Hollywood Archive 27; /RGR Collection 40, 159; /TCD/Prod/DB 41; /Ted Thai/The LIFE Picture Collection 177

Eyevine: Andre D. Wagner/New York Times/Redux 53

Getty Images: 14; /Evan Agostini 136, 145; /Archive Photos 153; / Neilson Barnard 157; /Roberta Bayley/Redferns 100-101; / Edward Berthelot 189; /Bettmann 69, 70, 82; /Tim Boxer 96; /Michael Buckner/Variety via Getty Images 140; /Larry Busacca 143; /Mike Coppola 118-119; /Richard Corkery/ NY Daily News Archive via Getty Images 83, 147; /Chalkie Davies 91; /James Devaney/ WireImage 19; /Steve Eichner 106-107; / Steve Eichner/WWD/Penske Media via Getty Images 178; /Express Newspapers 168; /Fairchild Archive/Penske Media via Getty Images 49, 174; /Billy Farrell/Patrick McMullan via Getty Images59; /Deborah Feingold 173; /Chuck Fishman 176; / Valentina Frugiuele 201; /David Gahr 85, 86-87; /Noam Galai/Getty Images for Central Park Tower 45; /Ron Galella/Ron Galella Collection via Getty Images 121, 123, 129; / Steve Granitz/WireImage 102-103; /Scott Gries/ImageDirect 117; /Frazer Harrison/ FilmMagic 154; /Rose Hartman 57; /Rose Hartman/WireImage 198; /Arturo Holmes 182; /Horst P. Horst/Conde Nast via Getty Images 50-51; /Dimitrios Kambouris/Getty Images for The Met Museum/Vogue 126, 130, 132-133, 135, 156 right, 185, 190, 202; / Rob Kim/Getty Images for Tribeca Festival 76; /Bob King/Redferns 60; /Keith Major/ Contour by Getty Images 46-47; /Jeffrey Mayer/WireImage 137; /Kevin Mazur/ WireImage 73, 125; /Jamie McCarthy/ WireImage 184; /Michael Loccisano 113; /Jamie McCarthy 193, 194; /Catherine McGann 66-67; /Lexie Moreland/WWD via Getty Images 104-105; /Paul Morigi 80; / Sonia Moskowitz 62-63; /Cindy Ord/Getty Images for SCAD 56; /Paramount Pictures/ Sunset Boulevard/Corbis via Getty Images 9, 25; /Al Pereira/Getty Images/MIchael Ochs Archives 138; /Jose Perez/Bauer-Griffin/GC Images 197; /PL Gould/IMAGES 54, 94-95; /Robin Platzer 122; /Todd Plitt/ Contour by Getty Images 181; /Michael Putland 34; /Jack Robinson/Hulton Archive 92; /Donna Santisi/Redferns 99; /Francesco Scavullo/Condé Nast via Getty Images 164; /Lawrence Schwartzwald/Sygma via Getty Images 146; /Jerry Schatzberg 97; / Sam Shaw/© Shaw Family Archives/Getty Images 37; /Michael Stewart 6; /Allan Tannenbaum 88; /TheStewartofNY 150; / Victor Virgile/Gamma-Rapho via Getty Images 175; /Santi Visalli 110, 169; /Theo Wargo/FilmMagic 35; /Susan Wood 180; / Art Zelin 163

Shutterstock: 13; /ADC 186; /Everett 109; / Stephen Lovekin/BEI 126-127; /Madison McGaw/BFA 142; /Moviestore 31; /Erik Pendzich 65; /Splash News 156 left; /THA 16